Engaged Observer

Engaged Observer

Anthropology, Advocacy, and Activism

EDITED BY
VICTORIA SANFORD
AND
ASALE ANGEL-AJANI

FOREWORD BY
PHILIPPE BOURGOIS

RUTGERS UNIVERSITY PRESS

NEW BRUNSWICK, NEW JERSEY, AND LONDON

Second paperback printing, 2008

LIBRARY OF CONGRESS CATALOGING-IN-PUBLICATION DATA

Engaged observer : anthropology, advocacy, and activism / edited by Victoria Sanford
and Asale Angel-Ajani; foreword by Philippe Bourgois.
     p.   cm.
     Includes bibliographical references and index.
     ISBN-13: 978-0-8135-3891-4 (hardcover: alk.paper)
     ISBN-13: 978-0-8135-3892-1 (pbk.: alk.paper)
     1. Anthropology—Philosophy. 2. Political anthropology. 3. Anthropological
ethics. 4. Social conflict. 5. Violence. 6. Social advocacy. 7. Social justice.
I. Sanford, Victoria. II. Angel-Ajani, Asale.
     GN33.E65 2006
     301.01—dc22   2006005654
                                          CIP

A British Cataloging-in-Publication record for this book is available
from the British Library

Manufactured in the United States of America

CONTENTS

PART THREE
Trauma, Violence, and Women's Resistance in Everyday Life

PART FOUR
The Engaged Observer, Inside and Outside the Academy

ACKNOWLEDGMENTS

This book would not have been possible without the patience of the contributors. We thank them for their support. We are honored to work with such committed individuals who have stayed the course over many years fighting for justice in the communities in which they work. The dedication of our editor Kristi Long diligently guided us through the early stages of manuscript production. We owe her our deepest gratitude. We are lucky to have worked with Adi Hovav and everyone at Rutgers University Press who helped us cross the finish line. We are especially thankful to Philippe Bourgois for writing the preface to this volume. His work is exemplary of the kind of engaged observing that inspires many anthropologists. We extend a special thanks to Faith Martin for copyediting the manuscript and Nick Likos, at New York University for performing technological miracles. The two anonymous reviewers gave us excellent comments on the first draft of this book and we thank them for their insight. We thank James Curley for generously allowing us to use his photograph for the cover of the book. We are appreciative for the assistance provided by the Virginia Foundation for the Humanities and the Gallatin School at New York University. Finally, we thank our families, Raul Figueroa Sarti, Gabriela Figueroa Cuevas, Valentina Figueroa-Sanford, and Alan J. Hanson for their love and support.

FOREWORD

Anthropology in the Global State of Emergency

PHILIPPE BOURGOIS

This volume challenges anthropology, the social sciences—and anyone who reads university press books—to engage critically with the urgent crises faced by the socially vulnerable under the global lie of democracy and neoliberal prosperity in the 2000s. The articles raise problematic questions about politically structured suffering. They examine both the responsibility of those who wield power and the painful, everyday experience of those who bear the brunt of social inequality. The editors have dared combine the discursive, self-reflexive insights raised by the more philosophically oriented postmodern critiques of anthropology from the mid-1980s and early 1990s with a contemporary commitment to being politically meaningful in the here and now, so as to 'ferret out' an understanding of truth that can speak to power.

During the last two decades of the twentieth century, the social sciences benefited from the unmasking of ethnographic authority and the deconstruction of the culture concept— especially its essentializing and orientalizing tendencies. The omniscient and invisible Western narrator with a totalizing vision of the exotic other was a pathetic anthropologist, a product of Enlightenment discourse arguing, at best, for a kinder, gentler administration of colonialism. There were notable exceptions in the early twentieth century, such as Franz Boas, who dedicated his scientific endeavors to combating racism and who also eloquently opposed collaborating with U.S. militarism. The professionalization of the discipline in the mid-twentieth century and its postmodern philosophical turn in the late twentieth century defanged critical analysis within anthropology and resulted in political paralysis. Ethnographers, for the most part, succumbed to their class and institutional logics. At the level of theory they became most creative and polemic with respect to denouncing textual-methodological inadequacies and to elaborating disciplinary mea culpas, rather than to elucidating the meaningful fault lines of power relevant to the people they study.

It is easier for suburbanized intellectuals in air-conditioned offices to vent textual angst than to analyze the workings of institutionalized power at the top of
the social structure or to cross uncomfortable class and cultural boundaries at
the bottom. Anthropologists respond to institutional rewards and constraints,
and during the final decades of the twentieth century they became skillful
development consultants in the applied sphere, or articulate authors of philo-
sophical-textual autocritiques in the corridors of elite universities.

There is a silver lining to anthropology relative to other scholarly disciplines,
however. Over the past century we differentiated ourselves from other social
science and humanities approaches through our dedication to participant-
observation fieldwork coupled with an inconsistent, destabilizing faith in cultural
relativism. The core methods and practices of anthropology often involve long-
term interpersonal contact across major social power parameters—class, ethnicity, and gender most frequently. Well-trained, self-reflexive scholars are often
jolted emotionally by the human face of their research topics, and sometimes
break out of the bourgeois intimate apartheids that define common sense in academia. Relativism often impedes our ability to write against injustice—and it
may encourage us to limit ourselves to argue about culture or to question the
meaning-of-what-was-meant—but, when combined with participant observation
methods, we are confronted ethically with the problem of the stakes of our writing. In other words, engaging theory with politics in ways that are relevant to the
people we study emerges vitally from our method and from our reflexive sensibility, even if it contradicts the institutional logics of scholarly privilege, academic
socialization, and abstract philosophical relativism.

The organizers of this volume urge us to engage with political stakes that
matter to the people who bear a disproportionate toll of the suffering caused by
the inequalities that power imposes. Most of the authors in the collection argue
that we need to build self-reflexive theory with an awareness of the politics of
representation in order to "get the facts straight." But they insist on conducting
ethnographies of actually existing social suffering, and their texts cannot be
pretty stories because oppression tends to be a solvent of human dignity. Reality exists, and it hurts most people even if it is shaped discursively and even if
we have trouble defining it philosophically. Similarly, suffering—however it is
defined at the everyday level—takes the form of blood, sweat, tears, angst, pain,
and premature death, as is revealed in the wide range of ethnographies of violence and oppression in this volume.

Ethnographers cannot presume to speak on behalf of the world's socially
excluded, but writing against inequality is imperative. Denouncing injustice and
oppression is not a naïve, old-fashioned anti-intellectual concern or a superan-
nuated totalizing vision of Marxism. On the contrary, it is a vital historical task
intellectually, because globalization has become synonymous with military intervention, market-driven poverty, and ecological destruction. It is impossible to

understand what is going on anywhere without paying attention to the power dynamics that shape inequality everywhere.

Many of the authors in this volume purposefully address the "legacies of the hidden histories of the Cold War." Their commitment to giving ethnography political teeth as well as theoretical depth and self-reflection is timely. The current historical epoch, arguably, is not just more of the same. It is not yet another form of poverty, or merely a conjunctural political-logistical-economic dislocation. A militarized version of empire has filled the Cold War void and is increasingly constraining the physical movements and ideological values of patriotic citizens, disciplined soldiers, and righteous victims who become explosive fodder for crusades. At the same time, corporate monopoly capital has never been more powerful. Globalization has lumpenized—in a Marxist sense of the term—an ever larger proportion of the world's population, rendering it redundant to the productive sectors of capitalism and to the workings of biopower, in the Foucaultian sense of the term. This is taking place at tremendous human cost. Modernity brought us industrial-scale genocide; development has augmented social inequality; technology brought us diseases of civilization and ecological wastelands; revolutions have betrayed hopes; and democracy has served to hide Walter Benjamin's realization that "everyday is a state of emergency" for most people on earth. The outcome of global patterns of oppression at the level of the individual has become increasingly violent and abusive. Progress, science, development, democracy, and the individuation of responsibility have rendered an ever larger proportion of citizens disposable and have institutionalized lumpen abuse.

The suffering produced on the margins of the contemporary economic global disorder as well as in the epicenter of metropolitan empire is ugly and complicated. As a discipline, anthropology, largely missed the macro facts of colonialism, capitalism, genocide, and revolution over the past century, despite being an eyewitness to those processes. Let us not repeat history today. The kinds of engaged ethnographies called for by this book seek an understanding of the responsibility for the ways power structures suffering. By informing fieldwork with critical theory, anthropologists can make the connections between macro forces and intimate social relations, emotions, and dispositions so that individuals are no longer misrecognized as having to be worthy victims or blameful agents.

At the same time, ethnographers must, of course, remain humble. Anthropology's unique relationship to participant-observation methods informed by cultural relativism does not protect us from the seductions of scholastic banality and political dogma, or even from ethnocentrism. It does, however, raise the stakes of the topics we pursue, because in the contemporary world those who explore the divides that are imposed by class, culture, gender, and sexuality—whether they are studying up, down, or both—will be surrounded by violence if they keep both eyes open. The contradictory politics of ethnography—both textual and carnal—force ethnographers into the nitty-gritty of witnessing human interaction and practice in an embodied manner.

Anthropologists cannot escape physically, ethically, and emotionally the suffering or the brutality of their research subjects and the historical epoch in which they live. An ever-larger proportion of the world's population survives precariously in refugee camps, rural wastelands, zones of ecological devastation, shanty towns, housing projects, tenements, prisons, and homeless encampments as a direct result of superpower military intervention and monopoly capital economic fallout. Although academics still may benefit from arguing cautiously over how to write effectively against unequally distributed suffering, violence, and abuse (as well as culture), this volume's authors are already immersed in the contemporary fray with ethnographies that combine a practical politics of solidarity with reflexive theoretical critiques to engage the high stakes of everyday life.

Engaged Observer

Introduction

VICTORIA SANFORD

Quitate el ropaje del pudor para decir
con libertad y déjate guiar por el
corazón.

–Vera Grabe, *Razones de Vida*

Most of the women and men I know who work in war zones and on the front lines of conflict never meant to go there. By there, I mean into the heart of the conflict—not just its geography or its physicality, but into the very everydayness of war, misery, and social struggle. Most of us ended up in these zones by looking for an explanation for some kind of disruption or dislocation of the everyday. Indeed, despite the fact that specific locales may be labeled as dangerous (by police departments, embassies, national governments, and international institutions), those who live in these zones of "danger" have a different scale of referents in the face of variable insecurity (Osorio Perez, forthcoming). The seemingly inexplicable and yet mundane everyday life is what draws us in to these zones where "no one goes" but where real people actually make and remake their everyday lives as best they can. Whether refugee, exile, undocumented immigrant or internally displaced person, survivors of massacres, genocide, and other crimes against humanity must face the daily challenge to remake everyday life (Sanford 2004). Whether in refuge from violence or struggling in its midst, the everyday needs of human life must be met in order to survive (Nordstrom 2004). In the end, these very survival strategies challenge our initial conceptions of the everyday as well as our research practices.

For example, in 1982 my mentor Philippe Bourgois began fieldwork in a Salvadoran refugee camp in Honduras to explore peasant ideologies of revolution. Much to his surprise, "the refugees desperately wanted foreigners to reside in the camps with them," as did the church and United Nations organizations working in the camp (1990: 48). In short order, he was invited to accompany the refugees crossing the border back to their village in El Salvador. Recalling the experience, Bourgois writes: "My 48-hour visit to El Salvador was prolonged into a fourteen-day nightmare when the Salvadoran military launched a search and

1

destroy operation against the region. . . . The population was composed of a typ-ical cross-section of peasants . . . grandmothers, grandfathers, young and middle-aged men and women, pregnant mothers, suckling infants, children, and so on. . . . We were all the target of the Salvadoran air force and army"(49).

Bourgois survived the assault and returned to the United States, where he described his experience in expert testimony to Congress, an opinion editorial, and an interview with the *Washington Post*: "A young woman gave birth on the sec-ond night of our flight. She was up and running for her life the next day, along with the rest of us. Those of us who were young and healthy were lucky. It was the law of survival at its cruelest: the slow runners and the elderly were killed" (50).

Shortly thereafter, Bourgois was accused of having violated the ethics of anthropology by: illegally crossing a border; not notifying his dissertation com-mittee of his decision to explore a new and potentially dangerous research site; violating the privacy of research subjects (including those soldiers shooting at Bourgois and the other civilians from helicopters) by contacting the media and human rights groups; and potentially jeopardizing future research opportuni-ties for colleagues in Honduras and El Salvador by violating immigration laws and "calling attention to government repression in public forums" (50). Signif-icantly, as Bourgois writes, "had I not gone to the media with my testimony of human rights violations, anthropological ethics would not have been violated in as serious a manner. . . . By remaining silent I would not have violated anyone's rights to privacy nor have threatened my colleagues' access to the field, nor offended my host country" (50). Nonetheless, Bourgois was obliged by his "own personal sense of moral responsibility . . . to provide public testimony" (50). Although perspectives on the professional responsibility of the researcher in the field have shifted significantly since Bourgois's experience in El Salvador, anthropologists and other social scientists continue to struggle with these ethi-cal issues. Indeed, as a founding editor of the University of California's Public Anthropology Series, Bourgois himself has remained a public intellectual at the forefront of scholarly endeavors in engaged research.

How do ethics, scholarship, and the rights of communities collide? How do ethical obligations of the researcher shift in war zones and areas of ongoing con-flict? How does this affect one's scholarship and one's own worldview? And what are the implications for the academy? Advocacy, activism, and the response of the academy are the fault lines of engaged anthropology. Philippe Bourgois, like other public intellectuals before and after him, challenges narrow interpreta-tions of anthropological ethics "premised on a highly political assertion that unequal power relations are not particularly relevant to our research" (51). Although the recent scholarly emphasis on public anthropology and activist anthropology might indicate that these concerns are new, Bourgois and other engaged researchers are following a tradition of public critique largely begun by people of color, immigrants, and women who have often been on the front lines of public debates challenging unequal power relations (Dubois 2005; Wells 1912; Malcolm X 1965; Davis 1983; Said 1978; Arendt 1968; Yasui 1987).

Politics, Ethics, and Advocacy

Anthropologists have raised ethical issues relating to advocacy and politics since the early twentieth century. For example, during World War I, Franz Boas condemned anthropologists spying for the U.S. government. And during World War II, Malinowski warned that anthropologists "should not act as spy or agent provocateur," but rather "should equally study the motives, intentions, and ways of action of the European community" (Pels 1999). In the 1990s, ethical codes in anthropology became hotly debated topics in anthropological associations in the United States, Britain, Holland, Sweden, Germany, Denmark, and France (1). In his "Prehistory of Ethical Codes in Anthropology," Peter Pels suggests that "the cultural politics of modern ethics is built around the discursive oscillation between the absolute denial of politics that is implied by ethical standards, and the equally absolute affirmation of politics that the necessarily partial use of these ethical standards bring with it" (2).

Indeed, a case in point appears in the 1971 American Anthropological Association Code of Ethics: the section on Responsibility to the Public, which affirms the politics of research by highlighting the professional obligation of researchers to contribute their expertise to public policy debates. The 1971 code states: "As people who devote their professional lives to understanding people, anthropologists bear a positive responsibility to speak out publicly, both individually and collectively, on what they know and what they believe as a result of their professional expertise gained in the study of human beings. That is, they bear a professional responsibility to contribute to an 'adequate definition of reality' upon which public opinion and public policy may be based" (AAA 1971). In the Responsibility to the Public section of the revised 1998 Code of Ethics, what had been a "positive responsibility to speak out publicly" became optional—here, the discursive oscillation to which Pels refers. In place of the "positive responsibility," the 1998 Code stated that: "Anthropological researchers should make the results of their research appropriately available to sponsors, students, decision makers, and other non-anthropologists. . . . Anthropologists may choose to move beyond disseminating research results to a position of advocacy. This is an individual decision, but not an ethical responsibility" (AAA 1998).

Thus, while recognizing the politics of inequality that might drive the researcher to take an ethical position, the 1998 code makes the ethical responsibility "optional." Yet, as Pels points out, "Western ethics discourse is not only suffused with notions of rights, responsibility and individual freedom, but also of protest (against illegitimate arrogations of rights) and unmasking (of false ethical frameworks and identities)." Citing Foucault's work on truth and power, he further challenges us to recognize that the relationship between politics and ethics becomes all the more complex when claims to "truth, openness and objectivity that are grounded *scientifically*" (emphasis in original) are brought into the mix because "truth shares with ethics the need for individual responsibility" (3).

In *Fearless Speech*, Michel Foucault traced a genealogy of truth as a societal concept back to the writings of Euripides and the practice in ancient Athenian democracy. He argued that truth, rather than being defined by a Cartesian system of evidence, is grounded in the risk one will take to speak truth to power out of a sense of duty. Within this schema, the requisite characteristics of truth are: courage in the face of danger, a duty to speak, risk in speaking, speaking to power, and a social or moral status from which to speak the truth (2001: 11–32). In this way truth goes far beyond breaking official silence, because underlying the duty to speak the truth is the belief that there is a corrective quality to truth when it is spoken to power (Sanford 2004). And truth can be politically transformative because "truth is a thing of the world: it is produced only by virtue of multiple forms of constraint. And it has regular effects of power" (Foucault 2001). Thus it is not surprising that issues of truth and power permeate most aspects of field research from methodology to writing ethnography. As Skidmore poignantly notes about her work with frightened Burmese citizens in her chapter in this volume, "The bond formed between anthropologist and informant is necessarily deep as we are both in danger when we speak truth to each other." And these truths bring a significant weight of responsibility to the anthropologist and worry to informants because "Burmese people must trust that I will safely take my notes out of the country and that I will never identify them or put their family into jeopardy. Sometimes this causes a large amount of anxiety, especially when the cities are undergoing curfew or other heightened 'security' measures." Reflecting on the implications of research in such conditions, Skidmore asks, "How could one justify a research methodology or project in contemporary Burma in which these turbulent lives are peripheral to the research questions at hand?"

In his work on the Ok Tedi Mine in Papua New Guinea, Stuart Kirsch suggests that "activism is the logical extension of the commitment to reciprocity that underlies the practice of anthropology" (2002: 178). Kirsch reminds us that our first commitment is to the communities in which we work. Further, he makes a convincing argument for the uses of anthropological field research in local struggles for social justice—particularly struggles with large transnational corporations. Focusing on his participation in a legal and political campaign to stop ongoing pollution of rivers and forests as well as assist communities in gaining compensation for damages already caused by the mines that were dumping more than 80,000 tons of tailings and other mine wastes into the local river systems each day, Kirsch makes a compelling argument about the inextricable links between ethics and advocacy. Following Strathern and Stewart (2000: 55), he suggests that the recognition of proprietary rights of communities to knowledge that was produced "*in interaction with the communities themselves*" (emphasis in original) clarifies the obligations of anthropologists to the communities who have contributed to the anthropologist's understanding of local conditions and interests. He concludes that "the resulting commitments may mandate engagement and advocacy on our part, rather than a scholarly, neutral stance. The notions of right and wrong can be invoked not only in relation to the truth, but also with regard to the cause of social justice" (2002: 193). In this volume, the contributors consciously struggle with notions of truth and social justice, especially the conflicting truths of those with power and those who are marginalized by it. In the end, our research has taken us to places of engagement regardless of our initial intentions. Our experiences in the practice of anthropology point to ethical engagement as a primary responsibility of the researcher rather than an optional mode of dissemination.

Anthropology and Unequal Power Relations

This book is a meditation on the contradictions one confronts when conducting field research in zones of social conflict and in ambient violence—the very terrain of unequal power relations and struggles for social justice. Through ethnographies of survival, the authors offer their own reflections on the role of anthropology. These reflections are themselves grounded in engaged research with survivors of war, occupation, marginalization, incarceration, displacement, dispossession, and massacres in Africa (Angel-Ajani), Italy (Angel-Ajani), Chiapas (Hernandez and Speed), Guatemala (Sanford and Warren), Vietnam (Sanford), Colombia (Sanford and Civico), Palestine (Collins), El Salvador (Silber), Burma (Skidmore), France (Bosia), Cambodia (Culbertson), and the United States (Davis and Bosia). These seemingly disparate themes and sites of field research lead to common thematic underpinnings such as:

- the human experience of rural to urban and forced urban to rural migration
- the limits of political democracy without economic and social reforms
- the lived results of neoliberal development schemes and agrarian colonization projects

In *A History of Bombing*, Sven Lindqvist reminds us that numerical and percentile representations of economic and population growth hide the fact that economic growth is mostly experienced in the already wealthy world, and population growth primarily in poor countries and communities. He writes: "Throughout this century, it has been clear that the standard of living enjoyed in industrial countries cannot be extended to the world's population. We have created a way of life that must always be limited to a few. These few can make up a broad middle class in a few countries and a small upper class in the rest. The members know each other by their buying power. They have a common interest in preserving their privileges, by force if necessary. They, too, are born of violence" (2000: 186).

It is the very unequal power relations produced by wealth that enable anthropologists to travel the world and carry out research. We are few and we are privileged. The authors in this volume struggle with this position of privilege as we seek to understand the marginalization of the communities we study. Moreover, recognition of these unequal power relations enable us to problematize not only the conditions in the communities in which we work but also our own conditions as researchers and our role in these relations of inequality. Our ethnographic method gives us the lived experiences of those hidden behind the numbers of economic and population growth.

Indeed, the authors in this volume go beyond a mere counting of the numbers of dead, disappeared, marginalized, landless, and displaced. Each ethnographic essay brings the people of the field sites back into the conversation with the researcher who self-consciously struggles with the unequal power relations and contradictory privileges of the ethnographer at work in the field. Angel-Ajani writes in this volume: "We fail to fully question the conditions that make our work possible as well as critically assess the consequences of our ethnographic production." These critiques move beyond self-conscious reflections of the researcher in the field to challenge official discourses about development, democracy, and peace-building. They heed Bourgois's call "to venture into the 'real world' not just to 'interview' people but to actually participate in their daily life and to partake of their social and cultural reality" (1990: 45).

Issues of truth, the role of the academic, the contract of testimony, the politics of memory, and the race, gender, age, and social position of the researcher are common points of concern for the authors in this volume. Violence, experience, access, representation, witnessing, and analysis are not abstract theoretical issues for these authors. On the contrary, they are tangible and immediate to the lives of those who live in the communities where we work and they are as much markers for our practice as researchers as they are a framework in which we each try to build an intellectual context in territories where survivors are often denied not only agency but their very subjectivity. On the basis of her work in Burma, Skidmore meticulously details the urgency to document lived experiences of ongoing state violence to prevent academic dismissal of citizen subjectivity—dismissal that ultimately supports the military regime's historical denial. Specifically, she sees ethnography as playing an important role in highlighting the various subjectivities that are recreated under authoritarianism in order to identify the potential forms of political agency. And, as she concludes, "The problem is with speaking to the present, not the past."

There is also a concerted effort to trace our intellectual genealogies and our own lived experience not only as anthropologists and field researchers but also

as political subjects with histories that have shaped us as human beings and as *bias*
anthropologists. Indeed, as Angel-Ajani suggests, perhaps our own subject positions raise different and difficult questions in our research and analysis. Likewise, Hernandez Castillo points to the "double challenge" of academics writing on violence: developing theoretical explanations without losing the meaning of the experience of violence for social subjects. Just as Hernandez Castillo challenges academics to develop intellectual contexts relevant to real life, Angel-Ajani highlights the way scholars often feel forced to "clean up" the messiness of social conflict by combining theory with emotional distancing. With great candor, Angel-Ajani writes, "I know that through the incorporation of 'theory' I have learned to water down difficult emotional moments so as not to appear too sentimental."

Ethnographies of Survival

Each chapter offers a self-reflective essay on engaged observation and the anthropological project, but field research and its representation are at the same time in conversation with what can be called ethnographies of survival. For example, both Collins and Silber reveal the limits of political democracy without economic and social reforms through, respectively, poignant ethnographies of contemporary life marked by regret, detachment, and personal isolation of the former Intifada youth in Palestine and the remarginalization of women survivors through the crushing bureaucracy of democratization in El Salvador. In her work with postrevolutionary women living in a repopulated community in a former combat zone in El Salvador, Silber pushes not only to develop a context but also to maintain the ambiguity and contradiction of postwar El Salvador. Working with former Intifada youth in a Palestinian refugee camp and exploring the contradictions of popular memory of Intifada as a living event, Collins raises similar questions about the "conflict between an idealized (albeit tragic) past and an unsatisfying present." In both cases, as suggested by Angel-Ajani, the lived experiences of survivors offer a path to understanding the production of new subjectivities.

Moreover, as Davis argues in her work with battered women, low-income and poor women, and young girls of color, the most marginalized and silenced members of society are those who live out their lives at the very center of policy. Thus she writes of institutional time and the "peculiar regulation of poor people" through the required meeting of social service mandates—in order to meet one's daily needs, one must submit to the hyperengagement and micromanagement of one's life by social service agencies and a constant ritual of waiting for this engagement or management. It should not, therefore, be surprising that Davis's critique of the neoliberal project at home mirrors the findings of Hernandez in Chiapas or Silber in El Salvador. In each case, poor women experience the very agencies supposedly designed to serve them as vehicles of control and revictimization.

Throughout this volume, the authors meditate on truth, the contract of testimony, the politics of memory, and the moral imperative to witness and listen. These reflections are significant for each of the contributors. Although Skidmore has never lost sight of her positioning as an outsider, living in Burma to conduct field research under the "gaze" of the Office of the Chief of Military Intelligence heightened her identification with Burmese informants as she became fearful of the military regime and, like most Burmese, sought to hide her thoughts, feelings, and actions. To be an engaged anthropologist in such conditions is not to be taken lightly. Skidmore notes that it is not an easy decision and "as the mother of two young children, it is a decision I constantly reevaluate."

Speed writes of her activist position supporting human rights work in Chiapas while simultaneously conducting field research. She acknowledges how her own position as a feminist, anthropologist, and activist enriched her field research and analysis. Seven months pregnant at the time of a brutal massacre in Chiapas that became part of her research, she writes: "Feeling my daughter move in my womb, I felt physically ill with the horror of what had happened. . . . While the violence at Acteal was a message to all, the threat to women specifically edged forcefully to the front of my consciousness." This type of transformative experience for the researcher is implicit in other chapters as well and, sometimes, the researcher is compelled by circumstances to take a position on the veracity of the truth claims of communities in which we work (see, for example, Hernandez, Davis, Angel-Ajani, Sanford, Skidmore, and Bosia). This positioning of the researcher is not without contradiction.

The Politics of Witnessing in War and Pain

In "Excavations of the Heart," I suggest that individual, communal, and national memories of "bare life" (Agamben 1998; Benjamin 1978) in ambient violence offer trajectories of meaning for survivors, perpetrators, bystanders, and others who later come on the scene to witness the reconstruction of everyday life amid the remains of a violent past. Further, it is one's location on a given trajectory of meaning that locates one's structure of understanding—which ultimately shapes the contours of "understandable" truth. This is not a relativistic argument that all truths are equal. Structures of understanding serve as a kind of filter; one that does not always, or easily, allow for the absorption or processing of truth—particularly difficult, painful, grotesque truths that can so rupture the structures of understanding that an individual, communal, or national trajectory of meaning in the world is forever shifted. I consider my own life experiences growing up during the Vietnam War and my field research in Guatemala

[handwritten margin note: Gugulethu – many involvement in PAC – life through apartheid are structure of understanding today Robben Island]

and Colombia to develop a theoretical framework for structures of understanding and argue for engaged anthropology.

Based on her vast experience as researcher and director of the Institute on Violence and Survival at the Virginia Foundation for the Humanities, Roberta Culbertson offers reflections, both philosophical and practical, on the study of postwar cultures. In particular, she underscores the importance of explorations of survival and the contributions these explorations can make to seemingly intractable debates about survival, truth, memory, and reconciliation. Throughout her essay, and like others in the volume (see Collins, Bosia, and Skidmore), the language of memory and identity are cornerstones to her exploration. Just as Collins found incomplete memory to be relevant, Culbertson finds that a "faulty" memory does not negate one's knowledge of place or ability to move through it. She further suggests that because war is an embodied experience, and thus a visceral memory, survivors often experience "perpetual alarm and a sort of half-life of limited hard awareness" after conflict, rather than a sensation of peace. Significantly, Culbertson believes that the perspectives, analytical tools, experience, and perception of engaged researchers can help us to better understand the metaphysical dimensions of survival and, thus, the very world in which we live.

A commonality in these truth-encounters is that researchers working in marginalized communities often find the people with whom they work labeled as subversive, deviant, or criminal. These very stereotypes cast doubt on the veracity of testimonies. Working with African immigrant women incarcerated in Italy, Angel-Ajani found that despite having little knowledge of the operations of carceral systems, society "imagines and even pleasurably envisions powerfully vivid images of crime, criminals, and prison life." Like Hernandez-Castillo, she experienced colleagues doubting the truth of testimonies because the testimonials were given by women in prison, by women labeled as criminal by the state. In "Expert Witness," Angel-Ajani offers a provocative discussion about the anthropologist as witness and the anthropologist as police. Her essay cautions us to remember that the recovery of truth, assembling of evidence, and providing our own testimony before our peers remains a powerful space in anthropology despite ongoing debates about representation and the practice of field research.

In her essay on the politics of engagement in Burma, Skidmore addresses the issues confronted by the engaged anthropologist in Burma and by scholars of Burma in the academy. She provides a self-reflective view of conducting field research under authoritarian rule and points to the easily elided conflicts of interest under which some political scientists with lucrative contracts have conducted "research" for international companies with investment interests in Burma. Not surprisingly, these researchers have provided reports to international lending agencies that urge financial cooperation with Burma's military regime. Skidmore also acknowledges that these same scholars have not only dismissed her ethnographic work about the political subjectivities and social suffering of the Burmese people under dictatorship but have also attacked Skidmore's work as "lurid," "emotive," and "full of dead facts." Skidmore concludes that this type of academic posturing does much violence to Burma and the Burmese people, and makes ethnographic work in Burma all the more important because "being an engaged anthropologist is to advocate for the histories of terror and misery to be retained in the contemporary world." Skidmore's work reminds us that "never again is now" (Kellner 1998: 235).

Lessons from Agents of Change

In "Moral Chronologies: Generation and Popular Memory in a Palestinian Refugee Camp," Collins examines what happens to popular memory when mass mobilization gives way to the logic of political negotiation and state building, and when the generational solidarities of "youth" give way to the economic and social pressures of "adulthood." He presents a collection of personal narratives of former Intifada youth and suggests that, taken as a group, these narratives comprise a moral chronology of the Intifada "that is rooted in a markedly different interpretive framework from the linear, triumphant story associated with official nationalism." It is a poignant moment when he writes of the realization of these former Intifada youth that "while they may not always be young, they may always be refugees, and the suspicion that because of this, they may always be poor."

Michael Bosia uses discursive analysis to refocus research methodologies on the physical experience of the politics of AIDS in "In Our Beds and Our Graves." He argues that any representation of AIDS that removes the physical experience from the center of sexual identity and HIV leaves little opportunity for understanding the emergence of barebacking (intentional intercourse without condoms) and other forms of unsafe sex. He sees a definitive link between testimony and understanding. He suggests that what is revealed in testimony is "the sense of the physical as meaningful, a sensitivity to the body as the location of pain and pleasure, as the origin of social and political ostracism or action." Indeed, he points to the discourse that has removed physical experience from the nature of the disease as the heart of the tension in AIDS politics today, because without physical experience, AIDS politics is no more than a politics of representation.

Significantly, though Bosia is a political scientist, he believes that the tension in AIDS politics today can best be addressed through testimony and ethnography. He writes: "We must avoid theories and sciences that search for the general, simply deconstruct the social, take knowledge for granted, find in the body only the location of subjectivity and thus isolate social action as primarily a creation of social forms." While not discounting the importance of representation, he challenges us to include the physical experiences that "drive our most intimate sense of belonging and community." He argues that "empathy for physical experience gives meaning to our studies of social action."

Many of the ethnographic essays in this volume self-consciously reflect upon the contract of testimony. Aldo Civico's "Portrait of a Paramilitary" may be one of the most disturbing essays on the anthropologist's relationship with so-called informants. Civico takes us through his field experience from the fear of his first clandestine meetings with heavily armed Colombian paramilitaries to the development of a familiar rapport, or even comfortable ease, with a paramilitary leader. He writes of this very personal experience of developing a kind of friendship with and discovering the human dimension of a paramilitary leader who terrorized Colombian villages and barrios and ordered at least one known massacre. Still, he asks himself and his readers, "Is it possible to have benevolent feelings for someone whose ideas and deeds I not only disapprove, but I despise and abhor forcefully?". Civico tells of the reciprocity of listening and reflecting with this paramilitary leader as well as the personal loss he felt when the leader disappeared and was presumably killed. He writes: "After all, participant-observation is not possible without being physically present and personally involved."

Trauma, Violence, and Women's Resistance in Everyday Life

In "Fratricidal War or Ethnocidal Strategy?" Hernandez Castillo carried out field research on a brutal massacre of indigenous women in Chiapas and listened to survivor testimonies of the atrocities and mutilation of female massacre victims. The Mexican media reported on particular cruelties carried out against pregnant women. Soon after, a rumor began to spread that the atrocities were exaggerated by human rights groups and the media. Academic circles picked up these same unsubstantiated rumors and soon the national magazine *Proceso* repeated these rumors as fact. Hernandez found herself compelled to defend the truth. Although she had numerous survivor testimonies, it was autopsy reports that confirmed the atrocities to those who doubted the truth-quality of the testimonials. Hernandez Castillo concludes that the contestation of rumors, practices, and discourses of terror has become a priority in contemporary research.

In "Indigenous Women and Gendered Resistance in the Wake of Acteal," Shannon Speed analyzes the testimonies of women who have participated in acts of resistance. She also interrogates the images of these women—media images that circulated nationally and internationally, as well as official discourse about them. She explores the gendered nature of these indigenous women's acts of resistance and how they have been understood and responded to in within a gendered ordering of the world and their significance for women's rights in Chiapas and beyond. As she draws on debates in new social movement theory, feminist theory, and resistance theory, she argues that: women's resistance is a gendered response to gendered violence; this resistance constitutes a new form of participatory citizenship that has emerged in new political spaces resulting from the Zapatista uprising; indigenous women's resistance has blurred binary categories such as feminine and feminist; and public discourses about women's resistance silenced both the voices and the experiences of those involved in the resistance. Speed's insistence on the centrality and importance of a gendered analysis resonates with Hernandez-Castillo's research in Chiapas and also with Silber's experience in postwar El Salvador. Like Speed, both Hernandez Castillo and Silber offer an analysis of institutional violence where the state has little to no regard for the lives and personal integrity of civilians—particularly women.

On the basis of extensive ethnographic research in the former conflict zone of Chalatenango, El Salvador, Irina Carlota Silber responds to Angel-Ajani's concern about cleaning up ethnography for the academy. Silber challenges those who would compartmentalize former revolutionary women as either "agentless victims" or "heroic mother fighters." She resists the ease with which others have written about the "demoralization of women's participation" as she offers a "corrective to more celebratory work on women's social movements." She fills the gap between these binary representations by highlighting the gendered limitations of societal reconstruction in postwar El Salvador. She heeds Bourgois's call "to check the impulse to sanitize and instead clarify the chains of causality that link structural, political, and symbolic violence in the production of everyday violence" (2001: 29–30). She does this by juxtaposing the societal construction of "deviant community women" to the ambiguities of unresolved injustices of the past with the bureaucracy-laden dangers and opportunities of the new democracy. Like Collins, Silber finds the deepest community contestation in the gendered coming-of-age stories shared in testimonies of survival. Like Angel-Ajani, she sees new subjectivities in lived experiences.

The Engaged Observer: Inside and Outside the Academy

The essays in this fourth and final section of the book offer two different entry points to engaged anthropology: Kay Warren meditates on the dilemmas presented by engaged anthropology, and Dana-Ain Davis makes a passionate case for politically engaged anthropology.

Seeking to take on the dilemmas confronting engaged anthropology, Kay Warren reaffirms the "importance of the ongoing examination of our roles as anthropologists and the sociopolitical contexts from which our work emerges." In the same way that Collins notes the importance of the generation of community members when collecting field testimonies, Warren points to the significant impact that our own historico-intellectual generation plays in how we conduct anthropological analysis and how we teach anthropology. She suggests a genealogical approach to theory and practice as a means for recognizing how our own generational belonging affects our work. She expresses a concern that the work of anthropology (a concern found in other disciplines as well) has become regionally compartmentalized, and notes with irony that the same people uninterested in reading "outside their region" are "eagerly and critically consuming works on glob-alization." No doubt, we must cross the borders of our own area literature to better understand our discipline as well as the world in which we live.

In the final essay of this volume, Dana-Ain Davis challenges us to cross theo-retical borders as well, as she interrogates her own positioning as a black feminist anthropologist and politically engaged academic. In this way, she responds to War-ren's call to place ourselves generationally through our own intellectual genealo-gies and further challenges us to recognize our responsibility to bring our research to bear in the service of social change when our agendas are tied to issues of inequity. She thoughtfully describes the relationship between academics and practice in her own research experiences as an illustration of politically engaged anthropology. Like others in this volume, she consciously seeks to challenge the "homogenous views" of the communities in which she works—specifically the ways in which women on welfare, black women, and battered women are por-trayed in the academy and beyond. Davis acknowledges that her work as a politi-cally engaged anthropologist began the moment she was asked to do something to help make a difference. She explains, "My accountability was a moral and political issue, not so much because I am in academia, but rather because my responsibil-ity as a moral agent is no different from the responsibilities of others. . . . I am, first and foremost, a person concerned about fairness and equity. Concerned that the voices of those on the margins be centered."

Engaged Anthropology

As Collins notes in his work on Intifada youth, Alessandro Portelli's observation about the timing of the researcher in the life of the research subject can produce different outcomes, analyses, and reflections on the part of the research subject. Pointing to scholars who survived academia marked by the Cold War, Warren indicates that analytic shifts can be found in research and its representation depending upon the generation of the scholar. Thus timing in the life of both the researcher and the research subject may yield different outcomes for each. Still, there is an underlying resonance cutting across all the chapters of this book from Vietnam to Guatemala, from Palestine to Burma, from Cambodia to Italy, from former Intifada youth to Zapatista women, from gay men in Paris to poor women in New York, from former Salvadoran revolutionary women to Colombian para-militaries; that resonance is the desire to be heard and contest official histories. In this way, the chapters of this book also serve to mediate between politics and the economy, the Cold War and globalization, and neoliberal triumph and utopian dreams of revolution. The accretion of marginalized voices transforms experience into collective memory. The representation of lived experience in engaged anthropology subverts official memory, institutional time, and homog-enized culture. As Tischler Visquerra suggests, the subversion of official time opens the door to a multiplicity of time and experience which, in turn, allows for the inclusion of diverse subjectivities with new visions of the past, present, and future (2005). In this way, changing political, economic, and cultural subject positions are central to the lived experiences represented in this volume.

It seems that, as many of the authors in this volume suggest, in attempts to encapsulate a culture, anthropologists often seek to categorize and compartmentalize rather than problematize experience. This is particularly dangerous when one seeks to reveal truths about violence, survival, and social conflict, for it is a slippery slope to reifying survival, difference, and terror, and thereby eliminating all possibilities for understanding. As Davis indicates, advocacy and activism, if not the initial impetus for research in zones of social conflict, are its inevitable outcome when one achieves an understanding of the everyday lived experience of violence and survival. It is not uncommon within the academy for lived experience to be dismissed as unscientific or not relevant to real, objective scholarship. This is completely backward, because it is the academy that needs to be relevant to the reality of lived experience. Advocacy and activism do not diminish the validity of one's scholarly research. On the contrary, activist scholarship reminds us that all research is inherently political—even, and perhaps especially, that scholarship presented under the guise of "objectivity," which is really no more than a veiled defense of the status quo. And, as Bourgois reminds us, the challenge of ethnography is to "elucidate the causal chains and gendered linkages in the continuum of violence that buttresses inequality in the Post-Cold War era" (2001: 5).

REFERENCES

AAA (American Anthropological Association). 1971. "Statements on Ethics". http://www. aaanet.org/stmts/ethstmnt.htm.

——. 1998. "Code of Ethics of the American Anthropological Association Approved June 1998." http://www.aaanet.org/committees/ethics/ethcode.htm.

Agamben, Giorgio. 1988. *Homo Sacer: Sovereign Power and Bare Life*. Stanford: Stanford University Press, 1998.

Arendt, Hannah. 1968. *The Origins of Totalitarianism*. New York: Harcourt.

Benjamin, Walter. 1978. "Critique of Violence." Translated by Edmund Jephcott. In *Walter Benjamin: Reflections*, edited by Peter Demetz. New York: Schocken Books.

Bourgois, Philippe. 1990. "Confronting Anthropological Ethics: Ethnographic Lessons from Central America," *Journal of Peace Research* 27.1: 43–54.

——. 2001. "The Power of Violence in War and Peace: Post-Cold War Lessons from El Salvador" *Ethnography* 2.1: 5–37.

Davis, Angela. 1983. *Women, Race, and Class*. New York: Vintage Books.

Dubois, W.E.B. 2005. *The Souls of Black Folks*. New York: Simon and Schuster.

Foucault, Michel. 1980. *Power and Knowledge: Selected Interviews and Other Writings*. New York: Random House.

——. 2001. *Fearless Speech*. Los Angeles: Semiotext(e).

Grabe, Vera. 2001. *Razones de Vida*. Bogota: Editorial Planeta.

Kellner, Hans. 1998. "'Never Again' Is Now." *In History and Theory*, edited by Brian Fay, Phillip Pomper, and Richard Vann. Malden, Mass.: Blackwell.

Kirsch, Stuart. 2002. "Anthropology and Advocacy: A Case Study against the Campaign of the Ok Tedi Mine." *Critique of Anthropology* 22.2: 175–200.

Lindqvist, Sven. 2000. *A History of Bombing.* New York: New Press.

Malcolm X. 1965. *Malcolm X Speaks: Selected Speeches and Statements.* New York: Merit Publishers and Betty Shabaz.

Nordstrom, Carolyn. 2004. *Shadows of War: Violence, Power, and International Profiteering in the Twenty-First Century.* Berkeley: University of California Press.

Osorio Perez, Flor Edilma. Forthcoming. "From Ruptures to Uncertain New Beginnings: Lessons of Persistence from the Displaced in Colombia's War." In *Markings: Violence and Everyday Life in Colombia*, edited by Victoria Sanford.

Pels, Peter. 1999. *Professions of Duplexity: A Prehistory of Ethical Codes in Anthropology.* http://www2.fmg.uva.nl/gm/articles/pp1999.htm.

Said, Edward. 1978. *Orientalism.* New York: Vintage Books.

Sanford, Victoria. 2004 "Contesting Displacement in Colombia: Citizenship and State Sovereignty at the Margins." In *Anthropology in the Margins of the State*, edited by Veena Das and Deborah Poole. Santa Fe: School of American Research.

Strathern, Andrew, and Pamela Stewart. 2000. "Creating Difference: A Contemporary Affiliation Drama in the Highlands of New Guinea." *Journal of the Royal Anthropological Institute* 6.1: 1–15.

Tischler Visquerra. 2005. *Memoria, Tiempo y Sujeto.* Guatemala City: FyG Editores and Instituto de Ciencias Sociales y Humanidades BUAP.

Wells, Ida. 1912. *Ida B. Wells Tells about Lynchings.* New York: African Islamic Mission.

Yasui, Robert. 1987. *The Yasui Family of Hood River, Oregon.* Yasui Desktop Publishing.

PART I

The Politics of Witnessing in War and Pain

1

Excavations of the Heart

Reflections on Truth, Memory, and Structures of Understanding

VICTORIA SANFORD

It is possible to develop an intimacy
with the most disturbing of things.

–Kazuo Ishiguro, *A Pale View of Hills*

A Village in My Mind

The house is the first image. It stands alone. Light brown tufts of grass tightly thatched over bamboo walls. There is a simple awning at the entrance, which has no door. A promise of emptiness within. This is the close-up of the hut. My image. My memory of his memory. It is in a village. Surrounded by green rice paddies and an enormous clear blue sky.[1]

The house is always empty, eerily untouched. There is pandemonium in the village. Women screaming and running with their children. Explosions and billowing smoke that fills the sky. The women and children are small. Smaller still as they run past the burning huts. The men in green camouflage are giants. Soldiers outnumber villagers. They wear sunglasses and helmets. The fleeing women wear delicate *mu las* (Vietnamese leaf hats) that hang by a string from the front of their necks and bounce off the backs of their simple peasant clothing as they try to flee. The men are U.S. soldiers. They shout louder than the women cry. I know their voices will triumph. Few villagers will escape. All the villages burn. This is any village, anytime, anywhere. This is a village in Vietnam. This is the image he gave to me.

He was a twenty-six-year-old war veteran. In 1972, after three years as a foot soldier in Vietnam, the only person my brother-in-law trusted with his confessions was a twelve-year-old girl. Each night, he drank to numb the pain of booby-trapped children, burned villages, and mass graves. In his stupor, he would describe each army action and always with great detail. The child accepting the gift. The explosion. Setting fire to the thatched roof. Sometimes he laughed and seemed to delight in my horror. Those days I hated him. But just as often as he laughed, there were nights when he cried, gasping for air and choking on his words. He told me he did not want to kill anyone; that he had to tell someone the truth, that I was the only one who would listen and understand. On those nights, I felt as much sorrow for him as I felt for the people in that village. It was a crescendo of powerlessness. Mine, because I could not make his pain go away. His, because he could not forget his crimes. The villagers, because they could not escape.

I was his confidant. Through his drunken tirades, I learned of the vulnerability and fear of the victimizer. Of the bitterness of shame. The powerlessness of guilt. These encounters were a foreign invasion that ruptured the security of my world. An emotional violence to the dailiness of my childhood. Each night, he would turn on the television, tune in to *Star Trek*, and start to drink. As the Starship Enterprise ventured out into unknown galaxies, my brother-in-law described how U.S. soldiers tricked Vietnamese children into carrying booby-trapped packages back to their village; how the exploding package ripped up the children, scattering their body parts. He told me that girls my age prostituted themselves for food, but that often these girl prostitutes were traps for U.S. soldiers. In my mind, Vietnam was a place where unarmed, hungry children frightened big American men who wore grenades around their waists and carried machine guns.

I was never afraid of him. I never avoided these conversations. I never told anyone about them. Despite my horror at his crimes, I was drawn to his conflicting representations of truth and meaning, and the emotional power of my own visceral responses. I hated him when he laughed. I pitied him when he cried. In the crescendo of powerlessness, I felt the privilege of being his confessor. His stories introduced what Primo Levi called the "grey zone" into the neat black-and-white world of "the domino theory and stopping communism" (a.k.a. "why we were in Vietnam") which I was given at school and by the television news over dinner each night. I felt the power of accompanying him as he wrested from oblivion his contradictory truths: the fears, secrets, and vulnerabilities of U.S. soldiers in Vietnam.

Yet within a few years, my memories of his memories faded with his departure from my life through alcoholism and divorce. I used to believe that he got drunk to forget Vietnam. Now, I believe he drank to remember. Only the anesthesia of alcohol allowed him the safe space necessary for memory. Only through the numbing of self-medication was he able to find the strength to confront oblivion—his own, his family's, his country's. Three decades later, I still carry with me the image of that village and struggle to understand truth, memory, and oblivion.

As an anthropologist conducting research on human rights, truth, and memory in Guatemala, my research has focused on the exhumation of clandestine cemeteries in isolated Maya villages (Sanford 2003a and 2003b). To participate in the exhumation of a clandestine cemetery is to walk on the edge that divides memory from oblivion. Massacre survivors, forensic anthropologists, and international human rights advocates, each in our own way, fight the oblivion of Guatemala's social memory through excavations of the heart by giving and witnessing testimonies of survival, and through exhumations of mass graves of massacre victims that provide forensic evidence and scientific corroboration to survivor testimonies.

In this chapter I explore truth and memory through ongoing narratives of the Vietnam war, La Violencia in Guatemala, and contemporary efforts to come to terms with each. I suggest that individual, communal, and national memories of "bare life" (Benjamin 1978; Agamben 1998) in ambient violence offer trajectories of meaning for survivors, perpetrators, bystanders, and others who later come on the scene to witness the reconstruction of everyday life amid the remains of a violent past.[2] Further, I suggest that one's location on a given trajectory of meaning determines one's structure of understanding—which ultimately shapes the contours of "understandable" truth. This is not a relativistic argument that all truths are equal. Rather, I am suggesting that structures of understanding serve as a kind of filter; one that does not always, or easily, allow for the absorption or processing of truth—particularly difficult, painful, grotesque truths that can so rupture the structures of understanding that an individual, communal, or national trajectory of meaning in the world is forever shifted.[3] Finally, I want to propose that neither structures of understanding nor trajectories of meaning are stagnant rather they are in constant flux and often mutually redefining motion, which challenges the rules of engagement for (and has serious implications for the responsibilities of) researchers and advocates alike. With these thoughts in mind, I close this chapter with some reflections on the challenges the current war in Colombia presents to engaged research and public anthropology.

Exhuming Truth in Rural Guatemala

Evidence produced by exhumations is legally recognized. It is concrete. It is real. You can touch it. It is the bones of the victims we pull out of the earth. In the case of Plan de Sánchez, like most massacres, the army claimed there had been a battle with the EGP (Guerrilla Army of the Poor-Ejército Guerrillero de los Pobres). The 1994 exhumations clearly showed that the vast majority of the 168 victims of the 1982 massacre were women, children, and the elderly. Moreover, the forensic evidence unquestionably proved that skeletons in the grave were victims of a massacre, not an armed confrontation.

Yet, even as bones are pulled from the earth and analyzed scientifically, the quantification of truth remains ethereal. Every day that I have spent in exhumations in villages throughout rural Guatemala, campesinos from other villages (elderly women, elderly men, young women and men, children, entire families) have come to witness the excavation of the graves.[4] Inevitably, they would tell me that they needed an exhumation in their village because they too had suffered a massacre. I would always ask them how many people had died, and the response was always the same: "Casi todos" (nearly everyone). Sometimes they meant all of the men in their family. Sometimes they meant all of the women. Sometimes they meant nearly everyone in their village had been killed.

"A True War Story Is Never Moral"

In *The Things They Carried*, Tim O'Brien writes, "You can tell a true war story if it embarrasses you. If you don't care for obscenity, you don't care for truth" (1990:77). It was the obscenity of truth that challenged our society to come to terms (however haltingly and incompletely) with U.S. intervention in Vietnam. The national trajectory of meaning of the Vietnam war helped to reshape national structures of understanding of war. At its most simplistic and least objectionable, or in other words as a product of the media for mass consumption, the lessons of Vietnam were simple: first, U.S. involvement in war should not involve the loss of life for young U.S. soldiers; second, successful military intervention would be measured by military objectives and limiting the loss of life of U.S. soldiers. A third, more critical lesson challenges the mass destruction of civilian lives and complete decimation of Vietnamese villages and their inhabitants, which has implications for contemporary proxy wars regardless of the level of involvement of U.S. soldiers. Despite popular emphasis on lessons one and two, the critical lesson seeps in and out of popular memory through films like *Apocalypse Now*, *Full Metal Jacket*, *Platoon*, and eyewitness nonfiction and fictional accounts such as *Dispatches* (journalistic nonfiction, Herr 1991), *The Things They Carried* (U.S. soldier's "nonfiction" novel), and *The Sorrow of War* (North Vietnamese soldier's novel, Ninh 1993). It is this seepage that has pushed national trajectories of meaning to such a degree that it is possible at one and the same time to believe that it was both wrong and inevitable to kill women, children, elderly, and other unarmed civilians. This seepage also allows for recognition of the My Lai massacre, but the emphasis on lessons one and two inhibits a national recognition of the ordinariness of My Lai and instead leaves it in the national consciousness as an ambiguous and tragic example of "when things go wrong." Thus revelations in April 2001 about former senator and current New School University president Bob Kerrey leading his squadron of Navy Seals into the Vietnamese village of Thanh Phong and killing thirteen to twenty unarmed women, children, and elderly was framed in the *New York Times Magazine*, which broke the story, as "What Happened in Thanh Phong—On the night of Feb. 25, 1969, in a tiny Vietnamese hamlet, something went horribly wrong" (Vistica 2001).

Although the exact circumstances of the mass killing are contentiously disputed by Kerrey, his former squad members, and at least one survivor/witness, what happened in Thanh Phong is a true war story regardless of if, when, and how Kerrey gave the order, how far away the shooting began, if enemy fire was received before the squadron fired, if Kerrey helped hold down an elderly man as he was stabbed to death, or if the squadron rounded up women, children, and the elderly and then killed them. What happened in Thanh Phong is a true war story because "you can tell a true war story by the way it never seems to end. Not then, not ever" (O'Brien 1990: 83). This recent revelation reminds the U.S. public that Vietnam is a true war story that never ended for Kerrey, the members of his squad, or the American people—and certainly not for the Vietnamese who survived. Largely missing from analyses of contradictory truths and memories of the Thanh Phong massacre are the voices of survivors, and the lone survivor's voice that is heard is, for the most part, discounted.

Pham Thi Lanh is a sixty-two-year-old woman who survived the Navy Seals' massacre in Thanh Phong. More than three decades later, she was interviewed by *60 Minutes II* about the incident, and her testimony affirmed claims by Gerhard Klann, one of Kerrey's former commandos, who has charged Kerrey with ordering the slaughter. In the *60 Minutes II* interview, Lanh said she saw the squad use knives and guns to murder women, children, and an elderly man. When interviewed by *Time*, she gave the same testimony, then added that she had not actually seen the killing and in the words of *Time*, "had *only* [my emphasis] heard the screams [of those being killed] and later seen the bodies" (Johnson 2001). Lanh is quoted as saying, "I heard screams, 'Help! They're killing us!' So, I crept quietly outside, and I saw them there, lying dead with their heads nearly cut off." *Time* writer Kay Johnson concludes, "What isn't clear is whether villager Pham Thi Lanh is an honest witness, a propagandist, or just an old woman with hazy memories." The same article notes that Kerrey admits that "an atrocity took place," but "swears it was accidental." Then, goes on to say that Kerrey "and his supporters argue that Lanh's account shouldn't be believed because she was a communist revolutionary married to a Viet Cong soldier, and because her stories have been offered to journalists while Vietnamese government officials sat nearby." Among those killed by Kerrey and his squad were Lanh's three sisters, a sister-in-law, and four of her nieces and nephews. The day after the massacre, Lanh and several other villagers dug a mass grave where they buried her relatives and the others killed by Kerrey's squad. "You can tell a true war story if you just keep on telling it. . . . [A] true war story is never about war. . . . It's about love and memory. It's about sorrow . . . and people who never listen" (O'Brien 1990: 91).

Kerrey's Memories, Kerrey's Anguish

Though Kerrey recognizes that he could be subject to court-martial if the Pentagon were to pursue an investigation of the Thanh Phong massacre, he claims that he did not come forward with this case earlier because he "did not want to make his own personal anguish public any more than other Americans want to dredge up the nation's agony again" (Johnson 2001). To Gerhard Klann's testimony that Kerrey ordered the killings, personally helped Klann cut the throat of an elderly victim, and that no incoming fire prompted the carnage, Kerrey says, "Klann's got a memory of what happened. I've got a memory of what happened. They're both vivid. They're both awful." When first asked by Gregory Vistica in 1998 about Klann's revelations, Kerrey said, "It's not my recollection of how it happened. I'm not going to make this worse by questioning somebody else's memory of it. But you would operate independently in this type of situation. I mean, it would not surprise me if things were going on away from my line of sight that were different than what I was doing." For Vistica's 2001 *New York Times Magazine* article, "Kerrey began to qualify his original story," then, "later, after that interview and as we were departing, Kerrey attacked Klann's credibility." (Vistica 2001: 66). If Kerrey cast doubt on the credibility and/or self-interest of Klann and survivor Lanh, he also carved out a space of flexible inaccuracy for himself by saying, "It's entirely possible that I'm blocking a lot of it out" (54).[5] Thus in Kerrey's structure of understanding, any holes in his story, unlike any in Lanh's or Klann's, would be due to trauma rather than lack of credibility.

In 1998, Kerrey told Vistica, "There's a part of me that wants to say to you all the memories that I've got are my memories, and I'm not going to talk about them. We thought we were going to fight for the American people. We came back to find out that the American people didn't want us to do it. And ever since that time we've been poked, prodded, bent, spindled, mutilated, and I don't like it. I've got a right to say to you, it's none of your damned business. I carry memories of what I did, and I survive and live based upon lots of different mechanisms" (51–52). Though initially reluctant, Kerrey eventually talked "willingly," but "not because a public accounting will help me, but because it just might help someone else" (52). Further, Kerrey said, "It's going to be very interesting to see the reactions to the story. I mean, because basically you're talking about a man who killed innocent civilians" (52). Nonetheless, Kerrey seized the opportunity to cast doubt on the victims themselves. Referring to the names of fallen U.S. soldiers listed on the Vietnam Memorial in Washington, he said, "There are people on the wall because they didn't realize a woman or a child could be carrying a gun" (68).

"In other cases you can't even tell a true war story. Sometimes it's just beyond telling" (O'Brien 1990: 79). Here, O'Brien is playing with words. It is not about our ability to detect a true war story; rather it is about the teller's ability to communicate it. Here, I would suggest that both trajectories of meaning and structures of understanding come into play. Although Kerrey is right that his memories are his own, he knows that he may ultimately be subjected to laws that punish war crimes and compel testimony. His story is a true war story even if it is beyond his telling. I suggest it is beyond his telling because his presentation is limited to the structure of understanding of the soldier's story, which not only excludes but also negates the survivor's structure of understanding.

In media coverage of his story, beyond Gerhard Klann's condemnation of the massacre in which he participated, the lone voice of opposition in the U.S. comes from Barry Romo, national coordinator of Vietnam Veterans against the War. "Everything is backwards," Romo told *Time.* "People shouldn't be looking at Kerrey as a victim but at the families of the Vietnamese who were killed. If Kerrey killed them by accident, and knew it, then he owed them some reparation. If he did line them up and shoot them, then you don't get away with murder because you wear a uniform" (Vistica 2001: 31). Thus, Romo seeks to create a new trajectory of meaning which allows for incorporation of both the soldier's and the survivor's structure of understanding.

Romo has a point. The U.S. government and media support the punishment of war criminals when they are Serb, Iraqi, or members of Al Qaeda, but Kerrey is portrayed as an anguished victim (which from a humanistic perspective he was, in that all youth who are thrown into war are victims), but Kerrey and the other members of his squad were also victimizers (and war criminals under international humanitarian law). Moreover, the rhetoric of suspicious peasants, women, and children neither began nor ended in Vietnam. This same rhetoric was used by the CIA, which conflated political affiliation with ethnic identity in order to justify the annihilation of complete indigenous peasant communities in Guatemala: "The well-documented belief by the army that the entire Ixil Indian population is pro-EGP hase created a situation in which the army can be expected to give no quarter to combatants and non-combatants alike" (CIA 1982, 3). I have never been to Vietnam and I don't know Bob Kerrey or Pham Thi Lanh. Still, I want to think about how different our national structure of understanding would be if we honored the survivor's testimony instead of discounting it because she is a Vietnamese peasant woman whose husband may have been a Viet Cong soldier. This isn't such a stretch. Indeed, we can use the context of the U.S. soldier's experience, our national trajectory of meaning (which is widely regarded to have traumatized Kerrey and others) to think for a moment about the space in which Pham Thi Lanh and the other unarmed women, children, and elderly were trying to carry on some semblance of daily life or, in the words of Agamben, "bare life" (1998).

Vietnam war correspondent Michael Herr writes that the U.S. soldiers in Vietnam and their military actions were "charged with hatred and grounded in fear of the Vietnamese" (1991: 39). According to the *New York Times Book Review,* Herr's highly acclaimed book *Dispatches* is "the best book to have been written about the Vietnam War." As a correspondent, Herr writes, "I stood as close to them [the U.S. soldiers] as I could without actually being one of them and then I stood as far back as I could without leaving the planet. Disgust doesn't begin to describe what they made me feel, they threw people out of helicopters, tied people up and put dogs on them" (67). One soldier told him, "We had a gook and we was gonna skin him" (66).[6] Another said, "We'd rip out the hedges and burn the hootches and blow all the wells and kill every chicken, pig, and cow in the whole fucking village" (29). Marines pointed out one man to Herr and "swore to God they'd seen him bayonet a wounded North Vietnamese soldier and then lick the knife clean" (35). Herr wrote about the "kid who mailed a gook ear home to his girl and could not understand why she had stopped writing him" (148). Another soldier told Herr, "I'm so fuckin' good 'n' that ain' no shit, neither. Got me one hunnert 'n' fifty-se'en [157] gooks kilt. 'N' fifty caribou. Them're all certified" (179). "It comes down to gut instinct," writes Tim O'Brien. "A true war story, if truly told, makes the stomach believe" (84).

Memory, Oblivion, and Truth(s)

True war stories are not limited to Vietnam, and my stomach believed in Guatemala from the very first day I began to work with the forensic team in Plan de Sánchez, where nausea, dizziness, and sweaty hands accompanied me as I listened to survivor testimonies. During the second week of work, a delegation of some forty Achi-Maya women and one elderly man came to our work site early in the morning on June 28, 1994.[7] Doña María appeared to be the leader of the group, although her father Don Miguel was treated with great deference by the entire group. They had walked six hours from Xococ, a village in the valley on the other side of the mountain, to report that on June 26 Xococ civil patrollers had damaged several sites of clandestine cemeteries in their village.[8] Doña María feared the civil patrol had removed skeletal remains in an effort to destroy any evidence that might subsequently be uncovered should an exhumation take place in Xococ in the future. They came to request that the forensic team investigate the sites to determine if the remains of their loved ones had been taken.

That same morning, I accompanied several members of the forensic team, the local justice of the peace, and the Xococ delegation to survey the grave sites. Plants used by the survivors to mark the graves had been cleared. Though the graves had obviously been disturbed and fragments of a human rib were found mixed with topsoil, the team determined that the skeletons had not been removed. The women asked the justice of the peace to put up an official sign like the one at our work site in Plan de Sánchez, which said: "Do Not Touch. Site of Legal Investigation by Order of the Justice of the Peace under Protection of the National Police." The judge explained that the sign could only be issued by the court when an exhumation began. He also commented on the conspicuous absence of the men of Xococ. The women explained they were absent because of the civil patrol. They said that while some men from Xococ wanted the graves exhumed, the military commissioner did not.[9] Thus, no patrollers accompanied the team on the site visit because those who did not oppose the exhumation feared those who did.

As an anthropologist, I was very interested in meeting with and interviewing these women from Xococ because of their courage in organizing themselves to request an exhumation against the will of the men in their community. When I mentioned my interest in returning to Xococ to interview the widows, Doña María enthusiastically supported the idea. "All you need to do is come to the village plaza, use the megaphone, and say, 'que vengan las viudas' [widows come here]," she said. "And we will all come."

Later that day, when I spoke with the priest in Rabinal, the municipality to which Plan de Sánchez and Xococ belong, Padre Luis did not believe Doña María. He believed the story of the widows of Xococ was an army plot, some kind of trick to sabotage the work of the forensic team. "Don Miguel is with the army," he told me. "Don Miguel cannot be trusted because he is a leader of the civil patrol and he likes it. He opposes the guerrillas." Padre Luis was convinced that the visits to Plan de Sánchez and the delegation's request for a speedy exhumation were a part of an army plot to trick the forensic team into exhuming civilians killed by the guerrillas or guerrilla combatants killed by the army—either of which would support army claims of armed confrontations with the guerrillas rather than army massacres of unarmed civilians.[10] Moreover, the priest reminded me, "the Xococ civil patrol committed the massacre in Rio Negro," a nearby village. The priest had lived with these communities for years. "I know these people," he reassured me.

For the priest's interpretation of events to be correct, the civil patrol of Xococ, as well as the many widows who traveled to Plan de Sánchez and accompanied us in our survey work in Xococ, would all have had to have been in collusion with the army in the orchestration of a huge lie to the forensic team, the local judge, human rights ombudsman, national press, and the residents of Plan de Sánchez and other surrounding villages. Although I was not convinced by the priest's interpretation, it was present in my mind ten days later as I prepared to visit the widows of Xococ.

Although Kathleen Dill (another anthropologist working in Rabinal) and I had originally made plans to travel to Xococ with the justice of the peace and local human rights ombudsman, this trip was canceled because the ombudsman never arrived. Kathleen and I made arrangements to rent a truck and driver to take us to Xococ, wait for us, and bring us back to Rabinal. Although the judge claimed he couldn't go because of his workload, we sensed he was fearful about entering Xococ without the security of the ombudsman's bodyguards. Kathleen and I were relieved to learn that on this particular day there was a livestock fair in Xococ, which meant that there would be a lot of activity in the village and our arrival would seem a little less extraordinary. We were warned by the judge and forensic team that traveling alone to Xococ could be dangerous, and were given a very long list of extremely contradictory safety tips. In the end, we decided to take lots of pictures and pretend we were tourists in the village. The women of Xococ had invited us, and we wanted to honor their invitation.

Although we were not necessarily expecting to be welcomed by everyone in Xococ, we were shocked that people leaving the fair ignored us. Women I had crossed a river with the previous week looked at the ground as they passed us. As we entered Xococ, we immediately knew why. Xococ was occupied by the army. Soldiers were everywhere in camouflage with grenades around their waists and machine guns in hand. We took pictures of children's dances and livestock at the fair. We were most concerned about endangering anyone in Xococ. After we had been in the village about thirty minutes, Doña María motioned to us to follow her out of sight and earshot of the soldiers. She invited us back to her house.

Entering her home through the cornfield out back rather than from the door at the front, we sat in the darkness with all doors and windows closed. She told us the soldiers had been in Xococ since they had presented their petition for a speedy exhumation. The civil patrol had gone to the army base to request troops in hopes of discouraging local villagers from pursuing the exhumation. Doña María was trembling with fear. Local villagers were blaming her for the occupation. Everyone was scared.

We passed more than an hour discussing her options: fleeing to Guatemala City; denouncing the occupation to the national and international press; and/or seeking support from CONAVIGUA—an organization of indigenous widows of the disappeared. Still, to her question, "What should I do?" I had to answer honestly, "I don't know."

Nonetheless, knowing there were options (however limited) calmed her significantly. Then, she began to tell me her story, not in the form of an interview but as an unloading of pain to someone who seemed to understand. She told me that in March 1981, when her husband and fourteen other men were working in the fields, a blue Toyota full of judicial police raced into Xococ.[11] They drove through the fields rounding up the men, accusing them of being guerrillas, and killed them. Local villagers buried them at the sites of their deaths. These were the graves that had been disturbed by the patrollers.

Later that day, I spoke with Padre Luis. Although he was clearly concerned about the army presence in Xococ, he maintained his initial interpretation that somehow this had to be some kind of conspiratorial army plot.

Negotiating a Field among Many Truths

Everyone has a truth, and often more than one. Whatever the number, each truth represents certain interests particular to the individual. Although I do not find the truths of Doña María and Padre Luis to be consistent with one another, I do believe that each represents an honest interpretation based on different memory and experience of the same events—based on different structures of understanding that result from different trajectories of meaning. I offer my interpretation, one which I believe allows for the coexistence of two contradictory versions of the same event which are expressions of structures of understanding that are derived from different trajectories of meaning.

For the priest, his truth about Xococ begins on March 13, 1982, when, under army order, civil patrollers from Xococ massacred seventy seven women and hundred children from Rio Negro.[12] This massacre is the lens through which Padre Luis sees Xococ. As an anthropologist in the field, the Rio Negro massacre is not the lens through which I see Xococ; it is a point of epiphany. It is a naked encounter with humanity's dark side. In fact, it seems to me that the practice of fieldwork is a spiritual experience with nakedness, where the disciplined "normal" becomes out of place and thus challenges the anthropologist (or anyone else in the field) to begin to peel the onion—that is, to begin to make sense of one's own self and the many daily acts and interpretations that customarily guide one through daily life. Fieldwork displaces structures of understanding and disorients trajectories of meaning.

It also raises the question of truth. Initially I believed that the issue of truth was compelling because of the very subject matter of my research. Having conducted fieldwork in zones of conflict since 1994, I have come to realize that the issue of truth is ever-present in all aspects of research—whether the researcher chooses to acknowledge this presence is the critical issue. In her book *Framer Framed*, Trinh Minh-ha writes on and of truth: "Being truthful: being in the in-between of all definitions of truth" (1992: 13); "Reality and Truth: neither relative nor absolute" (25); "Interview: an antiquated device of documentary. Truth is selected, renewed, displaced and speech is always tactical" (73); "Of course, the image can neither prove what it says nor why it is worth saying it; the impotence of proofs, the impossibility of a single truth in witnessing, remembering, recording, rereading" (83). Trinh's interrogation of truth touches off much of what I believe is problematic in representation on the intellectual level, but also on the emotional level. For me, this is finding internal balance rather than shutting down, as I dig and pull bones out of the mass graves before the relatives of victims, witness the sixteenth testimony of survival of the day, or listen to the priest tell me that the fear-stricken woman who sobbed before me embodied deceit.

Trinh's "in-between" space is a place for recognition of my own limitations and contradictions even when I cannot name them; somehow keeping sight of the tactics of my own research and agenda, and not forgetting that others have their own. Sometimes, as in the case of the priest, it is easier to fill in the outline of my own agenda than it is to recognize that although I might be able to demonstrate the validity of my hypothesis, this hypothesis may have little to do with the daily lives and needs of the communities in which I work—perhaps that is another of the "in-between of all definitions of truth." Of course, it is wholly paternalistic and/or naive to believe that those who provide information do not also have their own agendas. It is not, however, an attempt to somehow measure the sincerity or honesty of those interviewed; nor is it a relativistic position.

The hidden frame for many discussions about truth in fieldwork, particularly with indigenous populations, is the underlying assumption of the "noble savage." This was the case when on another occasion Padre Luis told me that the Achi do not desire revenge (which they collectively told me they did when I asked the surviving men of Plan de Sánchez what they wanted from the exhumation). A leader of an international human rights mission in Guatemala once commented, "The problem with these people is that they aren't yet civilized." Likewise, in Colombia, an international human rights worker from Europe told me that Black Colombians lacked sexual morality, whereas a white U.S. academic commented on the "predatory sexuality" she sensed when talking with Black Colombian youth. The hidden frame behind these comments is infused with colonialist racism and also assumes the "wily Indian," "unpredictable savage," or "sexual deviant" stereotype when an indigenous Guatemalan or Black Colombian shares an experience that somehow counters the "respected authority" (in this Guatemalan case, the authority being the priest). Thus, Doña María is "suspect" and must be lying, laying a trap, or has been duped by the "bad guys," and therefore is not authentic because the priest and/or the outside anthropologist know better who truly represents the indigenous community and what "these people need."

Lata Mani has pointed out that the static framing of agency around the "binary opposition of coercion and consent" is "limited and analytically unhelpful" (1990: 20). Moreover, the researcher viewing the world through this binary lens has little chance of encountering the multiple locations of truth. Truth is not fleeting, it is constant; yet it is heterogeneous and quite subject to tactical interpretations that vary with time and place, among other factors. A massacre survivor in Rabinal explained, "In other times, there was no way to say what had happened even in measured words because they were always nearby surveilling us" (Avila Santa María 1998: 42).

In *Framer Framed* (1992), Trinh says, "I want to find a book that speaks truthfully of Vietnam because everything I read either praises or blames but always in an absolute, black and white, clear cut manner" (1992: 87). The same could be said of most literature on Guatemala. Binary representations of the bloody military versus the liberating guerrillas or the evil ladino versus the innocent Maya tell nothing of the daily struggles for "bare life" confronted by real people in Guatemala. "The witnesses go on living to bear witness to the unbearable" (67). How can an outsider ever hope to understand, much less convey a level of terror so great that neighbors massacre neighbors and the exhuming of skeletal remains feels like a celebration of peace, a resurrection of faith, an excavation of the heart, an act of love? In such circumstances, it is easy to romanticize the Maya community and culture as "other," as "exotic," as somehow having a different level of tolerance in the face of violence based on cultural difference and more than 500 years of conquest. One of the women interviewed in *Framer*

Framed said, "to glorify us is, in a way, to deny our human limits" (72). It seems that often, in attempts to encapsulate a culture, anthropologists seek to categorize and compartmentalize, rather than problematize experience. This is particularly dangerous when one seeks to reveal truths about violence and survival, for it is a slippery slope to reifying survival, difference, and terror, and thereby eliminating all possibilities for understanding.

Moreover, institutions such as the state and the church, are able to naturalize themselves because of their positions of power. Thus, when doing fieldwork with survivors on the margins, there is always the danger of going to the center of institutional power without realizing that one is there. One could easily travel among the many divisions within indigenous villages in Guatemala without recognizing the role of historic power structures in these divisions. In the case of Xococ, this adds up to Padre Luis being a Spanish liberation theologian and Don Miguel being a principal of *costumbre* (respected religious leader). Moreover, the colonial relationship of the church to the Maya and all its baggage should not be assumed to have disappeared. Everyone has truths that represent interests and power relations grounded in history and practice.

To understand state terrorism in Guatemala, "we need to 'use' the past to construct a knowledge that is 'situated' and 'partial' in its politics" (Mankekar 1993: 238). It seems to me that this "politics" is what Mani, following Mohanty, calls "the politics of simultaneously negotiating not multiple but discrepant audiences, different 'temporalities of struggle'" (Mani 1990: 6). Thus, if the negotiation of multiple locations of truth(s) with all their discrepancies, rather than binary oppositions of truth, become the lens through which we see the world and how we perceive ourselves in it, we are less likely to accede passively to Padre Luis's interpretation as the one truth, on the basis of his "authority" and the ease with which a U.S. academic can communicate with a Western priest who is a Spaniard, an intellectual, and a theologian.

Structures of Understanding I

Issues of authority and subjectivity matter to all who work in the field trying to contextualize and sometimes categorize the meaning of surviving genocide and other crimes against humanity.[13] Ramiro Avila Santa María, an Ecuadorian human rights lawyer and a MINUGUA (United Nations Mission in Guatemala) legal advisor, travels to El Petén during his weekend off to take in the tourist sites, including the Tikal ruins. There, he meets a Maya priest who says: "We gather here each year, priests from all over the country to celebrate Maya ceremonies and, in this way, little by little, we recover our sacred places and our culture. *¿Y usted, qué hace?* (And you, what do you do?)"

In his thoughts, Ramiro structures the Maya priest's identity and his own: He (the Maya priest)

- does not read Spanish, but reads *the nahual*
- indigenous, *q'eqchi'*
- peasant who burns the earth to farm
- Maya priest
- has four sons; two who did not die as nature orders but as the tyrant ordered

I (a visitor in this land)

- read Spanish, but do not understand what I read nor do I know

what I write

- ladino, Latin American
- lawyer
- bureaucrat: I sign papers; respond to calls; greet; give information; I don't sign papers; don't respond; don't greet, don't inform

Ramiro answered the Maya priest with his structure of the moment. He preferred to use the action of what he was doing, the "unbearable noun: *turista*." Thus, he responded evasively, which allowed him the time to continue thinking about his condition. Remembering that the priest had said the other Maya priests came from all over the country, Ramiro asked, "Where are you from?"

When the priest responded that he was from San Cristobal, "Have you been there?" Ramiro was relieved because "we finally had something in common." With a smile, Ramiro said, "Of course, I live in Cobán" (which is near San Cristobal). And Ramiro continued to consider his identity and that of the priest:

I

- if I put on a uniform, am a military officer
- if I put on my blue vest and carry my radio, am from MINUGUA
- if I put on a stethoscope, am a doctor
- if I put on a suit, am a lawyer
- if I put on sunglasses and pants, am a tourist

He

- if he demands his land, is a communist
- if his sons are catechists, is a guerrilla
- if he farms his land, is subversive
- if he is indigenous, is fucked—no matter what he puts on.

When the priest asked Ramiro what he did in Cobán, Ramiro told him *todo mi rollo* and gave him his business card. The card has the seal of the United Nations and is imprinted:

> *MINUGUA*
> Guatemala
> *Ramiro Avila Santamaría*
> Legal Advisor

with address, telephone, and fax numbers, email
Misión de las Naciones Unidas
para la Verificación de los Derechos Humanos en Guatemala
(United Nations Misión for the Verification of Human Rights in Guatemala)

Structures of Understanding II

Three months later in the MINUGUA office in Cobán, the secretary told Ramiro, "A señor who says he met you in el Petén is looking for you." Ramiro responds, "I will come down." He recalls, "I said this with all the self-importance that those who are sought out by others have."

After smiling, greeting one another, and remembering their encounter in Petén, Ramiro and the priest sat down. In Ramiro's words, "The priest looked at the ground with the sadness of those who suffer when they see a fallen tree." The priest began to tell his story to Ramiro (the MINUGUA legal advisor in the Cobán office, no longer the tourist in el Petén):

"I am bored." (Followed by prolonged silence.)

"In 1982, army soldiers carried away my two sons who were catechists. 'What debt do they have?' I asked the soldiers who took them. 'I don't know,' they answered, 'we are following orders.'

"I went to the military base. I talked to another soldier. 'I don't know,' he said. I talked to the lieutenant, to the captain, to the colonel, to the general. With different tones of voice and skin color, they responded to me, 'I don't know.'

"I got bored knocking on the doors of army bases, jails, and the ministry of the military. All this for two years and I got bored. So I went and asked if they had seen my sons in the morgue, in the hospital, at the Red Cross. I asked people I knew, people I didn't know, and neighbors what they might know. 'I don't know,' they told me in the morgue, the hospital, the Red Cross and as did the people I knew and didn't know and the neighbors some who surely know something and some who surely don't know anything. I did this for six years and I got bored." (Followed by silence. Profound, obscure silence.)

Ramiro was "completely aware that the priest was not bored, that I was one more door and that he had placed some kind of hope in me. I felt my impending powerlessness when I asked him, 'What can I do for you?' "

"How can I find my sons?" he asked the MINUGUA legal advisor as he looked straight into Ramiro's eyes for the first time. Ramiro recalls, "I held my head in my hands, I looked at the ground and very quietly, I told him, 'I don't know.' "

What We Do Already Know

Joseph Conrad's *Heart of Darkness*, from which Sven Lindqvist draws his title *Exterminate All the Brutes* (1996), is the vehicle both for taking the reader through his study of European genocide in Africa and also for accompanying Lindqvist in his own modern expedition through the Congo. He closes his journey and his book with the following insight:

> And when what had been done in the heart of darkness was repeated in the heart of Europe, no one recognized it. No one wished to admit what everyone knew.
>
> Everywhere in the world where knowledge is being suppressed, knowledge that, if it were made known, would shatter our image of the world and force us to question ourselves—everywhere there, *Heart of Darkness* is being enacted.
>
> You already know that. So do I. It is not knowledge we lack. What is missing is the courage to understand what we know and draw conclusions (172).

I would like to close this essay with some reflections on Sven Lindqvist's challenges to what we already know, our structures of understanding, trajectories of meaning, and some of the questions that have been raised in the narratives of life experiences with the Vietnam war and La Violencia in Guatemala.

We know that collective memory is a political process. Beyond the personal memories of survivors of violence, we know that U.S. intervention in Vietnam in the 1960s and U.S. military aid to Central America in the 1980s escalated violence against leaders of civil society and destroyed local communities, effectively dismantling peaceful alternatives. We know that the strengthening of local community structures and civil society is key to peacebuilding and postwar reconstruction. One conclusion we can draw from the political memory of Vietnam, Central America, and elsewhere is that effective peacemaking offers citizens alternatives to violence for the resolution of political conflicts. With Vietnam and Guatemala in mind, I would like to shift from memories of violence past to the current war in Colombia. We know that entire communities in Colombia have begun to identify themselves as peace communities, rejecting the militarization of the Colombian army, paramilitaries, and the guerrillas. In Colombia, while twenty civilians lose their lives and 680 citizens flee political violence each day (CODHES 2005), the U.S. government, in 2001 alone, provided more than $1.3 billion in military aid to Colombia, increasing its fleet of combat helicopters to sixty—twice as many helicopters as the Guatemalan army used in its scorched earth campaign that resulted in the total destruction of 626 villages and ultimately took the lives of 200,000 Guatemalans.

At this writing in May of 2005, it is estimated that more than 3 million Colombians have been internally displaced by the war (CODHES 2005). According to refugees in Ecuador and internally displaced Colombians, these violent displacement operations are joint maneuvers between the paramilitaries and the army. The army frequently uses planes and helicopters to bomb civilian areas, forcing the inhabitants to flee, while paramilitaries carry out ground maneuvers, destruction of physical community, threats and assassination of those deemed by paramilitary lists to be "subversive" or potentially so (Sanford 2003e and 2003f).

In the Uraba-Choco region of northern Colombia, where I have conducted research since 2000, the paramilitaries control municipalities through alliance with, or representation of, local economic power interests. They act in ways consistent with racketeers or mob bosses, charging for protection and operating like Pinkertons with carte blanche. The guerrillas dominate the mountains, the paramilitaries control the rivers and municipalities. The guerrillas are around the rivers and the paramilitaries are around the mountains. The civilians are everywhere in between the guerrillas, paramilitaries, and the army.

The key to paramilitary success in gaining control of the Uraba-Choco region was to violently attack river communities, ultimately displacing more than 45,000 people. The fifty-nine peace communities that exist today represent some 12,000 displaced people who have returned to their lands.

While staying in the peace community of Costa de Oro during the summer of 2001 with Asale Angel-Ajani, we witnessed the tremendous pressures to which communities are subjected. On a humanitarian mission with a social service team from the Diocese of Apartado that accompanied the displacement of the communities of Andalucia and Camelias from a combat zone to Costa de Oro, we were stopped by the guerrillas several times. We were also forcibly removed from our boats at gunpoint by several dozen paramilitaries who twice detained our group—once for about an hour and once for about thirty minutes. The first time the paramilitaries commanded us to beach our small boats on the riverbank, they ordered us into a corridor they had cut into the jungle, and shouted at us to "run like cattle." As we ran into the jungle, some fifty-three paramilitaries with machine guns and mortar launchers said, "Here are the cattle. What shall we do with them?" However, when they saw our international faces, they began to say, "Good morning, don't worry. We won't do anything to you." This did not, however, stop them from attempting to separate several young men from our group. Father Honelio intervened, telling the commander that if they wanted to talk with one of us, they would have to talk to all of us, effectively informing the commander that if the paramilitaries wanted to kill one of us, they would have to kill all of us; because as Honelio explained, "We will not be separated as a group." At this, the commander ordered a dozen or so paramilitaries to try to engage the guerrillas on the other side of the river in an exchange of mortar and machine-gunfire. Had the guerrillas responded, the paramilitaries would have had more choices of how to handle us—because civilians often die in crossfire. Fortunately, the guerrillas did not respond.

This is not to paint the guerrillas as innocent actors. We were frequently told, "Both sides kill. The paras kill everyone, the guerrillas are more selective."

Indeed, when we were there, the paras were seeking to gain territorial dominion by displacing the peace communities, and the guerrillas were seeking to regain territorial dominion by prohibiting villagers in the war zone from displacing.

Shortly after our departure in August, the paramilitaries seized control of several key communities, entered Costa de Oro, and occupied Curvarado—the last town you pass as you head upriver to the peace communities in the heart of the war zone. Paramilitaries killed several Curvarado functionaries, including the municipal secretary who had participated in one of the accompaniment missions. In early September of 2001, the paras were seizing peace community lands, and killed four residents of Puerto Lleras and claimed their land while threatening to kill anyone else who challenged them. That same September, the guerrillas tightened control on river tributaries under their command—as well as prohibiting the diocese teams from entering some communities. In late October of 2001, the paras forcibly recruited two boys from Costa de Oro and the guerrilla ambushed a platoon of paramilitaries, killing at least thirty paramilitaries and reclaiming the territory and populations that the paras had conquered one month earlier. In Curvarado, the guerrillas killed a peasant branded as a paramilitary collaborator. In late October, residents of Costa de Oro were very worried because one of their leaders was on the FARC's list of people to be assassinated. On November 10, Father Honelio and another priest were prohibited from entering Costa de Oro, which was then under definitive guerrilla control. At the time, one observer expressed fear that the paramilitaries would respond to the guerrillas with an even more severe attack on the communities. Indeed, on December 5, 2001, there was a major battle between the guerrillas and the paramilitaries in the town of Rio Sucio in which several hundred civilians were killed, and which caused another wave of displacement of those fearing even greater retaliatory battles. On Christmas Day, 2001, the guerrillas killed two youth leaders in Costa de Oro.

From 2001 to 2002, a series of violent attacks against peace community youth leaders culminated with the assassination of Edwin Ortega, who represented the youth of peace communities internationally and was an outspoken advocate of the right of youth to resist forced recruitment. Rather than abandon their organizing project, peace community youth gathered on October 22, 2002, to restructure their organization, because "It is only through our organization that we have the possibility of a future. Alone, only weapons await us" (Sanford, 2006).

Since November 2002, a negotiating commission (comisión negociadora) has been traveling to all the communities of the Lower Atrato. The peace communities celebrated their sixth anniversary in October 2003 with a general assembly of peace communities followed by an international anniversary celebration. A central focus of both the assembly and celebration was the right of youth to organize for peace. "We are here because we want a positive future," explained Luis. "We refuse to be targets of the armed actors. We refuse to carry their guns. We want our right to peace respected" (author interview, Costa de Oro, October 17, 2003). In October 2004, the peace communities celebrated their seventh anniversary despite paramilitary, army, and guerrilla tactics of confinement that impeded many communities from actually attending the celebration (author interview, Bogotá, November 12, 2004).

Indeed, we already know enough. We must find the courage to take the lessons learned in our studies of the sequelae of violence and insist that international aid be used to strengthen peaceful alternatives, not escalate wars that disproportionately take the lives of civilians. Throughout the world, survivors come forward to give testimonies not only to denounce a violent past but also to claim a future of peace. Let us not stand by idly waiting for future research opportunities on violence that is currently in the making. We need to move beyond reporting human rights abuses and become effective advocates for peace (Messer 1993). Our fieldwork experiences, research methodologies, and cultural analyses place us in a unique position (Magnarella 1994) to problematize structures of understanding and trajectories of meaning in theory as well as contribute to peace and social justice in practice. As anthropologists, public intellectuals, and human rights advocates, it is our moral obligation not only to share our analytical conclusions about memories of violence but also to place them in new frameworks of understanding for the prevention of violence, so that our research honors the international plea of *Nunca Más*, Never Again

NOTES

1. This essay greatly benefited from the critical feedback and thoughtful comments on earlier versions from Asale Angel-Ajani, Kathleen Dill, Purnima Mankekar, John Collins, Eric Weiss, Michael Bosia, Helena Pohlandt-McCormick, John Mowitt, Wendy Weiss, Arif Dirlik, and participants in the Legacies of Authoritarianism MacArthur workshop at the University of Wisconsin. I especially thank Ramiro Avila Santa María for generously sharing his own writing and insights on La Violencia in Guatemala. Research and writing of this essay was made possible by support from Fulbright-Hayes, Inter-American Foundation, Peace and Life Institute, MacArthur Consortium, Bunting Peace Fellowship, and Rockefeller grants. All opinions and errors are, of course, my own.

2. See Roberta Culbertson's thoughtful essay on this topic in this volume.

3. See Sanford 2003c.

4. Between 1994 to 1998, I spent some twenty-four months in rural Maya villages before, during, and after exhumations. With the Guatemalan Forensic Anthropology Foundation, I participated in exhumations in Plan de Sánchez, Panzós, San Andrés Sacabajá, Acul, El Tablón, and San Martín Jilotepeque, as well as a preliminary site visit to Xococ.

5. In this volume, Angel-Ajani, Silber, Castillo Hernandez, and Davis, among others, amply demonstrate that casting doubt on victims is a structural tactic of marginalization.

6. Gook is a derogatory term used by U.S. soldiers to dehumanize the Vietnamese.

7. The Achi are one of the twenty-one distinct Maya ethnolinguistic groups.

8. The civil patrol was an army-mandated and controlled, compulsory paramilitary organization composed of all men in rural villages. They were responsible for carrying out all army orders. Begun in the early 1980s, they were not officially disbanded until the signing of the peace accords in December 1996.

9. The military commissioner was the army-appointed civilian commander of the civil patrols charged with implementing army orders and accountable to the army.

10. More than 200,000 Guatemalans were killed or disappeared, and there are 626 known massacres of rural villages. Fully 87 percent of victims were Maya. The Commission for Historical Clarification attributed 93 percent of the violence to the Guatemalan army and 3 percent to the guerrillas.

11. Many Guatemalans, both indigenous and ladino, use the terms *judicial police* and *death squads* interchangeably.

12. For more on Rio Negro, see Sanford 2003a.

13. "Structures of Understanding I and II," drawn from Ramiro Avila Santa María's, 1998 unpublished memoir. Used with kind permission.

REFERENCES

Agamben, Giorgio. 1998. *Homo Sacer: Sovereign Power and Bare Life.* Stanford: Stanford University Press, 1998.

Americas Watch. 1984. "Guatemala: A Nation of Prisoners." *Americas Watch Report,* June. New York: Americas Watch.

———. 1986. "Civil Patrols in Guatemala." *Americas Watch Report,* August. New York: Americas Watch.

———. 1988. "Closing Space: Human Rights in Guatemala." *Americas Watch Report,* May 1987–October 1988. New York: Americas Watch.

———. 1989. "Persecuting Human Rights Monitors: The CEJ in Guatemala." *Americas Watch Report.* May. New York: Americas Watch.

———. 1990. "Messengers of Death: Human Rights in Guatemala." *Americas Watch Report,* November 1988–February 1990. New York: Human Rights Watch.

———. 1993. *Clandestine Detention in Guatemala.* New York: Americas Watch.

Americas Watch and Physicians for Human Rights, 1991. *Guatemala: Getting Away with Murder.* New York: Human Rights Watch.

Amnesty International. 1981. "Guatemala: A Government Program of Political Murder." *New York Review of Books,* March 19, 38–40.

———. 1982. "Guatemala: Massive Extrajudicial Executions in Rural Areas under the Government of General Efrain Rios Montt." *Special Briefing,* July. New York: Amnesty International.

———. 1987. *Guatemala: The Human Rights Record.* London: Amnesty International Publications.

———. 1989. *Guatemala: Human Rights Violations under the Civilian Government.* London: Amnesty International Publications.

———. 1990. *Annual Report.* London: Amnesty International Publications.

———. 1991. *Guatemala: Lack of Investigations into the Past Human Rights Abuses: Clandestine Cemeteries.* London: Amnesty International Publications.

———. 1992. *Human Rights Violations against Indigenous Peoples of the Americas.* New York: Amnesty International.

———. 1998. *Guatemala: All the Truth, Justice for All.* April. New York: Amnesty International.

Avila Santa María, Ramiro, 1998. "Structures of understanding." Unpublished Manuscript.

Benjamin, Walter. 1978. "Critique of Violence." Translated by Edmund Jephcott. In *Walter Benjamin: Reflections*, edited by Peter Demetz. New York: Schocken Books.

Black, George. 1984. *Garrison Guatemala*. London: Zed Books.

Bommes, Michael, and Patrick Wright. 1982. "Charms of Resistance: The Public and the Past." In *Making Histories: Studies in History-Writing and Politics*, edited by Richard Johnson. Minneapolis: University of Minnesota Press.

Butler, Thomas, ed. 1989. *Memory, History, Culture and the Mind*. Oxford: Basil Blackwell.

Cali, Francisco. 1992. Author's interview, San Francisco, March 26.

CIA (Central Intelligence Agency). 1982. "Document Secret 65–41," February 5. Declassified January 1998.

CODHES (Consultoria para los Derechos Humanos y el Desplazamiento). 2005. "Desplazamiento y Conflicto Armado—La política del Avestruz." CODHES Informa— Boletín informativa de la Consultoria para los Derechos Humanos y el Desplazamiento, Bogota, no. 58. May 1.

Commission for Historical Clarification (CEH). 1997a. Draft Report on El Valle Polochic. Guatemala City: CEH.

———. 1997b. MINUGUA/CEH Interviews in Panzós. Guatemala City: CEH.

———. 1999a. *Guatemala Memory of Silence—Conclusions and Recommendations*. Guatemala City: CEH.

———. 1999b. *Guatemala Memoria del Silencio*, vols. 1–12. Guatemala City: CEH.

———. 1999c. Guatemala Memoria del Silencio. http://hrdata.aaas.org/ceh/report/english/intro.html.

Das, Veena. 1987. "The Anthropology of Violence and the Speech of Victims," *Anthropology Today* 4.3: 11–13.

———. 1989. "Subaltern as Perspective." In *Subaltern Studies VI—Writings on South Asian History and Society*, edited by Ranajit Guha. Delhi: Oxford University Press.

———, ed. 1990. *Mirrors of Violence: Communities, Riots, Survivors in South Asia*. Delhi: Oxford University Press.

———. 1997. "Language and Body: Transactions in the Construction of Pain." In *Social Suffering*, edited by Arthur Kleinman, Veena Das, and Margaret Lock. Berkeley: University of California Press.

———. 2001. "Documentary Practices: State and Everyday Life on the Peripheries." Paper presented to School of American Research Seminar on "The State at Its Margins: Comparative Ethnographies of the Modern State in Africa, Latin America and South Asia." Santa Fe, April 22–26.

EAFG (Equipo de Antropología Forense de Guatemala). 1995. *¡Nada Podrá contra la Vida!* Guatemala City: EAFG.

———. 1996. *EAFG Anuario No. 3, 1994–1995*. Guatemala City: EAFG.

———. 1997. *Las Masacres de Rabinal*. Guatemala City: EAFG.

FAFG (Fundación de Antropología Forense de Guatemala). 2000. *Informe de la Fundación de Antropología Forense de Guatemala: Cuatro Casos Paradigmaticos Solicitados por la Comisión para el Esclarecimiento Historico de Guatemala*. Guatemala City: FAFG.

Herr, Michael. 1991. *Dispatches*. New York: Vintage International.

Ishiguro, Kazuo. 1982. *A Pale View of Hills*. New York: Vintage International.

Johnson, Kay. 2001. "When Hell Visited the Village—Scene of the Killings." *Time*, May 27, 33.

Lindquist, Sven. 1996. *"Exterminate All the Brutes": One Man's Odyssey into the Heart of Darkness and the Origins of the European Genocide*. Translated by Joan Tate. New York: New Press.

Magnarella, P. J. 1994. "Anthropology, Human Rights and Justice." *International Journal of Anthropology* 9.1: 3–7.

Mani, Lata. 1990. "Multiple Mediations: Feminist Scholarship in the Age of Multinational Reception." *Feminist Review* 35 (Summer): 24–41.

Mankekar, Purnima. 1993. "National Texts and Gendered Lives: An Ethnography of Television Viewers in a North Indian City." *American Ethnologist* 20.3 (August): 543–563.

Manz, Beatriz. 1988. *Refugees of a Hidden War: The Aftermath of Counterinsurgency in Guatemala*. Albany: State University of New York Press.

McGeary, Joanna, and Karen Tumulty. 2001. "The Fog of War." *Time*, May 7, 25.

Messer, Ellen. 1993. "Anthropology and Human Rights." *Annual Review of Anthropology* 22: 221–249.

Mohanty, Chandra, Ann Russo, and Lourdes Torres, eds. 1984."Under Western Eyes: Feminist Scholarship and Colonial Discourses." *Boundary Two* 12.3–13.1 (Fall): 333–358.

———. 1991. *Third World Women and the Politics of Feminism*. Bloomington: Indiana University Press.

Montejo, Victor. 1987. *Testimony: Death of a Guatemalan Village*. Willimantic, Conn.: Curbstone Press.

———. 1999. *Voices from Exile: Violence and Survival in Modern Maya History*. Norman: University of Oklahoma Press.

Ninh Bao. 1993. *The Sorrow of War*. New York: Riverhead Books.

O'Brien, Tim. 1990. *The Things They Carried*. New York: Penguin Books.

Popular Memory Group. 1982. "Popular Memory: Theory, Politics and Method." In *Making Histories: Studies in History-Writing and Politics*. Minneapolis: University of Minnesota Press.

Sanford, Victoria. 1993. "Victim as Victimizer: Indigenous Childhood and Adolescence in Guatemala's Culture of Terror." M.A. thesis, San Francisco State University.

———. 1997. "Mothers, Widows and Guerrilleras: Anonymous Conversations with Survivors of State Terror." Uppsala: Life and Peace Institute.

———. 1999. "Between Rigoberta Menchu and La Violencia: Deconstructing David Stoll's History of Guatemala." *Latin American Perspectives* 10926. (November): 38–46.

———. 2000a. "From *I, Rigoberta* to the Commissioning of Truth: Maya Women and the Reshaping of Guatemalan History." *Social Justice* 27.1 (June): 128–151.

———. 2000b. "Testimony and Truth: The Gendered Struggle for Guatemalan History." *Mujeres y Latinas*, Fall, 22–37.

———. 2001. "From *I, Rigoberta* to the Commissioning of Truth: Maya Women and the Reshaping of Guatemalan History." *Cultural Critique* 47: 16–53.

———. 2003a. *Buried Secrets: Truth and Human Rights in Guatemala*, New York: Palgrave Macmillan.

———. 2003b. *Violencia y Genocidio en Guatemala*, Guatemala City: FyG Editores.

———. 2003c. "'What Is Written in Our Hearts': Healing Fragmented Communities in the Guatemalan Highlands." In *Political Transition Politics: and Culture*, edited by Paul Greadyo. London: Pluto Books.

———. 2003d. "The 'Grey Zone' of Justice: NGOs and Rule of Law in Post-War Guatemala." *Journal of Human Rights* 2.3 (Fall): 393–405.

———. 2003e. "Learning to Kill by Proxy: Colombian Paramilitaries and the Legacy of Central American Death Squads, Contras and Civil Patrols." *Journal of Social Justice* 30.3: 1–19.

———. 2003f. "Peacebuilding in the War Zone: The Case of Colombian Peace Communities." *International Journal of Peacekeeping* 10.2: 107–118.

———. 2006. "The Moral Imagination of Survival: Displacement and Child Soldiers in Colombia and Guatemala." In *Troublemakers or Peacemakers? Youth and Post-Accord Peace Building*, edited by Siobhan McEvoy. Notre Dame: University of Notre Dame Press.

Smith, Carol. 1984. "Local History in Global Context: Social and Economic Transitions in Western Guatemala." *Comparative Studies in Society and History* 26.2(April): 193–228.

———. 1990a. "The Militarization of Civil Society in Guatemala: Economic Reorganization as a Continuation of War: Military Impact in the Western Highands of Guatemala." *Latin American Perspectives* 17.4: 8–41.

———, ed. 1990b. *Guatemalan Indians and the State, 1540 to 1988.* Austin: University of Texas Press.

———. 1999. "Why Write an Exposé of Rigoberta Menchú?" *Latin American Perspectives* 26.6 (November): 15–28.

Spivak, Gayatri. 1988a. "Subaltern Studies: Deconstructing Historiography." In *Selected Subaltern Studies*, edited by Ranajit Guha and Gayatri Spivak. New York: Oxford University Press.

———. 1988b. "Can the Subaltern Speak?" In *Marxism and the Interpretation of Culture*, edited by Cary Nelson and Lawrence Grossberg. Urbana: University of Illinois Press.

Trinh Minh-ha. 1992. *Framer Framed.* New York: Routledge.

Vistica, Gregory. 2001. "What Happened in Thanh Phong." *New York Times Magazine*, April 29, 50.

Warren, Kay. 1993. *The Violence Within: Cultural and Political Opposition in Divided Nations.* Boulder: Westview.

———. 1998. *Indigenous Movements and Their Critics: Pan-Maya Activism in Guatemala.* Princeton: Princeton University Press.

Zielbauer, Paul. 2001. "Memory Molds Story of War for Vietnamese-Americans." *New York Times*, May 8, A14.

2

Scholarship, Advocacy, and the Politics of Engagement in Burma (Myanmar)

MONIQUE SKIDMORE

April 26, 2005: A polythene bag is placed on the ground near a trash bin outside the Hla Bettman clothing shop in Mandalay's central Zeygyo market. It detonates at 4:15 in the afternoon, killing twenty-three-year-old Ma Moe Kyi from Sone Village, who was shopping at the clothing store, and an unidentified forty-five-year-old female market porter. Sixteen other people were injured, according to casualty figures given by staff at the Mandalay Hospital. The following day, Buddhist monks were asked to perform ceremonies designed to ward of evil spirits and the ghosts of those who had died in the explosion. Earlier that morning forty-four-year-old Khin Maung Lay had died from exposure to fumes inhaled while carrying injured people from the market. A week later, nineteen-year-old Myint Myint Aye, a worker in the Rising Sun textile store next door to the bombsite, also succumbed to her injuries in Mandalay Hospital (*Burma Issues* 2005; DVB 2005a, b, c, d; Myo Lwin 2005; *USA Today* 2005).

May 7, 2005: Eleven days later, on a busy Saturday afternoon, three bombs are detonated in Burma's capital city, Rangoon (Yangon). Two bombs targeted grocery shoppers; the other bomb was detonated at a Thai business expo taking place at the Yangon Convention Centers. Like the Mandalay market bombing, the fatalities and injuries that occurred at the Junction 8 and Dagon shopping Centers had women and children as their main casualties. The bombs were detonated in five-minute intervals. Some have said that the terror campaign was executed with military precision.

The death count from these acts is impossible to know, as the military regime forbids medical staff from giving out information, and the regime's own figures are notoriously low. Official figures are 23 dead and 162 injured. The Thai prime minister, Thaksin Shinawatra, sent a C-130 military plane for the 122 Thai nationals attending the trade fair, and the Thai government reports at least 21 people died from these three bombings. Three Thais were injured, and four

42

Malaysians. One injured Malaysian, Goh Cha Watt, was part of a Lutheran Church group who were in Burma for a week to visit an orphanage and set up a children's camp. The *Asia Times* reported eyewitness accounts of the bombings and of Rangoon General, Insein, and North Okkalapa hospitals where injured people were initially treated:

> Within hours of the multiple bombing, witnesses at all three blast sites said they had seen dozens of casualties—many of them missing limbs or heads—and numerous blackened corpses. An eyewitness who was at the General Hospital in Rangoon . . . said the casualties overwhelmed the hospital's capacity and had to be laid on concrete floors. The witness, who asked not to be identified, reported seeing "nine or ten" people killed in the explosions who had been taken to the morgue, as well as many victims, including children and the elderly, who had lost body parts (*Asia Times* 2005).

Bombings are nothing new in Burma. There are many each year; usually it's a hydropower plant or a rail line being blown up, sometimes it's a small explosion near a Western embassy or a general's house, or even a military-built new pagoda. No one pays them much attention anymore. A few bombs have targeted the generals and their families, but in the main assassination attempts against members of the ruling military council are rare. Until recently there have been very few bombing campaigns that targeted civilians. Almost unremarked upon, a series of bomb blasts have occurred in public areas in the past few months. For example, on March 19, 2005, a bomb exploded in the Panorama Hotel in Rangoon. Two days earlier a bus was bombed in Rangoon and an unexploded bomb was defused in a bus terminal. In June of 2005, four bombs were detonated close to Rangoon's central railway station, as well as one in a French café near Bogyoke Market, and one outside of the Southern Division Court (*Irrawaddy* 2005a). Bombers also targeted the Supreme Court in Rangoon on March 22 (DVB 2005c).

Burmese activist groups correctly point out that the kinds of civilians targeted are in general wealthy, and therefore have close links with the military regime. Military sites have also recently been targeted by bombers, and the bus that was bombed was owned by Myanmar Economic Holdings Limited, an army-dominated company that owns much of Burma's private enterprises (DVB 2005d). The fact that military-owned sites or by the military sites frequented the main ones targeted has prompted speculation among Rangoon residents that the bombs were planted by disgruntled former members of the military intelligence branch, which was disbanded in 2004, and whose employees were jailed or fled the country. The international media has ignored scores of such bomb blasts in 2004 and 2005.

The military council, the State Peace and Development Committee (SPDC), has accused many expatriate groups, rebel armies, Western organizations such as the CIA and political opponents in-country of exploding the bombs. In the first two weeks following the bombings, most Rangoon residents reckoned that the military regime had detonated the bombs in order to be able to portray itself as a victim of terrorism. Other rumors circulated in Rangoon teashops suggesting that the regime committed this violence to allow it to graciously hand over its chairing of ASEAN (Association of Southeast Asian Nations) later in the year to another country, or perhaps to chair ASEAN but to hold the meeting in Thailand, thus diffusing American and European diplomatic anger at ASEAN for allowing Burma to chair the meeting.

Some of the bombings in the past year have been the self-confessed work of Burma's own terrorist organization, the Vigorous Burmese Student Warriors (VSBW), and the military junta were quick to blame this organization. Following denial of the allegations by the VSBW, the military regime continued to deliberately conflate the aims and motivations of armed and nonarmed political opponents. In doing so it sought to remove suspicion from the Burmese military, to inculcate a state of vulnerability in the general populace, and to justify its heightened security and surveillance measures. Multiple forms of armed and nonarmed opposition and bombing campaigns against the military rule are currently occurring in Burma. The regime's obfuscation of this resistance, combined with the lack of attention paid by scholars to the violence that is occurring in Burma, has created a complex situation in need of analysis.

After the initial shock of the bombings, Burmese people were inundated with state propaganda vowing to find the culprits responsible for the carnage and offering a large reward for information leading to the arrest of the perpetrators. Teashop conversations vacillated between ongoing cynicism of the regime's words, and the beginning of doubts that the regime had truly committed this act against its own (urban) people. The rumor that the former prime minister and head of military intelligence Khin Nyunt was behind the bombing campaign, also circulated, as did various revenge scenarios metered out by his former intelligence operatives in hiding. There is an urgent need to write about such violence events from the perspective of Burmese people caught up in the violence, and within the context of the sociopolitical environment that has been created by the Burmese military regime. Not only are such histories of violence and suffering not being written but also the few attempts to document violence and human rights violations are often being subjected to a process of academic (and thus historical) denial and dismissal.

Burmese Scholarship

Anthropologists who work in Myanmar (Burma) are rare. It is not hard to be let into the country but it is difficult to be given permission by the Burmese military regime to stay there. International conferences about Burma are now held in Yangon (Rangoon), and the regime sends black saloon cars to ferry the conference speakers to and from their hotels. "Why do you go?" I ask the few anthropologists I know who attend these conferences. The answer is invariably, "Because it ensures our access and allows the regime to categorize us firmly as scholars and not journalists and activists." And that probably sums up why I've never gone to one of these in-country conferences.

It would be comforting for the regime to acknowledge that I am a scholar and to continue to give me access to my field site. The trouble is, each time I think up a topic, I have to drastically censor myself. I would have to make no mention in my paper of the atrocities perpetrated by the regime, the ongoing civil war, and the suffering, fear, and injustice that envelop the nation. Do anthropologists have a moral duty to speak out publicly about such atrocities? The premise that one can choose to be an engaged anthropologist (or not) is troubling to me. I can see that for specialists of, say, lacquer ware and mulberry tree papermaking techniques, this may not be an issue. Similarly, for historians of precolonial Burma, there is no one to interview and no reason to go to Burma other than to view archival material. The problem is with speaking to the present, not the past.

Critiquing a recent article of mine about fear in Burma (Skidmore 2003a), a reviewer pointed out that I had become an activist-by-proxy. This comment made me truly reflect for the first time about why I had chosen Burma as a field site and why I work on violence and fear. I had ostensibly gone to Burma to research a medical anthropological topic, but at McGill University in the 1990s we were all aware that the medical is almost always political and the juridical, political, and medical arms of the state are sometimes inseparable. Social suffering was a theoretical paradigm I was eager to explore in Burma, but I had imagined my graduate work focusing upon help-seeking behaviors and forms of healing sought by the populace, and that this hoped-for healing would not necessarily differentiate between traumas of the mind and body.

It was evident to me upon arriving in Burma that the whole nation was in distress and engaged in help-seeking behavior. I remembered the Kleinmans' line about needing to attend to the concerns of our informants in their local moral worlds (Kleinman and Kleinman 1994). Suddenly, studying Burmese medicine and the occult just didn't seem enough when clear and planned resistance to military rule was being promulgated on the streets and in the teashops of the major cities. I decided to stay in the capital cities and document the resistance and fear that were overlaying so many thoughts and actions at the time. I wasn't sure where I was going with the project, but I knew instinctively that I was following the "cultural grain," something that Evans-Pritchard advocated many years ago (Evans-Pritchard quoted in Rozenberg 2005), a method only half-consciously passed on to each new generation of anthropology students.

What didn't occur to me as a graduate student was that concerns for social justice motivated my choice to study anthropology instead of medicine, and it undoubtedly, at least sub- or unconsciously, motivated me to choose field sites such as post-Pol Pot Cambodia (Skidmore 1995, 1996) and Burma. As I compiled literature reviews in preparation for that first long stint of fieldwork in Burma, I read avidly the brutal history of the nation and the complexities of the Burmese cultural and religious systems as well as the tortured past and present of Burma's political history and bloody civil war against the military regime. For years the Burmese nationalist movement had created the political momentum necessary for independence from Britain, and I read with horror the usurpation of the fledgling democratic government first by a hand grenade lobbed into the parliamentary cabinet room and several years later by the military coup of General Ne Win.

I approached the study of the suffering of the Burmese people from the perspective of an outsider who, over time, came to live in Burma in a mode similar to that of most Burmese people. That is to say, I became fearful of the military regime and I hid my thoughts, feelings, and actions from the gaze of the Office of the Chief of Military Intelligence. This was the point where the reviewer realized I had become an activist-by-proxy. I had not been able to admit this to myself until then. Given some time to think about it, I realized the consequences were different from those of being an anthropologist who approached Burma on a par with any other field site, collecting my data and pursuing methodologies as taught in fieldwork courses and textbooks. From that time onward I was able to examine my own motivations more clearly, and I made the conscious, and therefore frightening, decision to continue to work in Burma on issues of fear, violence, and suffering.

Knowing that such work is subversive, illegal, and dangerous for my informants has created a series of ethical and methodological dilemmas that I have written about elsewhere (Skidmore 2004, 2003b). It has also created a series of dilemmas in the way in which I write about suffering and fear. Burma studies in the fields of political science and international relations has, in recent years, become increasingly politicized. Political scientists have taken lucrative contracts to work for multinational organizations that have interests in Burma. Others have lobbied the U.S. government and the European Union to remove their sanctions banning business in Burma and Burmese exports. International conferences have occasionally been the scene of such public lobbying in the guise of scholarship, without the obvious conflicts of interest being declared. Several political scientists have argued that American sanctions prohibit them from gaining course materials necessary to teach about Burma. Both political scientists and international relations scholars and students have produced reports for international lending organizations that urge cooperation with the military regime (Taylor and Pedersen 2005). In their zeal to become "Burma experts," faculty at some universities have taken a pro-engagement stance toward the military regime (Bowring 2005), often in contravention to their own government's position of nonengagement with Burma.

The Burmese expatriate activist community has been damning in its condemnation of what it has labeled "pro-military scholarship" and in particular, against those political scientists and students known as the "Brussels Four" (*Irrawaddy* 2005b). To date, academics have rarely argued against such scholarship. My own ethnographic work about the subjectivities of Burmese people under dictatorship and the manifest social suffering occurring in Burma has become a target for a section of the Burma studies community. It has been described as "lurid," "emotive" and "full of dead facts" (Lambrecht and Mathieson 2005). The desire to be a "Burma expert" is leading some scholars and graduate students to a condemnation of ethnographic fieldwork as nonobjective and therefore inaccurate. There is much at stake here for such players. The international lecture and conference circuit is alluring to such authors, and discrediting in-country information creates the illusion that no one really knows what is occurring in Burma.

This kind of academic posturing does, to my mind, a great deal of violence to Burma and to Burmese people. To be an engaged anthropologist within the orbit of Burma studies is to be labeled a kind of fringe lunatic, the kind who would hang out with Burmese activists in Thailand and succumb to their emotional pleas for an end to the regime's rule. To gather data from the most disadvantaged sectors of Burmese society is, for me, an opportunity to give a voice to largely powerless people who have no recourse to justice and for whom universal human rights are incomprehensible, as they can never envisage how such rights would be accorded to them. But there is another reason to do ethnographic work in Burma, and that is to document the potential forms of political agency that exist in the various subjectivities that are created under authoritarianism. In this sense, being an engaged anthropologist is to advocate for the histories of terror and misery to be retained in the contemporary world. These alternate readings of political power, legitimacy, and moral authority have the power to puncture the hegemonic reading of past and present created by the military regime. They are not the political strategies documented by political scientists and international relations scholars, and they have no import on the global political stage. It seems important for some scholars to discredit the words, feelings, and actions of Burmese people, and it seems that to write about power in Burma is to be seen as a threat to such scholars: to be considered an activist and have a political agenda that interferes with some imagined view of objective fact gathering.

It is also worrying that scholars are choosing to interpret the war that has been waged by the Burmese military against its own populace since 1962 in terms of "security." The American government's belief in a "war on terror" has meant a reduction in the civil rights of people all over the world as governments have introduced legislation that allows increased powers of surveillance, arrest, and incarceration. The Burmese regime has sought to recast its attempt to permanently silence all those who resist its rule as a war on terror, one that requires the military to become engaged in securing the nation and its borders. Some scholars are borne along by the regime's tide of seemingly reasonable, pragmatic, long-term strategic planning goals, and choose not to investigate the means by which dissent is put down.

To many such scholars, the Burmese military regime is the only institution that emerged at the end of the 1950s with enough strength to pull the country together and form a government. The place of violence, of fear, of both genocidal and low-level intensity conflict is unwritten. The 2005 bombings of crowded public spaces will also be interpreted as a small part of the collateral damage involved in creating a unified country that can participate in international affairs and in the global economic and development marketplace.

The Ethics and Risks of Fieldwork in Burma

The perils of conducting ethnographic research in Burma on any issues that can somehow be regarded as political or "sensitive" are manifest. In 2002 I applied for my latest "official" research visa for 2002–2003, as I would not have been able to conduct fieldwork in rural areas of the country without permission. The visa was initially denied, even after I had used all of my previously successful networks and strategies for gaining a research permit. Finally the visa was signed by the former prime minister and chief of military intelligence, General Khin Nyunt. After signing my visa, Khin Nyunt warned me: "You are an angel of light come to help the Burmese people. You obviously have very high karma and your fate is linked with that of the nation. It would be a shame to lose that karma and go to hell from associating with negative political elements" (Khin Nyunt, personal communication 2002). Phone tapping, physical surveillance, luggage searches, and recourse to informants are ways in which the movements of anthropologists are monitored and curtailed in Burma. I was being warned off doing any of the things we both knew to be illegal in authoritarian Burma and, although phrased in a mild manner, it was a chilling reminder that fieldwork in Burma always carries significant risks to myself and my informants.

Government officials who read the signature on the research visa forms were incredulous. The letters to various government officials came in a manila folder with "Top Secret" stamped in the upper right-hand corner. No one could pronounce Khin Nyunt's name: it came out as a kind of squeak, the last part of the name seemingly swallowed. Eyes bulged with apprehension and several officials asked me about my personal connection to Khin Nyunt and my "real agenda." "Great," said my husband, when I told him about my day, "another ethical dilemma for you." And he was right. I was causing fear in people who were just trying to do their job. Ever day, thousands of Burmese people weigh their involvement with the regime. By wanting to conduct research I had just made life more fearful for some people. There is no easy answer; I still don't know if I've made the right choice. In this particular case, I tried to minimize my contact with government officials.

Burmese people always carefully weigh their involvement with me. Khin Nyunt's belief that my fate is somehow intertwined with that of the nation is a statement that has also been made to me by medical, religious, and magical healers in the past decade. In my last period of prolonged fieldwork in Burma, I asked magical and religious healers if I could record our conversations. "Certainly," they invariably replied, "If you don't mind me recording you." Ancient tape players were used to record our conversation and at some point in the conversation I inevitably needed to provide my informants with batteries or tapes. When I asked for informed consent before interviewing these healers, I was almost always asked if I would use the knowledge passed on to me for good purposes, refrain from harming anyone armed with this knowledge, and if I had a pure heart. Continuously, Burmese people place upon my shoulders the burden of disseminating knowledge of their beliefs and life experiences in ways that are ethically appropriate and that contribute to a better future for Burma.

It's not an easy burden, and asking questions related to the political situation invariably causes some degree of fear. Knowing about people's political views and activities can occasion a variety of negative emotions and behaviors in my informants. A fellow anthropologist who works on Burma, Christina Fink, once told me that she remembers a meeting we had in Rangoon in 1996 when I expressed frustration at having to continuously tear up my field notes. Informants would spend a sleepless night tossing and turning before coming to my house at first light and demanding I destroy the notes I had made of our conversations. The bond formed between anthropologist and informant is necessarily deep, as we are both in danger when we speak the truth to each other. But this intensity exists only for that one issue; otherwise we know little about each other. In particular, Burmese people must trust that I will safely take my notes out of the country and that I will never identify them or put their family into jeopardy. Sometimes this causes a great deal of anxiety, especially when the cities are undergoing curfew or other heightened "security" measures.

Diplomats and Burmese people whom I had come to regard with great affection have accused me of being a spy. Many people have become so cynical under the current regime that they find it hard to envisage my motivations as being other than negative or egotistical. The affective milieu is one of heightened suspicion and sometimes paranoia, and gathering information in order to pass it on to political masters is a familiar norm. The bonds I form in the field (and attempt to reforge each year) often wither and snap under the weight of fear and anxiety that my leaving Burma occasions. Nightmares are created with my leaving the field, carrying the secrets of frightened people with me.

Subjectivity and Political Agency: Writing against Terror

To be an engaged scholar under conditions of authoritarianism and in a climate of fear is not an easy decision to make. As the mother of two young children, it is a decision I constantly reevaluate. It is not a decision I was aware of needing to make when I was in graduate school, but it is one that carries a weight of responsibility to oneself, one's family, and one's informants and their families. That responsibility begins with ensuring safety and ethical conduct, and ends with a commitment to portray the experiences of one's informants as powerfully as possible.

As Burma's ongoing bombing campaign shatters lives and instills fear in Burmese people who must constantly negotiate public spaces with a new feeling of vulnerability, I wonder how I can render a decade of witnessing suffering, misery, and terror in Burma in such a way that it will not become bound up in the chapter of Burma's history to be known as "attempts at resistance to military rule." Already some of my writings are glossed over by political scientists as being in-depth accounts of this specific moment and thus not representative of the ongoing nature of Burma's state of emergency. As an engaged anthropologist I seek to write not only against terror but also against the homogenizing weight of political forgetting.

The Burmese military regime has been writing propaganda, but it has also been writing violence, terror, and its own version of history into the very bodies of Burmese people since at least 1962. Burmese people respond by creating subjectivities under authoritarianism that hide political agency in a variety of forms. The regime is aware of the potential of some of these forms of subjectivity, and it attempts to crush the healers, teachers, and community leaders who advocate forms of subjectivity at odds with the regime's requirement of "disciplined democracy" from its "model citizens." In the following pages I describe some of these forms of subjectivity. In writing about the potential political agency embedded within them, I consciously write about the politics of everyday life in order to provide a different record from that created by successive military juntas. I also record these forms of subjectivity and political agency to deny nonengaged scholars the ability to dismiss the words and experiences of Burmese people. Both processes inscribe forgetting into the historical record, and both do violence to Burma and its people.

Following Benjamin (1983), Burmese forms of subjectivity, particularly those that lead to political agency, can constitute a potent weapon with which to pierce the future era of disciplined democracy and its associated linear historiographies. Such subjectivities are necessarily created within the framework of disciplined democracy. Forms of political agency arising from Burmese subjectivities are acknowledged by the military regime as requiring monitoring and, wherever possible, eradication. My argument here draws on Michael Taussig's writings on the anthropology of violence (Taussig 1980, 1987, 1991, 1992, 1997, 1999, 2003, 2004) and about the creative potential of writing against terror. I accordingly draw upon the forms of emergent subjectivity that Burmese people deploy to invest their repressive situations with hope and the possibility for change.

Domains in which memory can live and in which counterhegemonic subjectivities can be constituted and refined are actively crushed by the regime. The intelligence services, the Ministry of Information, the Department of Psychological Warfare, the Department of Propaganda, the Press Scrutiny Board, the system of reportage all the way from the Ten House Leader to the State Peace and Development Council, the parastatal organizations, the four-decade-long civil war, and the dominant political reportage of the generals versus a federal alliance of prodemocracy parties—all act to force narrative linearity upon history. This politics of forgetting attempts to channel the political agency and subjectivities of Burmese people.

For example, in the 1990s, the urban centers of Yangon (Rangoon) and Mandalay were transformed with the forcible removal of hundreds of thousands of residents to rice fields on the outskirts of the cities. The area became known as the "New Fields" (Allot 1994), and the residents began their new lives with virtually no compensation for the houses, apartment buildings, and businesses they left behind. The changes in living arrangements, quality of life, and economic prospects severely affected many families. Increased rates of sexual assault, commercial sex work, alcoholism, domestic abuse, and sexual barter (Skidmore 2003a) in the New Fields constitute evidence of the breakdown of many traditional social structures. Residents were sundered from a Buddhist cosmology where they had lived close to main Buddhist infrastructures such as the pagoda complexes on Mandalay Hill and the Mandalay Fort and its surrounding monasteries and pilgrimage halls (Dhamma yon).

In the following fifteen years, garment factories opened and closed in industrial zones meant to employ these formerly urban workers. Hospitals, roads, and schools were opened or extended, and the markets in these townships have grown. Boom industries have developed in land speculation, money lending, gambling, and prostitution. In contrast to this reality, the history of this area, as written by the regime, is of a phenomenally successful "huts to highrise" scheme, where urban residents are given modern accommodation and provided with employment opportunities and an ability to partake in the development of the nation (Skidmore 2004: 84–97). It is in the narrow lanes of these relocated townships that I first conducted ethnographic fieldwork and where I came to learn about a particular form of subjectivity and its radical political potential.

I already had an inkling that the regime was worried about forms of authority other than itself, and in particular, forms of charismatic authority. The

demonization of Daw Aung San Suu Kyi in the regime's newspapers is unceas-
ing, but it's not just prodemocracy politicians who are viewed as threatening, it
is also charismatic religious leaders and healers. Burmese people need no remind-
ing of this fact. Almost everyone in Rangoon can tell you about the well-known
healer, Saya San, who led a peasant rebellion against the British in the 1930s
(Herbert 1982). Rangoon landmarks memorialize key figures in the fight for
Independence in the 1940s and early 1950s, when fiery monks such as U Wizara
rallied the population, in part through recourse to the Buddhist foundations of
Burman culture. Army of God Twins, Johnny and Luther Htoo, led God's Army in
southeastern Burma and were believed to create magical bullets that made
themselves and their troops invincible (Ingram 2001). Religion and medicine
are two areas of knowledge and praxis that the regime knows can lead Burmese
subjects to collective political action.

Burmese beliefs in causality and order means that things happen when a
variety of necessary events and forces align to bring a particular path of possibility into existence. This tenet is one of a web of associated epistemological
understandings of the structure of time, matter, and place that have pre-Buddhist
antecedents. In the Burmese framework of existence, power is a property that
moves through time and place and movement is rarely linear. All this means
that Burmese people have an extremely strong belief in the miraculous. This
belief forms the basis for the most potent types of political agency. When agents
of the Burmese regime scurry from place to place removing statues of weikza
(wizards), jailing mystics and those who practice both religion and medicine,
the regime is acknowledging the power of the Burmese belief in the miraculous
and its potential as a political threat to the state.

From the Burmese regime's perspective, the main problem with having a
repressed populace who believe in the miraculous is that the linear narrative of
state-making (that is, the belief in a forward-moving development into a peaceful, secure, prosperous, and modern nation) is at odds with the forms of temporality and causation that Burmese know to be true. A belief in the miraculous
means that at any moment something totally unexpected can occur, and the
path of the future will be changed. For the junta to convince Burmese people
that they are going to rule in perpetuity and everyone ought to give up trying to
resist them runs against popular wisdom. Burmese people know that power
exists in many forms across various domains and that the military regime controls only one form of power in this particular moment.

Individual strategies for escaping from the oppressive present involve dissociation, both physical and mental, and are very common in Burma. The population of the central valleys and deltas hide their consciousness from the
regime and wait out its ascendancy. State-making falters because for dissociative subjects, this form of being-in-the-world bears little similarity to the linear
nature of the state's historical projects. Burmese see history as just another

version or string of events that happened along one path of causality, making history a complex and contentious issue. In addition to the many histories of Burma's minority groups, alternate readings of history are also based upon an adherence to religious, cosmological, and occult time frames. These latter forms of temporality and causality are framed by the subjunctive mood, where different modes or levels of the present can fuse in particular moments to alter the course of the future.[1]

The strong belief in the miraculous is the most important example of the Burmese subjunctive mode. As the nation has become progressively impoverished, Burmese increasingly turn to the miraculous as a strategy for improving their daily lives. The construction of an ornate temple in Rangoon in which supernatural imagery is stressed is evidence of this phenomenon (Bekker 1989). *Dagò*, the manipulation of sacred power through objects associated with the Buddha (Kumada 2002), is also reported in times of political and economic crisis, as are increased encounters with Nat spirit mediums (Brac de la Perrière 2002) and ornate funerary and other rituals associated with the movement from one world to another (Robinne 2002). The creation of new Nat spirits, the reported thickening of the right side of Buddha images after the democracy leader, Aung San Suu Kyi, touched a particular Buddha image (Houtman 1999), and the reported appearances of a poltergeist at the site of the origin of the 1988 prodemocracy uprising (Leehey 2000) are small, everyday occurrences that reveal the deep Burmese belief and investment in the miraculous as a source of potential political and religious salvation. The millions of Burmese who have, since the failed democracy uprising, moved to meditation centers (Jordt 2001), monasteries and nunneries (Kawanami 2002), and semi-autonomous Buddhist areas such as that overseen by the late Thamanya Sayadaw (Tosa 2002; Rozenberg 2002) are further examples of the increasing disengagement that Burmese have with the world of authoritarian power. Instead, Burmese people have engaged in realms where forms of supernatural authority and power hold the potential for changes in the material and psychological conditions of one's daily life.

Waiting, wandering, denying, and forgetting—this is how the people of the New Fields characterize their lives and the strategies they enact to stay sane and ward off the feelings of rage, impotence, and despair. Many Burmese people whom I have spoken to in central Burma adopt a strategy of waiting, in which they describe their "minds'" leaving temporarily, while waiting for change. In Burmese Buddhism the enduring part of consciousness that remains after death and moves through the cycle of reincarnation to its eventual release through enlightenment is conceived of as a butterfly spirit. These butterfly spirits are released by an oppressed populace out into the cosmos, where they congregate in various alternate dimensions and planes of reality. Burmese people suspend this-worldly history by allowing their butterfly spirits to inhabit nontemporal dimensions or realms. The mundane world (*loka*) is deferred as Burmese butterfly spirits wander

Truth commissions must account for religion and ways victims deal

through other subjective realities. They shelter in these domains, waiting for an end to military rule.

At the Rangoon Drug Rehabilitation Unit, I interviewed fifty men and boys being forcibly detoxified of heroin, methamphetamine, and barbiturate addiction. The young male heroin addicts tell me that they send their minds to the kinds of places that they see on television or read about in books: leisure and entertainment precincts that don't exist in Burma. Their minds sleepwalk through these pleasurable domains until withdrawal symptoms rouse them back to full consciousness in the mundane world. In a similar way, young women and girls working in the sex industry in the New Fields tell me that they send their minds flying to their mother's hearts when they are engaged in sexual intercourse. The dissociative strategy denies their mind to the men they service, while allowing them to provide money for themselves and their families, keeping all alive.

Unemployed housewives of the New Fields feel that they live each day the same as the last. They tell me of the many ways they refuse to live in this present reality. They concentrate on the minutiae of everyday life; their conversations skim along the surface of daily events and conditions; emotional life is kept deliberately shallow, and they refuse to remember the past or plan for the future; they refuse to listen to news and current affairs; and they invest their time and attention in escapist pursuits such as the video hut and participation in the monthly lottery draws (Skidmore 2003a, 2004). The nature of the subjunctive mood that blankets central Burma, with its chief characteristic of possibility and the potential for immediate transformation, makes waiting a positive strategy for both suffering and survival.

A reading of the violent past must thus include the subjunctive mode as a dimension of lives lived through conflict. As Arias (1997: 825) has written about Guatemala: "the enormous changes experienced in Guatemala in recent years . . . force us to re-examine the inherent meaning of the space of subjectivity and the role of agency. In the end it is in these areas that systems of thought develop and knowledge that contributes to the renovation or restructuring of meaning emerges." He might also have added that it is in these spaces of subjectivity that forms of political agency may both arise and find shelter.

Engaged Anthropologist

I mentioned at the beginning of this chapter that the very question as to whether to be an engaged anthropologist (or not) is troubling to me. In such conditions of repression, terror, and civil war, there seems to me to be no ethical alternative to becoming engaged. This is especially true for anthropologists who take upon themselves the burden of conveying the most secret thoughts, fears, and experiences of our informants. This does not necessarily mean the kind of activism and advocacy on behalf of indigenous peoples that involves becoming engaged in the daily battles waged against an oppressive regime or system. This is the task of Burmese people, and the Burmese diaspora have been extraordinarily successful legal and cyber warriors (Danitz and Strobel 1999; Brooten 2004; Zarni 2005). Report upon report has been compiled by activist expatriate groups and by international human rights organizations about the atrocities perpetrated by the Burmese military regime against the people of eastern Burma (for example, SHRF and SWAN 2002; Apple and Martin 2003; WLB 2004). Thousands of stories of rape, torture, and the death of babies, infants, girl children, men, and women lie between their pages, and yet the Burmese regime denies any wrongdoing or any violation of the Geneva Convention (Po Khwa 2002; AFP 2003). Even highly credible evidence of chemical weapons usage by the junta (Panter 2005) goes barely mentioned in the international press, and on such issues the Burmese scholarly community is completely silent.

Silence is a powerful force in the contemporary world. Mechanisms such as censorship and fear, and motivations like greed and a desire for power, fame, and wealth cause individuals, institutions, and companies to remain silent on the ongoing campaign of terror waged by the Burmese regime against its own people. Academic silence seems to me to be completely unacceptable and a form of complicity in the politics of forgetting pioneered by dictatorial regimes.

The funerals for the seventy people confirmed by the *Democratic Voice of Burma* killed in the three bomb blasts in Rangoon on May 7 (DVB 2005) have been anything but quiet. Hundreds of Burmese people have attended memorial services held at the Yea Way and Htein Pin cemeteries, and such funerals are loud in order to ward off green ghosts and malevolent spirits of the unquiet dead who died "green" or untimely deaths. Curiously, the Burmese ruling council has been silent on the issues of consolation and compensation for the families of the victims, fueling even more teashop speculation that the regime carried out the blasts against the economic interests of its in-house opponents.

The discrediting of in-country information as emotive, exaggerated, anecdotal, or nonverifiable makes the ongoing bombing campaign seemingly inexplicable: too many possible actors, too many potential motivations. The bombings are thus largely ignored because of the apparent paucity of information about them. Not enough is known about Burmese people's actions under authoritarianism, it is widely believed, for analysis to be made about such broad opposition.

How can anthropologists in particular (and academics in general) fail to engage with the fear, suffering, and hope that infuse our conversations with repressed people? How could one justify a research methodology or project in contemporary Burma in which these turbulent lives are peripheral to the research questions at hand? Until such time as Burmese people are free to write against the politics of forgetting, I will continue to write about Burmese repression and Burmese ways of understanding and acting upon the world with a sense of indeterminacy and in the subjunctive mode. To maintain a polysemous, multivalent rendering of accounts of violence, to juxtapose the absurdities of authoritarian rule, and to render the subjectivity of our informants in vivid detail is to remain true to Michael Taussig's vision of the essential possibility of creative disruption. Surely the spirits of the men, women and children whose bodies were recently buried at Yea Way and Htein Pin cemeteries are deserving of this relatively simple task from academics who make their lives and reputations from commenting upon, and working amid, other people's misery.

NOTE

1. The theory of subjunctivization describes how human beings understand the ruptures to temporality and their sense of normalcy at moments of crisis and rapid change. Victor Turner (1990: pp) has described the "subjunctive mood" in the following way: "I sometimes talk about the . . . 'subjunctive mood' of culture, the mood of maybe, might-be, as-if, hypothesis, fantasy, conjecture, desire . . . a storehouse of possibilities, not by any means a random assemblage but a striving after new forms and structure." And as Edward Bruner (in Good and DelVecchio Good et al. 1994) notes, "to be in the subjunctive mode is to be . . . trafficking in human possibilities rather than in settled certainties." Like chronic illness sufferers, frightened and repressed Burmese people leave the future unemplotted so as to admit the possibility of miraculous change. The subjunctive mode is the mode of Burma. To live with the unexpected, and with possibility, is the normal modus operandi of the entire nation. It is only when one is "beyond fear," for example in the darkest moments of terror or despair, that one can no longer exist in a subjunctive mode (Skidmore 2003b).

REFERENCES

AFP (Agence-France Presse). 2003. "Myanmar Rejects Latest U.S. Rape Accusation." *Agence-France Presse*, April 7.

Allot, Anna J. 1994. *Inked Over, Ripped Out: Burmese Storytellers and the Censors.* Chiang Mai: Silkworm Books.

Apple, Betsy, and Veronika Martin. 2003. "No Safe Place: Burma's Army and the Rape of Ethnic Women." Refugees International, April. www.refugeesinternational.org/files/3023_file_no_safe_place.pdf.

Arias, Arturo. 1997. "Comment on Consciousness, Violence, and the Politics of Memory in Guatemala." CA Forum on Anthropology in Public. *Current Anthropology* 38.5 (December): 824–825.

Asia Times. 2005. "Junta Clamps down after Yangon Blasts." *Asia Times*, May 11.

Bekker, Sarah M. 1989. "Changes and Continuities in Burmese Buddhism." In *Independent Burma at Forty Years: Six Assessments*, edited by Josef Silverstein. Ithaca: Cornell University Southeast Asia Program.

Benjamin, Walter. 1983. *Das Passagen Werk.* Frankfurt au Main: Suhrkamp.

Bowring, Philip. 2005. "Chances for Reform in Myanmar Are Slim." *International Herald Tribune*, New Features, April 5.

Brac de la Perrière, Bénédicte. 2002. "Transmission, Change and Reproduction in the Burmese Cult of the 37 Lords." Paper presented at Burma Studies Conference, Burma-Myanma(r) Research and Its Future. Gothenburg, Sweden, September 21–25.

Brooten, Lisa. 2004. Human Rights Discourse and the Development of Democracy in a Multi-ethnic State." *Asian Journal of Communication* 14.2: 174–191.

Burma Issues. 2005. "Market Bomb Explosion Kills Two." *Burma Issues Weekly* 225 (April 21–27). http://www.burmaissues.org/En/BIWeekly2005-04-27-225.html.

Danitz, Tiffany, and Warren P. Strobel. 1999. "Networking Dissent: Cyber-Activists Use the Internet to Promote Democracy in Burma." *Virtual Diplomacy*. United States Institute of Peace, November 8. www.usip.org/virtualdiplomacy/publications/reports/ vburma/ vburma/vburma_intro.html.

DVB (*Democratic Voice of Burma*). 2005a. "Bus Stop Bomb Spreads Fear in Burma's Capital." *Democratic Voice of Burma News*, March 18.

———. 2005b. "Another Bomb Blast in Burma's Capital." *Democratic Voice of Burma News*, March 22.

———. 2005c. "Bomb Blast in Mandalay Kills at Least Two." *Democratic Voice of Burma News*, April 26.

———. 2005d. "Burmese Authorities Invited Buddhist Monks to Ward Off Evil in Mandalay." *Democratic Voice of Burma News*, April 27.

———. 2005e. "Burma Mandalay Blast Claims Another Life." *Democratic Voice of Burma News*, May 2.

———. 2005f. "More than 70 People Killed in Rangoon Blasts, Not 19 as Claimed by Junta," *Democratic Voice of Burma News*, May 2.

Feldman, Allan. 2004. "Memory Theatres, Virtual Witnessing, and the Trauma-Aesthetic." *Biography* 27.1: 163–202.

Good, Byron J., and Mary-Jo Delvecchio Good et al. 1994. "In the Subjunctive Mode: Epilepsy Narratives in Turkey." *Social Science and Medicine* 38.6 (March 15): 855–892.

Gutter, Paul. 2001. "Law and Religion in Burma." *Legal Issues on Burma Journal* 8 (April): 1–18.

Hale, Charles R. 1997. "Consciousness, Violence, and the Politics of Memory in Guatemala." *Current Anthropology* 38.5 (December): 817–838.

Herbert, Patricia. 1982. "The Hsaya San Rebellion (1930–1932). Reappraised." Melbourne: Monash University Centre for Southeast Asian Studies, Working Paper no. 27.

Houtman, Gustaaf. 1999. *Mental Culture in Burmese Crisis Politics: Aung San Suu Kyi and the National League for Democracy*. Tokyo: Institute for the Study of Languages and Cultures of Asia and Africa, Tokyo University of Foreign Studies.

Ingram, Simon. 2001. "God's Army Twins Captured." BBC News, January 17. www.news. bbc.co.uk/1/hi/world/asia-pacific/1121333.stm.

Irrawaddy. 2005a. "Death Toll Rising in Rangoon." *Irawaddy Online Edition*, May 8. http://www.irrawaddy.org/aviewer.asp?a = 4609.

———. 2005b. "Opposition groups scan 'Burma Day'." *Irawaddy Online Edition*, April 4. http://www.irrawaddy.org/aviewer.aspia = 4609.

Jordt, Ingrid. 2001. "The Mass Lay Meditation Movement and State-Society Relations in Post-Independence Burma." Ph.D. dissertation, Harvard University.

Kawanami, Hiroko. 2002. "Religious Ideology, Representation, and Social Realities: The Case of Burmese Buddhist Womanhood." Paper presented at Burma Studies Conference, Burma-Myanma(r) Research and Its Future. Gothenburg, Sweden, September 21–25.

Kleinman, Arthur, and Joan Kleinman. 1994. "How Bodies Remember: Social Memory and Bodily Experience of Criticism, Resistance and Delegitimation Following China's Cultural Revolution." *New Literary History* 25.3 (Summer): 707–736.

Kumada, Naoko. 2002. "Dago, Cosmogony, and Politics: Religion and Power in Burmese Society." Paper presented at Burma Studies Conference, Burma-Myanma(r) Research and Its Future. Gothenburg, Sweden, September 21–25.

Lambrecht, Curtis, and David Mathieson. 2005. "Casting Light on Opacity: An Argument for a Grounded Political-Economy Approach to the Study of Burma." Paper presented at Australian National University, April 27.

Leehey, Jennifer. 2000. "Censorship and the Burmese Political Imagination." Paper presented at Northern Illinois University, October.

Myo Lwin. 2005. "Bomb at Mandalay Market Leaves Two Dead." *Myanmar Times and Weekly Review* 14.264. May 2–8.

Pandolfi, Mariella. 1990. "Boundaries inside the Body: Women's Suffering in Southern Peasant Italy." *Culture, Medicine and Psychiatry* 14: 255–273.

Panter, Martin. 2005. "Chemical Weapons Use by Myanmar Army." *Christian Solidarity Worldwide*. www.csw.org.uk.

Po Khwa. 2002. "The Enemies of the People." *New Light of Myanmar*, September 12.

Redfield, Peter. 2004. "A Few of His Favorite Things." *Anthropological Quarterly* 77.2 (Spring): 355–363.

Robben, Antonious C.G.M., and Marcelo Suárez-Orozco, eds. 2000. *Cultures under Siege: Collective Violence and Trauma*. Cambridge: Cambridge University Press.

Robinne, Françoise. 2002. "Shamanistiz Practice in a Kachin Village." Paper presented at Burma Studies Conference, Burma-Myanma(r) Research and Its Future. Gothenburg, Sweden, September 21–25.

Rozenberg, Guillaume. 2002. "Reciprocity and Redistribution in the Quest foe Sainthood Burma." Paper presented at Burma Studies Conference, Burma-Myanma(r) Research and Its Future. Gothenburg, Sweden, September 21–25.

———. 2005. "Journey to the Land of the Cheaters." In *Burma at the Turn of the Twenty-First Century*, edited by M. Skidmore Honolulu: University of Hawai'i Press.

Sartre, Jean-Paul. 1972. *The Psychology of Imagination*. London: Methuen.

SHRF (Shan Human Rights Foundation) and SWAN (Shan Women's Action Network). 2002. "License to Rape: The Burmese Military Regime's Use of Sexual Violence in the Ongoing War in Shan State." May. www.shanland.org/HR/Publication/LtoR/ license_to_rape.htm.

Skidmore. Monique. 1995. "The Politics of Space and Form: Cultural Idioms of Resistance and Remembering." *Santé, Culture, Health* 10.1–2(Fall): 33–72.

———. 1996. "In the Shade of the Bodhi Tree: Dhammayietra and the Re-awakening of Community in Cambodia." *Crossroads: An Interdisciplinary Journal of Southeast Asian Studies* 10.1: 1–32.

———. 2003a. "Behind Bamboo Fences: Forms of Violence against Women Myanmar." In *Violence against Women in Asian Societies*, edited by L. Manderson and L. R. Bennett. London: RoutledgeCurzon.

———. 2003b. "Darker Than Midnight: Fear, Vulnerability and Terror-making in Urban Burma (Myanmar)." *American Ethnologist* 30.1: 5–21.

———. 2004. *Karaoke Fascism: Burma and the Politics of Fear*. Philadelphia: University of Pennsylvania Press.

Taussig, Michael P. 1980. *The Devil and Commodity Fetishism*. Chapel Hill: University of North Carolina Press.

Taylor, Robert, and Morten Pederson. 2005. "Supporting Burma/Myanmar's National Reconcilliation Process." Paper presented at the Burma Day conference. Brussels, April 5.

———. 1987. *Shamanism, Colonialism and the Wild Man: A Study in Terror and Healing*. Chicago: University of Chicago Press.

———. 1991. *The Nervous System*. New York: Routledge.

———. 1992. *Mimesis and Alterity: A Particular History of the Senses*. New York: Routledge.

———. 1997. *The Magic of the State*. New York: Routledge.

———. 1999. *Defacement: Public Secrecy and the Labor of the Negative.* Stanford: Stanford University Press.

———. 2003. *Law in a Lawless Land: Diary of a Limpieza.* New York: New Press.

———. 2004. *My Cocaine Museum.* Chicago: University of Chicago Press.

Tosa, Keiko. 2002. "Weikza: The Case of Tamanya Tang Hsayadaw." Paper presented at Burma Studies Conference, Burma-Myanma(r) Research and Its Future. Gothenburg, Sweden, September 21–25.

Turner, Victor. 1990. "Are There Universals of Performance in Myth, Ritual and Drama?" In *By Means of Performance: Intercultural Studies of Theatre and Ritual*, edited by Richard Schechner and Willa Appel. Cambridge: Cambridge University Press.

United States of America Department of State, Bureau of Democracy, Human Rights and Labor. 2005. *Burma: Country Reports on Human Rights Practice–2004.* February 28. http://www.state.gov/g/drl/rls/hrrpt/2004/41637.htm.

USA Today. 2005. "Bomb Explodes in Myanmar, Killing Two and Wounding at Least 15." *USATODAY.com.* April 26. http://www.usatoday.com/news/world/2005-04-26-myanmar-blast_x.htm.

WLB (Women's League of Burma). 2004. "System of Impunity: Nationwide Patterns of Sexual Violence by the Military Regime's Army and Authorities in Burma." Women's League of Burma. September. www.womenofburma.org/Report/SYSTEM_OF_IMPUNITY.pdf.

Zarni. 2005. "Trials of Total, and Pro-Boycott Burma Activism: Compiler's Note." Free Burma Coalition. http://freeburmacoalition.blogspot.com/2005/02/trials-of-toal-and-pro-boycott-burma.html.

3

War and the Nature of Ultimate Things

An Essay on the Study of Postwar Cultures

ROBERTA CULBERTSON

War

At the beginning of the twenty-first century, war knows few boundaries. Battle-fields and towns are superimposed. Wars wind tightly round the lives of citizens, who become their primary casualties. Soldiers fight across villages, using fami-lies as hostages and shields, and from those villages take children as their soldiers. Governments bomb their own citizens at the behest of other govern-ments, or under the guise of peacekeeping. Genocide is defined as war, and armies blossom everywhere, ragtag to computerized, national to warlord-run, supported by international markets in drugs and guns.

Nor does war honor other boundaries. It does not end with cease-fires or treaties, or even when the combatants are exhausted and impoverished. New wars reassert old war lines of skirmish, reinvoke historical wrongs in the service of new exigencies and demands, and employ child soldiers grown up as wars leap the bounds of their own time. In the most devastating cases, the thinking of war becomes the thinking of peacetime, and peace devolves into perpetual violence.

War today (perhaps it was always so, but perhaps not) bursts the bounds of the everyday and comes to occupy that ground for itself. The brutal lessons and expectations of war quickly replace the quotidian emotions of family and home, the warmth of familiar rooms, and innocent glances with wartime highs and devastations (Hedges 2003). Even the banal is roughed up by the metaphors and patterns of war: simple arguments take on the shape of conflict, and disagree-ments devolve into distrust and the demonization of the other. Afterward, war continually reappears in cultural and individual memories and denials in a strange malaise that passes from one generation to the next. The teachings and manner of war masquerade as contemporary truth and the immutable nature of things. We see the shadows of war in the long silences of postwar and in its mutual mistrusts. We see it in high rates of depression, anxiety, and dysfunction in places of "peace."

The answers to why war holds its power so fully for so long are often based in "common sense" or pathology. In the harder sciences, the longevity of war is attributed to the costs and politics of wartime or the social and demographic facts of war. From economic and political perspectives, war is useful to some, damaging to others. It opens markets and ensures them. It makes victims of most of those at ground zero but makes fortunes for those who supply it. The effects of war persist because wars destroy economies or reroute them along extralegal lines, and because armies still occupy the garrisons. The egregious pain of the aggrieved and harmed continues: poverty, exile, loss, and grief. The bounds of normal social life are breached in war, and in the gaps black markets and bribery make a guesswork and a mad chaos of life, which itself becomes a new kind of normalcy.

But there are other, more profound reasons for the longevity of war, ones that surpass even the psychological and the social, though they manifest most clearly in those domains. In its extreme moments war breaks the bounds of morality and the senses, exposing a world beyond the known and often destroying the most deeply held assumptions about the nature of the world. War exposes the nature of ultimate things without the mediating benefit of concepts and frames, and leaves a war-torn, shattered metaphysics. Its violence and boundary breaking confront the mind with the inexplicable and the intolerable. The substance of this inexplicable is not vacant but vastly different and almost impossible to describe. Its essence is detectable in the manner of a negative, in what is left behind. This experience of the ineffable in anguishing, excruciating circumstances shapes war-torn worlds by changing the very grounds of meaning.

After War

The injustices and crimes of wartime, for example, overwhelm the normal processes of justice and punishment; issues of culpability, restitution, and punishment remain open wounds in cultures unable to come to closure (Minow 1998; Murphy and Hampton 1988). Closure remains elusive not only for practical reasons but also because a host of questions remain unfathomable: what are we that we inflict and feel pain so terribly? What causes evil? Is there any ultimate accounting of right and wrong? Who decides? What is chance, what fate, and what choice? The list is lengthy, and it is the nature of war to have both posed them and removed comfortable answers.

What is the metaphysics of the war-torn world? Is there a metaphysics of war and survival that encompasses a significant and lasting break with peacetime patterns of belief and explanations of the unseen—that shapes and colors life thereafter, perhaps in ways unattended or misperceived or denied?

If so, what might be the lines of such metaphysics? How might we come to recognize them? Will they emerge in stories, dreams, and events? How will a war-torn metaphysics shape worldly decisions and plans?

If war produces a certain war-torn metaphysics, an experience of the ultimate nature of the world that differs from the unvoiced assumptions of the peaceful everyday, might it not be important to invoke that metaphysics to stop war or ameliorate its effects? Might not that metaphysics both suggest why war may continue—at least in part—and what might be done to dress its deepest wounds? Perhaps new enmities and reconstituted wars emerge not only from economic dislocations and political turmoil but also from a phenomenology of danger and suspicion that is more encompassing and tenacious than imagined, and that is itself rooted in a different view of how the world is fundamentally constituted.

The Institute on Violence and Survival at the Virginia Foundation for the Humanities explores this question of the metaphysics of the war-torn world through scholarship focusing on and interpreting survivor texts, accounts, reports, and other expressions of survivor realities. We construe the notion of "survivor" broadly to include victims, witnesses, and the perpetrators and instigators of war, taking from other work in the field the notion that in war most (not all) are in some sense survivors. This is so because war operates by its own logic, which destroys the more shallow human logics of economy, civil society, and personal intent by bursting their presumptions.

In several years of work with survivor materials, fellows and staff at the Institute have noted that survivor accounts, written and oral, are filled with, begin from, and suggest metaphysical themes. At the Institute, we support the development of this particular reading of survivor materials with the aid of survivors. This is not by way of privileging survivor discourse, but in order to make use of the close and intimate knowledges of those who know war in this way. We believe that such explorations may contribute to seemingly intractable debates about dimensions of the survivor experience—truth and falsehood, memory and moral wrong, reconciliation and revenge, denial and forgetting—by exposing their roots in the alteration of fundamental assumptions about the world in the course of war.

The Experience of War

War is perhaps the species' most overwhelming encounter with itself, though the nature of that encounter is in part to disappear in a welter of subsequent meanings and activities that glorify or deny war's primal existential moments. The survivor of war is fundamentally changed by his or her experience of the proximity of death, chance, and culpability, experienced not in everyday ways but as atrocities, as horrible deaths and impossible choices or consequences: "The thing that was very upsetting was the fact that we, as soldiers on the first line of defense, were unable to protect our civilians. That was the hardest psychological moment, because we thought that we should be those who they should fight, they should shoot at us, not at our children and wives" (Somali soldier "T," 1998–1999).

The survivor experiences grief, for example, but not ordinary grief (Eisenbruch 1991). Cultural bounds and practices prepare people for the death of one or many, but not for the death of thousands; for death by natural causes, but not death by humans using symbolically laden means such as dismemberment, evisceration, and impalement. When any of these methods becomes expected and bounded by countersymbols in a postmodern war it is replaced by more horrific methods—the point is the destruction of meaning and symbol, the overwhelming of the limits of perception and human tolerance.

The wounds inflicted in war penetrate and sunder the bounds of self and self-respect, of the expected and the simply human. The brutalized may become brutal, may be trained to be. Beyond those bounds of self, the lines of normal life continue to be erased until far from the border of one's country or one's former understandings one comes to an uneasy rest, and the truths of now and then ceaselessly crash against one another as loss.

In sum, the loose logic of war twists and subverts familiar meaning in ways planned and unplanned (Feitlowitz 1999). It breaks the bounds of normal thought and feeling, taking these into realms that are at once terrible and compelling. The events of war elude frames of word or image, becoming not so much unspeakable as unreferenced, detached, and resistant to normal definitions. Writing of Rwanda, Fergal Keane says: "I cannot write in terms of facts alone. So bear with me when the road runs down into the valleys of the heart and mind and soul. For this is a diary of an encounter with evil beyond any scope of reference I might have had when the journey began" (Keane 1995: 3–4). The demands of war throw the experience of the world into a formless place that is nevertheless full of the rawest feeling and pain. Life intrudes without the protection of limits, or having subverted them.

A common response to such frame-bursting experiences is the lyric poem, a body-based form of expression that does not rely on time, strict rules of grammar, or other elements of more formal speech, but uses its own intimate conventions—the use of metaphor, pun, the flesh, brevity—to communicate suffering by offering an imaginal experience of it. Although poetry may be considered "highbrow," it is in fact commonly appropriated as a form of expression that encapsulates horror—lodging it in the part of the mind that thinks as well as feels, that constantly reconfigures the world in the face of destruction—with the minimal tools of words. Whether the lyric poem in the Western sense is universal is debatable, of course, but in my experience at the Institute some form of expression that paradoxically holds the reader in beauty while offering him a taste of terror is taken up by many survivors across cultural lines. The love song, the prayer, the admonitory poem, the teaching tale, may all be adapted to the needs of the survivor, who thereby produces a crucial bit of ethnographic information on the nature of the war experience. The information contained in a poem or other lyric device provides an intimate, essential source of insight into the nature of war experience and its effect on perception of the ultimate (Orr 2002). Consider this excerpt from Siamanto's poem of the Armenian genocide, "The Dance":

> This incomprehensible thing I'm telling you about,
> I saw with my own eyes.
> From my window of hell
> I clenched my teeth
> and watched with my pitiless eyes:
> the town on Bardez turned
> into a heap of ashes.

The speaker sees horror beneath her window: several Armenian women are raped and set afire to the taunts of a group of soldiers. The burning women are called "brides," the gasoline "perfume," their nakedness, "wedding dresses." The account becomes extreme, terrible, almost unreadable:

> The twenty beautiful brides fell to the ground exhausted . . .
> "Stand up," they shrieked, waving their naked swords like snakes . . .
> Then someone brought to the mob a barrel of oil . . .
> O, human justice, let me spit at your forehead . . . !
> They anointed the twenty brides hastily with that liquid . . .
> "You must dance," they roared, "here is a perfume for you which even
>   Arabia does not have . . ."
> Then they ignited the naked bodies of the brides with a torch,
> And the charcoaled corpses rolled from dance to death. . . .

Words of love and marriage carry torture and death on their slim shoulders. Siamanto's poem ends:

> Like a storm I slammed the shutters
> of my windows,
> and went over to the dead girl
> and asked: "How can I dig out my eyes,
> how can I dig, tell me?"
> (Siamanto 1993)

Overwhelming Experience

Siamanto's poem is about a first terrible brush with war's power to ravage meaning, conveyed in a surfeit of emotion, agony, and moral outrage.

In time, as war drags on, the body's exhausted or hyperaroused responses to continued threat may reset the pattern of the everyday to include an insouciant or haunted intimacy with death and killing—perhaps as the soldiers in Siamanto's poem had found for themselves. This expectation at an existential level takes its toll, and makes of the world a different place from that in peacetime. Even apparent acceptance requires a view of life that is rooted in death and the fear of death—the ultimate metaphysical topic—though this is consistently suppressed or minimized: "A person can come in and see the war, fear the war, be scared of the violence—but their life, their very being, is not determined by the war. . . . I know everyone has suffered a loss in this war: a family member killed, a loved one captured and never heard of again. But it goes much deeper than this, to the very heart of the country, to my very heart. When I walk on the road, I carry nervousness with me as a habit, as a way of being" (Mozambican woman, quoted in Nordstrom 1997: 7). See what even this sensitive woman does: her response to the threat of death, loss, and deep harm to self and country she can only call "nervousness," not fear or terror. Her lamented habit betrays a creeping numbness to her own way of being, a sort of uneasy accommodation to her tenuous mortality.

At the edges of that "war being," just past the uncomprehended terrible, dart and press the inexplicable and unfathomable in a boundless universe beyond the bounds now broken. The experience feels at once unreal and super-real, at once more than the world has ever been and yet ungraspable, evanescent. For Siamanto's witness, this entails an overwhelming sense of terrible power or evil or wrong, to which the only response is a most violent form of denial—to want to dig out one's eyes. In the face of unbounded and very real horror, "human justice" is laughable. What is this horrible world? What other justice might there be that is equal to it? If none is felt or found, what does that fact say about the world?

At times the survivor of extremity, of the edge-experiences of war, encounters another form of extremity—the loss of all sense of understanding—a sudden conviction that things are not only not what they seem but also vast and incomprehensible. The contingency of each moment—or its complete design—is intolerably felt and not understood. The encounter is with what religious traditions refer to as "mystery." Wislawa Szymborska summarizes the power and the effect of the split second, the possibility of parallel worlds and the apparent randomness of eventualities, all agonizingly critical and unanswerable dimensions of life and death in the metaphysics of war:

Luckily there was a forest.
Luckily there were no trees.

Luckily a rail, a hook, a beam, a brake,
a frame, a turn, an inch, a second.

Luckily a straw was floating on the water.

Thanks to, thus, in spite of, and yet.
What would have happened if a hand, a leg,
one step, a hair away . . .

(Szymborska 1993)

The Roots of a War-Torn Metaphysics

The metaphysical encounters and confusions of survivors originate in the individual experience of two central and common events of every war: the breaking of the moral order that defines everyday life and defends it against the unbounded and absurd; and the overwhelming of the body's normal means of perception in the presence of pain or persistent fear. In this place of lost morality and overwhelmed perception something else may surface—the inexplicable. In the case of war, these two elements, which occur in nonwar circumstances in the context of crime, for example, are multiplied by the context of war itself. For these purposes, this context includes forced and often drastic changes in life circumstances, usually in the direction of dissolution or loss, the impossible juxtaposition of mutually exclusive categories of reality, and mass death. The result is overwhelming moral failures and impossible perceptions not just at the hands of someone outside social norms but often in the context of new or shattered norms, moral categories that seem to offer no redress for wounding. The overpowering combination is what torments Siamanto's witness: not just crime but a loss of moral groundedness; not just victimization but horror on a vast, society-wide scale and by design. This horror is visceral for victim and witness both, not only to the edge of sensory tolerance but beyond as well. In short, war often produces an experience of existence beyond the bounds of the moral and the sensual, and what is encountered there shapes life thereafter in particular ways.

Moral Affronts and the Dissolution of Everyday Reality

The following are empty synonyms:
man and beast
love and hate
friend and foe
darkness and light. . . .

I seek a teacher and a master
may he restore my sight hearing and speech
may he again name objects and ideas
may he separate darkness from light.

(Ròzewicz 1947)

Among the memories that most entangle the survivor are those that suggest he has done wrong by being insufficient to the task of being human. This is most often presented as the survivor's anguish, guilt, confusion, and sense of failure, but this sense of guilt and failure begs the question of standards. By what standards has the survivor failed? The agony in Auschwitz survivor Tadeusz Rózewicz's poem suggests that the question is more than a matter of social rules and ethics, even more than a matter of some violation of a person's expectations of himself. Survivors are not only angry with themselves for their failure to be brave or trustworthy or honest or careful; they feel they have broken rules that are ultimate and central to what it is to be human; rules that are foundational and unavoidable. They have failed basic, unassailable rules of human life, which address its sanctity, humans' mutual responsibility to keep one another alive, and an absolute abhorrence of death. Rules that are, in other words, transcendent, beyond daily expectations and explanations.

It is often suggested to survivors that the rules of a violent encounter must be different from the rules of an everyday exchange, and that the rules of war must be different from those of peace: "You can't blame yourself for your actions when you had no choice. That way you don't put the blame where it belongs; on the perpetrators, you take it on yourself. That accomplishes nothing, and it's wrong. Don't let the bad guys get off that easy! It was their fault, not yours!" (Strejilevich 1995).

But in general this is not acceptable to the survivor who is not politically trained. The survivor's sense of guilt and failure remains powerful and primary, and all memory is bound up to some degree in this sense of failure. This is because the rules by which survivors judge themselves (even more than they judge others) are rules they see as timeless, primary, immutable, and essential, and politics are at best a superficial balm.

Violent experiences first show their transcendent nature by pointing to rules and expectations about being human that surpass social categories or requirements, rules and expectations that seem to transcend ordinary reality and normal expectations. Transgressions are registered in the survivor's own mind, rather than by the society.

There are no tribunals for such failures; no one goes to jail for having failed in the ways survivors see themselves as failing. Even when these failures are clearly—to the objective eye—not matters of cowardice but the consequences of chance, self-preservation, failed efforts, and overwhelming force, the survivor still feels that he has failed, and that the court of public opinion is ignorant when it does not show him to the gallows. He holds himself to a standard that surpasses any everyday structure of morality, a higher moral standard that does not allow for human frailty.

In the poem, Rózewicz seeks a teacher to make sense of his new and intolerable understanding of the world, in which antonyms have become not only synonyms but "empty" ones, in which there seems to be no difference between man or beast, love or hate, in which all words and all meaning seem hollow. He has seen that ideas are not substantial or real but "mere words," "virtue and crime weigh the same." He feels this in himself—he is a man who was both "criminal and virtuous." He is anguished about his position in the world: a survivor led to slaughter with the rest, he is somehow morally at fault for having survived. There is no nihilism here, no cynical self-absolution, but rather anguish and grief—by virtue of some higher truth to which Rósewicz is appealing, and to which he feels accountable. He wants a teacher to explain this truth to him. Perhaps he doubts its existence; perhaps the appeal to a teacher is sarcastic. But still he is saying that something is amiss, something he cannot tolerate in himself or existence. Something calls him to account.

Anguish and guilt, then, this sense of having failed, are the first indication of survivors' discovery of the metaphysical. Guilt is the clear sign of grasping or intuiting fundamental, irrevocable, and always applicable laws of existence, to be found not on this earth or in human laws, or even in human action, but in some metaphysical place—in the out-reachings of the human mind to a god or a universal or natural order. This sense is within the mind and yet judges its actions by standards that feel beyond it, as if the mind does not end at the cranium but encompasses far more than can be seen.

Bodily Affronts and the Appearance of Unmediated Reality

War is perhaps the species' most potent encounter with itself because it is so embodied. It takes the body to the edges of its abilities to tolerate pain, fear, hunger, thirst, and confusion and generally holds it for long periods of time past these limits. Death weaves in and out, halted or advanced by chance or miracle, which become indistinguishable. Stopped one day by a bit of bread, the next by a chance warning, death is palpable in ways the comfortable do not encounter.

The biochemical environment of the body changes in war; it enters an advanced state of concentration in which all sensations unrelated to survival are discounted. What looks like numbness may in fact be a concentration on only certain "dangerous" stimuli, or evidence of the body's effort to hide in immobility. Much has been written about actual damage to the brain in the context of the persistent release of hormones that regulate the body's limited range of responses to threat: those processes damaged are those that provide impulse control and context (van der Kolk et al. 1996; van der Kolk 1987). The damage is irreversible, though it may be mitigated by pharmaceuticals or illegal drugs.

In moments of supreme danger or terrible witnessing, even the most prepared and trained body is psychologically compromised. The ego, it is said, confronted with the impossible likelihood of its own death or dissolution, ceases to take in sensory information as a form of protection, or takes it in only at primal action levels (run right, run left) that do not reach the sense of self. For this reason, it is generally remarked that survivors do not fully or accurately recall their most extreme experiences, those that take place beyond ego involvement with the sensoria (for example, see Riviere 1996 for a good account of repression and dissociation).

But at the Institute we have often remarked that survivors do describe such moments, albeit not necessarily in what is normally called description. The issue is how to discuss them, because the experiences or what is recalled of them "make no sense," or involve a self enacted beyond ego, a kind of embodied "other" self that took hold of the disintegrating biographical and socially and morally defined self:

> I said, "I think this is the end," because that was what I thought. I didn't know then that I would start shouting, "Damn it! I'm not going anywhere!" I didn't know then that the sudden wave of despair—this is the end! this is the end!—would come bursting forth in obscenities and profanities. I didn't know then that this litany of curses would help me more than the best identity cards and rubber stamps. "Get out!" he said, and pushed the papers off the table with his riding whip. The hall was empty. The blood drained from my face; the stairs spiraled below me. (Fink 1993: 60)

We wonder: perhaps the blankness and non-sense survivors sketch or even live out as flashbacks, misplaced emotions, and dreams are in fact pregnant and bursting with what is untold but not necessarily unknown about an experience beyond the self. Were Fink to ask questions of this moment in which she finds herself screaming at a Nazi officer with such effect that he lets her go, what might she conclude about who she had become at that moment? What might she make of the time-out-of time she had just inhabited when she found the stairs spiraling below her?

The answers to such questions are given sometimes in the language of memory and identity, dropping them back into the everyday and the given (Kleinman et al. 1997). Fink by this reading is both her disguise and her "self," and in war the identities move, submerge, and surface so as to keep her alive (Nordstrom 1997). The deep questions are about who she is then, really, where we might locate a moral being with responsibility, what we might eventually be able to tease out from her story as "the truth" (Kirmayer 1996; Riviere 1996). But perhaps Fink's "fictional" account (she was in hiding during the Holocaust, though this account does not purport to be her own—yet another layer of identity issues) is not only about memory and identity but also about how all such extreme events happen against a backdrop of the ineffable and not understood, often driven by the impossible and the miraculous. Perhaps the falling away of the staircase is not just fear and relief, but the falling away of the world.

Some Possible Dimensions of War-Torn Metaphysics

If we can say that the experience of war creates two incontrovertible encounters with the unbounded world—moral and physical—what can we see that people do with those encounters? Is this not the place for God, and redemption? How is this world described? How can everyday speech describe fully the experience of death, dismemberment, fear, the mockery and infliction of pain, the incomprehensible actions of one's own body, all by definition and fervent hope most crucially not everyday matters? "A man with a machete, halving a three-year-old." What does this accounting describe of the experience of witness, perpetrator and victim? What does it silence? One might grasp at one's traditions and religion to ground one at such moments, but, rooted as these are in the everyday, in the common and expected, they often desert or prove inadequate and irrelevant.

Fergal Keane has just encountered thousands of bodies in a churchyard in the now empty town of Nyarubuye, in Rwanda. In italics he writes, as if the words do not merit the status of his more "factual" information:

> How do I write this, how do I do justice to what awaits at the end of this road? As simply as possible. This is not a subject for fine words. . . . I look down to my left and see a child who has been hacked almost into two pieces. The body is in a state of advanced decay and I cannot tell if it is a girl or a boy. I begin to pray to myself. "Our father, who art in heaven . . . "These are prayers I have not said since my childhood but I need them now. . . . And then in front of me I see a group of corpses. . . . The bodies seem to be melting away. Such terrible faces. Horror, fear, pain, abandonment. I cannot think of prayers now. (1995: 78–79)

In his numbness, Keane suggests something about the response to moral violation and sensory surfeit: it includes silence, the perceived uselessness of most sources of comfort, but also a sense of something else. Keane suggests, in fact, an encounter with something that in another part of his book on the Rwandan genocide he calls "Evil," capitalizing it. He comes to feel that Evil is a thing, not an idea. But he does not know what to do with it or how to engage it—he can barely bring himself to speak of it. He assures us he does not want sympathy—as if sympathy should not be called upon to balance Evil or the suffering of it, as if we might begrudge him this easing of his own suffering. Or perhaps because he realizes that any effort on our part would be unavailing—he is now beyond our understanding and our universe and its particular close-by constellations.

Some who, unlike Keane, were not witnesses but victims report that something happened in the heat of war or the long debacle of the end of life as they knew it: a miracle, a visitation, the unexpected and impossible, a blessing, a space in which as life and even the most treasured duties and expectations fell away, the impossible intervened:

TELLER: A man came from the woods with bread. I was starving and could not move. I had given up! My children kept begging me to get up, but I couldn't. I didn't even want to! The man said, "take, eat this, the border is not far." I took and I ate this bread and the border was not far.

LISTENER: Was it real bread?

TELLER: What is this question? (Kauv 1988)

Ms. Kauv finds any question about this "bread" being real or not absurd; her look is not one of confusion or doubt or uncertainty but of exasperation—from her perspective, her place of understanding now, the question has no relevance. Yet in her metaphysics of war, Ms. Kauv does not feel resolved or even thankful. Though Ms. Kauv lives, she believes, by virtue of this encounter, the fact is not necessarily beautiful or redeeming. The point is that it happened and she is here now. Why is she here? Does it matter? Does she owe someone, or something? Like Keane, she cannot explain what she knows. Like Keane, she questions and objects more than accepts and defines. We are reminded of the cries, "where was God?" which posits either an empty and soulless universe or an evil one. In survivor metaphysics, the question is generally left open. Ms. Kauv does not become a mystic; she becomes haunted by the ill-explained edge between life and death and what is seen there.

The metaphysics of war are not comprehensive or redeeming metaphysical systems; they are metaphysical experiences. Though impossible events may mark a point at which a life was saved, a mistake avoided, the rules of nature suddenly and briefly reversed, this marks only a surprise inexplicable occurrence, a comment on cause and effect and perhaps on destiny or suffering. Perhaps survival is in fact a sentence of another kind, as Rózewicz says—to be dead would be easier than to confront and contemplate the long-lived, incomprehensible, and demanding reality of some salvation, of an incomprehensible reprieve that seems to beg response and gratitude—but how?

Many survivors cross-culturally report some terrible haunting that ties then to every subsequent now. They find themselves in an endless repetition of events, of inexplicable coincidences that replay the inexplicable moment. They live a life of such coincidences, in which horror and the inexplicable confront them with recurrent cosmic ironies. Here the encounter with an expanded world is not only problematic, mysterious and inconclusive, but also agonizing in its results not once, but again and again:

My husband was executed by a gun to the head. His head was destroyed by the gunshot. Just before, though we did not know the Khmer Rouge were coming, he made me promise to take care of our baby daughter if something should happen to him. As if he knew. He left me with that obligation in that awful place; at the time I said "yes, of course!" But this is what I do not understand: When my daughter-in-law died, in this country just two years ago, she made me promise before they left to go to dinner that I would take care of her baby if she should die. Then my boy called; they had been in a car accident. Her head was destroyed too; in death she looked just like my husband! And I now have a child to raise because I promised in a moment like that one a long time ago. As if she knew! It is the same! I want to know: why do these things keep happening? It is always the same! (Vatha 1997)

Survivor reports suggest, in short, that perhaps the collapse of a morally defined universe and of a universe defined by normal sensoria opens the door to a wider, boundless conception of the real in which all is shifting and paradoxical. It may take the form of blankness or the inexplicable; it may occasion numbness, but it is numbness in the face of something that cannot be encompassed. This is the realm of radical truth, as Michael Jackson might put it: "Truth is on the margins. . . . It makes its appearance fleetingly, when systems collapse and dogmas are exploded" (1995: 187). In the realm of radical truth, there are, it seems, no truths that comfort or explain.

Unintentionally, unexpectedly, and without frame, a participant in war at its traumatic edges thus confronts another means of human perception and thought altogether, and the world becomes a different place. It is a kind of dark enlightenment. But how to move from transcendence to meaning? It is not easily done. If little is recalled or can be said upon the step back from the abyss, the resulting affliction may be called repression. The recurring ways in which the haunting manifests itself in quenched desire for normal things and a deep sense of separateness will be called an illness. If no answers or frames for the experience present themselves, the survivor is left with a kind of haunting, a search for the meaning of transcendent experience that presents itself in other ways: perhaps with an obsession with the past which he mistakes for a desire for justice or a desire to forget. But perhaps the survivor is looking in the wrong place for answers.

Survivors as Unwitting Mystics

Religion scholar Jess Hollenback and some anthropologists have recently revived the study of mysticism, the attended-to, disciplined exercise of mystical thinking (Hollenback 1996). Hollenback suggests that certain acts of intention and focus produce a particular form of human experience, which can be described as different from everyday experience in the following ways: a mystical experience is a radical, trans-sensory metamorphosis of the subject's mode of consciousness; it provides a knowledge of what his tradition regards as ultimately real; it provides knowledge about matters of soteriological concern to his community; it is laden with affect; it is literal and metaphorical; it is fundamentally amorphous and its content historically and situationally conditioned; and it has its genesis in the recollective act. The "recollective" act, as Hollenback defines, is the result of single-pointed concentration or the escape from normal perception, precisely what survivors report in extremity.

Can perspectives and analytical tools like Hollenback's and those of the anthropologists of experience and perception (Jackson 1995) help us to more fully develop the dimensions of survivors' metaphysical thinking—the world or worlds they experience in changed states of consciousness, worlds that feel ultimately real, and that provide knowledge about matters of soteriological concern?

Perhaps such explorations and such discoveries can inform the discourse that now swirls about survival literature, survivor cultures, and survivor actions. Perhaps it can contribute to an understanding of survivors' curious gaps and overwhelming experiences and their embodied hauntings, and their obsessive moralizing about war or about those who harmed them in the course of war. Perhaps it can explain the preoccupations with evil on the part of some survivors, and the dead disinterest on the part of others in what evil they committed.

Perhaps a reading for the unseen and ultimate can contribute to the more sophisticated understanding of survivor accounts, and allow us to use those accounts to explore the possibilities of a problematic, compelling, different worldview and comprehension of ultimate things. Perhaps this, in turn, would allow us to inform other work on survivors, and to answer some of the more pressing problems of war and after.

What if, for example, moral issues of reconciliation and retribution could be informed by some knowledge of the hauntings of after-war? What if one brought survivors' concern with "soul loss" (as some survivors say it) to bear on questions of the disturbing encounter with the banality of evil? Might an understanding of survivors' possible conceptions of ultimate truths explain the impassioned pleas of some survivors for justice, or the curious conviction not only that there is no possible justice but that the concept is irrelevant?

And what if the difficulties of memory—false, blank, incomplete, impossible, unreliable—could be informed by the notion of a memory beyond the conceivable, a memory of immanence and boundlessness rather than a memory of specificity and event? What if the truth lies, as Jackson says, at the margins, and the survivor speaks not of what he saw on the ground but what he glimpsed beyond it? Then how might we take survivor narrative? What might be believed of what is so often discounted as overheated or imaginary, even by survivors themselves?

I don't believe it! But I was there, with my own eyes I saw the dark cloud cover our boat and keep us hidden from all the ships everywhere, all the

way out to the open sea. It was a miracle, or is it just that I dreamed it
somehow? Why did we all see it? Were we all hallucinating? I don't believe
it. I believe the cloud was there. I just don't know why. (Pham 1986)

An exploration of this dimension of survivor knowledge will require a slightly
different reading of survivor literature, accounts, art, and stories. It will require
a research agenda that asks about the unbounded. It will lead us to ask of survivors precisely how the unbounded world presents itself and interpenetrates
the everyday, the ways in which the apparently normal is not, how haunting is
not mere leftover superstition but real and abiding knowledge.

Many survivor accounts touching on this subject remain to be written. The
world the survivor knows is large, and largely haunted, thus often held close to
the chest, or armored against, or denied. Accounts of the ineffable are suspect
and simply beyond the bounds of common knowledge—there is nothing to do
with them. But if we were to court and encourage them, what might we find
about the metaphysical world of survival?

Perhaps we would find that it consists, at minimum, of the following: a singular, bursting event; the appearance of something or the collapse of everything;
a transcendent moment (which may be unrecalled in cognitive, describable
form); consequential miracles or unexpected turns of fate; and haunting after, as
in the repetition of patterns of coincidence. Such a world is not the normal world.
It makes demands, offers miracles, suffers from its repression under the cloak of
normalcy. It perhaps resurfaces as revenge or holy war or minor malice. Or perhaps, when attended to and recognized, it emerges as a healing force. Carolyn
Nordstrom, an ethnographer working in Mozambique, reports on a movement
among traditional healers, who are mystical thinkers by profession, to "take the
war out of people": "we walk with them, talk with them, reach into the earth with
them, coax a seed into food with them. We encourage them to do the ceremonies
that protect them and their families and lands, appease their ancestors, make our
community healthy and safe. You walk someone through these daily acts, with the
help of the healers, they learn what words can never convey" (1997: 218).

REFERENCES

Eisenbruch, Maurice. 1991. "From Post-Tramatic Stress Disorder to Cultural Bereavement":
    Diagnosis of South east Asian Refugees." *Social Science and Medicine* 33.6: 573–580.
Feitlowitz, Marguerite. 1999. *A Lexicon of Terror: Argentina and the Legacies of Torture*. London:
    Oxford University Press.
Fink, Ida. 1993. *The Journey*. Translated by Joanna Weschler and Francine Prose. New York:
    Plume, Penguin Books.
Forché, Carolyn. 1993. *Against Forgetting: Twentieth-Century Poetry of Witness*. New York:
    W.W. Norton.
Hedges, Chris. 2002. *War Is a Force That Gives Us Meaning*. New York: Anchor Books.
Hollenback, Jess Byron. 1996. *Mysticism: Experience, Response, and Empowerment*. University
    Park: Pennsylvania State University Press.

Jackson, Michael. 1995. *At Home In the World*. Durham: Duke University Press.

Kauv, Koeun. 1988. Personal, voluntary telling of an experience at the end of the Khmer Rouge regime to the author at a business luncheon.

Keane, Fergal. 1995. *Season of Blood: A Rwandan Journey*. London: Penguin Books.

Kirmayer, Laurence. 1996. "Landscapes of Memory: Trauma, Narrative, and Dissociation". In *Tense Past: Cultural Essays in Trauma and Memory*, edited by Paul Antze and Michael Lambek. London: Routledge.

Kleinman, Arthur, et al. 1997. *Social Suffering*. Berkeley: University of California Press.

Minow, Martha. 1998. *Between Vengeance and Forgiveness: Facing History after Genocide and Mass Violence*. Boston: Beacon Press.

Murphy, Jeffrie, and Jean Hampton, 1988. *Forgiveness and Mercy*. New York: Cambridge University Press.

Nordstrom, Carolyn. 1997. *A Different Kind of War Story*. Philadelphia: University of Pennsylvania Press.

Orr, Gregory. 2002. *Poetry as Survival*. University of Georgia Press. I am indebted to Greg for much of my understanding of the function of the lyric poem among survivors.

Pham, Tam. 1986. Personal telling to author, relating escape by boat from Vietnam.

Riviere, Susan. 1996. *Memory of Childhood Trauma: A Clinician's Guide to the Literature*. New York: Guilford Press.

Rózewicz, Tadeusz. "The Survivor." Available in a number of internet collections.

Siamanto. 1993. "The Dance." Translated by Balakian and Yaghlian. In *Against Forgetting: Twentieth-Century Poetry of Witness*, edited by Carolyn Forché. New York: W.W. Norton.

Strejilevich, Nora. 1995. Discussion with fellows at the Institute on Violence and Survival.

Szymborksa, Wislawa. 1993. "Any Case." Translated by Drabik and Olds. In *Against Forgetting: Twentieth-Century Poetry of Witness*, edited by Carolyn Forché. New York: W.W. Norton.

"T." 1998–1999. "Testimony of a Survivor, in People on War, a project of the International Committee of the Red Cross." Greenberg Research Inc. report on Somalia. The paragraphs containing this testimony, once on the Web site, were not included in the final report.

Van der Kolk, Bessel. 1987. *Psychological Trauma*. Washington, D.C.: American Psychiatric Press.

Van der Kolk, Bessal, et al. 1996. *Traumatic Stress: The Effects of Overwhelming Experience on Mind, Body, and Society*. New York: Guilford Press.

Vatha. 1997. Personal telling to the author in response to a question: "What do you still wonder about since that time?" Ms. Vatha is a survivor of the Pol Pot genocide.

4

Expert Witness

Notes toward Revisiting the Politics of Listening

ASALE ANGEL-AJANI

> One confesses—or is forced to confess.
>
> —Michel Foucault, *History of Sexuality*

A Confession

I am haunted by voices. There is one voice in particular that calls to me day in and day out, and unlike the loud rambling voices of the others that I hear, her voice is a distinct whisper that licks at my ears. I try to ignore the voices, but hers sits before me like a starving child. Her bloated stomach repels me. She cries to me at all hours. I hate to be alone with her, but she sits on my brain, pounding on my skull for attention. She keeps me up at night, and during the day her whispers make my skin crawl. I cannot be alone with her, and yet I dare not stray too far away.

Her voice demands to know if can I remember what it was like. She questions my memory's ability to return to that horrible place that is the prison. Can I, she wonders, walk back into my mind's eye and conjure up the images of the dark cold corners, the smells of cat shit, and the noise of heavy metal doors clanging shut? Can I return to the shouts of the angry guards or the embattled women? Can I remember the faces that held my deepest respect and affection, can I return to the women as they once were? Mostly, she wants to know if I will be able to live with myself for walking away from them.

She is teaching me that, maybe, for most people who work with "real live" flesh and blood, who negotiate the horrors that envelop people, maybe there is no salvation. It is one thing to do research safely from the archives and it quite another to make a living off of the everyday suffering of women.

Two or three things I know for sure: I cannot live with the fact that I peddle the flesh of women's stories for academic consumption, making them pretty, because the reality of their lives is too difficult to bear. I know that through the

incorporation of "theory" I have learned to water down difficult emotional moments so as not to appear too sentimental. Another thing that I know is that working with African women detained in one of Italy's largest female prisons, Rebibbia Femminile, numbed many of my emotional sensibilities. I am not certain that, despite my commitment (and my privilege) to struggle with these women for recognition and dignity, I have the strength to walk back into that space where the horrors of unspeakable trauma, institutional and societal violence, and individual suffering live. However, even though every moment was shaped by the institution and even small acts of resistance were bundled in reprisals, there were happy times, even feelings of utter joy. On very special days, many women were motivated by the promise of prospects for the future, for friendships and lives lived beyond the walls of Rebibbia. And on those days, I (and I am sure all of us) silently hoped that the world could be a different place for Black women who, forced by social conditions and their social positions, lived just beyond the confines of the fluctuating and unequal rules of dominant society.

I quickly learned that in spite of the lack of knowledge about how carceral systems actually operate, society imagines and even pleasurably envisions powerfully vivid images of crime, criminals, and prison life. These images are, of course, fed to people by academics and the media and because of this, stories of inmates, women inmates in particular, seem already familiar. "Incarcerated women" is the story that has already been told; they are old news. Both public and academic discourse about female criminals represents them as poor women of color, single mothers, and addicted to drugs. More sophisticated accounts identify imprisoned women often as survivors of physical violence and sexual abuse, who are less often detained for violent offenses than men. In spite of whatever truth these theories and ideas might hold, as imprisoned women, activists, and a few scholars have long argued, the lives of imprisoned women are much more complex than these mere "facts."[1]

When I began my research in 1996, I had, as a daughter of parents who had been incarcerated, long understood the quiet respect of not asking people who had been or were in prison why they were there. So, while I was in Rebibbia I did not ask. Because of this, I was shocked by some of the women's willing admission of what brought them to Rebibbia. I realized that because the prison officials introduced me as a researcher there seemed to be little question of why I was there and what information I was deemed as "needing to know." Many of the women had become very familiar with the rules and routine of being an interview subject. This unsettled me. Even though I knew that I was, by the nature of my position in the university, part of the machine that produced the often negative representations of prisoners to the world "outside," I hoped that I was more than just a narrator of other Black women's lives. I hoped I was more than just a mere anthropologist. I believed that I belonged to a group of activist-scholars who, through writing, research, and organizing are working toward the abolition of prisons as we know them and, through this process, exposing the broader racist, sexist, and classist social structures that criminalize and demonize poor Whites and people of color.

Firm in my commitment not to participate in furthering the criminalization of African women, whenever I shared my research I did not mention why women that I worked with in Rebibbia were imprisoned. Needless to say, this frustrated several audiences. I had failed the first duty as an anthropologist and as an academic. I learned that as an anthropologist, I had a *particular* professional duty to translate my observations about the lives of women who are forced to live in cages. But by discussing the toll that imprisonment, violence, and forced prostitution (among many other traumas) had on the lives of women—without ever having mentioned their crimes, or worse, by not confirming the veracity of some women's seemingly "outlandish" stories—I had not met the demands and expectations of my audience.[2] As much as representation and the practice of fieldwork have been debated, the anthropologist has not entirely rid herself of the role of "recovering the truth," the role of being the one who assembles evidence, and then testifies in a (court)room of her "peers."

Ethnographic Authority (again)

In the heyday of more reflective treatments about anthropology's troubled roots, Jim Clifford penned the influential essay "On Ethnographic Authority" in 1983. Although his essay encouraged questions about power and representation, anthropologists and other social scientists continue to be plagued with the unresolved quandary of ethnographic authority, so much so that save for a few recent ethnographies, many anthropologists have chosen to forgo the problem of authority by ignoring the question altogether. As it has been argued by mostly Native American, Black, and Latino anthropologists, it is one thing especially, as marginalized, racialized, and gendered voices within the discipline of anthropology to speak with authority, and it is quite another to speak authoritatively (Edmund Gordon, personal communication). As Faye Harrison argued in the groundbreaking publication of the Association of Black Anthropologists, *Decolonizing Anthropology*, "to recapture the authority . . . anthropology needs to confront both discursive and material power" (1991: vii). Although there have been many instructive monographs, edited volumes, and journal articles that attend to the issue of authority, representation, and power, I want to explore ethnographic authority through a discussion of the somewhat undertheorized notion of activist anthropology. Hale and Gordon argue that activist anthropology is "predicated on the idea that we need not choose between first-rate scholarship, on the one hand, and carefully considered political engagement, on the other. To the contrary, we contend that activist research can enhance the empirical breadth and the theoretical sophistication—as well as the practical usefulness—of the knowledge that we produce as anthropologists" (n.d.).

In this chapter I think through the promise and the limitations of engaged observation, especially the form of anthropological engagement some have called "witnessing." I will call attention to the ways that the act of anthropological witnessing is largely an attempt to (re)establish the authority of the ethnographer, without ever having to enter into this long-standing debate. I do not mean to suggest, however, that all ethnographers who evoke the figure of the anthropologist/witness are necessarily actively positioning themselves as authority. I believe that especially for ethnographers who work with and write about survivors of many forms of violence, the figure of the witness becomes a powerful space in which to authorize and legitimate the painful and often devastating histories that we anthropologists are allowed to listen to and sometimes see with our own eyes. Nevertheless, despite good intentions, we do not recognize both the responsibility of the witness and the many ways in which being called to act as a witness are not always noble. With the full-hearted embrace of the notion of the anthropologist as witness, we fail to fully question the conditions that make our work possible as well as critically assess the consequences of our ethnographic production.

I want to contemplate how we who are critical of the more traditional forms of social science data gathering and reporting often turn to courtroom metaphors, or worse. The metaphors that I will be discussing sit between the anthropologist as witness and the anthropologist as police. I question the political stakes of this slippage and attempt to grapple with the necessity, despite the growing silence in the discipline, for an anthropology that is steadfast in its commitment to "creating and consolidating a counter-hegemonic movement through active political struggle" that has at its roots heartfelt dedication and yes, even sentimentality (Gordon 1991: 155). This call for socially relevant and politically engaged anthropology is not new, of course. Black, Latina/o, and Native American anthropologists have long challenged the racist foundations that persist in the discipline, just as feminists have waged their critiques and formerly colonized subjects (and objects of the anthropological gaze) have poignantly debated the issues of the power differentials that continue to plague the field and the academy.

Between the Witness and the Police

The notion of the anthropologist as witness is widely used and often referenced, but not always under the sign of engaged observation. For some, the anthropologist as witness is what all anthropologists do. For others, the discipline of anthropology itself is a mode of witnessing. As Ruth Behar writes: "Anthropology . . . is the most fascinating, bizarre, disturbing, and necessary form of witnessing left to us at the end of the twentieth century" (1996: 5). Clearly Behar's sentiments about anthropology as a form of witnessing do not expressly speak about forms of engagement with the people who are subjected to the eye of the witness/ anthropologist. But she elevates the status of witnessing not only as necessary but also as seemingly one of the few viable options "left to us." Nancy Scheper-Hughes goes even further by positioning the witness as a noble actor. In the introduction to *Death without Weeping*, she argued that "the act of witnessing is what lends our work its moral (and at times its almost theological) character" (1992: xii). Scheper-Hughes's account of witnessing underscores a form of anthropological engagement that she implies is active and committed.

In similar fashion, the mission statement for the series on Public Anthropology published by University of California Press and edited by Robert Borofsky claims that "the series seeks to affirm ethnography as an important public witness of today's world." According to the statement, the goal of this series, titled "Public Anthropology," is to bring ethnographic analysis to the fore of "the world's public discussions" and to "position ethnography as a central way of knowing in public intellectual life." At the heart of ethnographic witnessing, then, at least for Borofsky, is the desire to heighten anthropology's status in the domain of public affairs and to return anthropology (as an expert witness of culture) to its former valorized place on the world scene.

Though very different, the articulations by Borofsky, Behar, and Scheper-Hughes of the witness firmly establish the centrality of the anthropologist by suggesting that as a witness she not only bears witness (was there) but has testimony to give. Although this is certainly provocative, it leads to at least two questions: what and for whom does this form of observation advocate, and who benefits from this mode of engagement?[3] What is true about both Behar and Scheper-Hughes is their desire, despite the increasingly scientific and "proof"-oriented environment that continues to plague anthropology, to write in a manner that surrenders "to the intractableness of reality" (Behar 1996: 2). As Behar herself notes, however, this is not the stuff from which Ph.D.s in anthropology are made.

Recently and in keeping with other scholars critical of the role of historians or anthropologists (Clifford 1983; Rosaldo 1987; Viswesaran 1994), Liisa Malkki (1997) explored alternative ways of positioning anthropologists in relation to the field and the written production of fieldwork. As Malkki writes: "In our fieldwork, as well as through our writing, we have long been oriented to look for the repetitive, the persistent, the normative—durable forms" (90). Through her work with Hutu refugees from Burundi living in Tanzania, she challenges more typical ethnographic norms that anthropologists are supposed to adhere to. Malkki, endorsing a notion by Dick Hedbige, suggests that we "think less in terms of ethnographic description than of witnessing." For Malkki, being a witness implies a greater sense of responsibility, presumably to the subjects of the ethnography. She writes, "being a witness implies both a specific positioning and a responsibility of testimony, 'a caring form of vigilance'" (94). Malkki goes on to argue that being a witness and giving testimony would be a "workable strategy" against producing the more typical ethnographic accounts of, "cultures, peoples, communities and ways of life" (95). While acknowledging that testimony and witnessing have convoluted and complicated meanings and origins, her notion of bearing witness is part of an end game, apparently (and perhaps rightfully) for the anthropologist. Bearing witness, or testifying according to Malkki "does not mean speaking for someone else; it is one's own testimony" (94). This raises the question, if witnessing is "one's own testimony" but still a form of caring vigilance, for whom is the anthropologist being vigilant?

The act of witnessing is not as uncomplicated as is often represented. It is not always about the person bearing witness, the anthropologist, or about an insider or outsider rendition of events. There are many forms of witnessing, from the ecclesiastical to the courtroom, but to cast the anthropologists and their "product"—the ethnography—as a form of witnessing may just confuse the ethical and the juridical, as Giorgio Agamben notes in *Quel che resta di Auschwitz*. With few exceptions, most anthropologists are third-party chroniclers of events who have not experienced (from beginning to end) what they write about.[4] As third-party chroniclers, the act of witnessing that anthropologists engage in is ultimately juridical in nature. Like material witnesses, anthropologists provide information about a "case," culture, or community that significantly affects the understanding (negatively and positively) of that community.

If the possibility of "anthropological witnessing" or the anthropologist as witness exists, then the question of responsibility and ethnographic authority must be grappled with, and as Agamben suggests, the act of witnessing must then be cast in the realm of the juridical. He writes: "The gesture of assuming responsibility is therefore genuinely juridical and not ethical. It expresses nothing noble or luminous, but rather simply obligation, the act by which one consigned one-self as a prisoner to guarantee a debt in a context in which the legal bond was considered to inhere in the body of the person responsible (1998: 22)." But is the role of the (academic) witness to be devoid of what some might call "ethical obligation" and others might call advocacy or activism? Consider too how scholars who write about witnesses who survived the *Shoah* discuss the problem of witnessing and responsibility. In *Suffering Witness: The Quandary of Responsibility after the Irreparable*, James Hatley (2000) calls upon those who write or think about violence and irredeemable wrongs to think about our responsibility, "to those who suffer within that moment." He urges us to think about responsibility by asking, "How have we been addressed by those who suffer? In what manner might we be in complicity with he or she who perpetrates this violence?" (2). Ruminating on the question of the ethical role of the witness, Hatley suggests a path for scholars troubled by violence. He writes:

> Burdened by the other's suffering, we are called upon not only to
> understand or, at the very least, to give a historical record of a particular

act of violence, but also and in the first instance to witness it. By witness
is meant a mode of responding to the other's plight that exceeds an epistemological determination and becomes an ethical involvement. One
must not only utter a truth *about* the victim but also remain true *to* her or
him. In this latter mode of response, one is summoned to attentiveness,
which is to say, to a heartfelt concern for and acknowledge of the gravity
of violence directed toward particular others. In this attentiveness, the
wounding of the other is registered in the first place not as an objective
fact but as a subjective blow, a persecution, a trauma. The witness
refuses to forget the weight of this blow, or the depth of the wound it
inflicts. (2–3)

If anthropologists were to aspire to being the kind of witness Hatley advocates, what might our practice (and product) look like? Would we, for example,
feel comfortable with conflating anthropological methods with the methods of
the police or the inquisitor, as Liisa Malkki (1997), and Kamala Visweswaran
(1994) have suggested? While Visweswaran self-reflectively ponders policing as
an anthropological method, recalling the debate that the anthropologist Renato
Rosaldo (1983) initiated over twenty years ago, Liisa Malkki's discussion of the
seeming similarities between "police work and fieldwork" invites us to examine
our anthropological intentions. What are the driving forces behind why we
study what we choose to study? What ultimate goals do we hope to achieve when
we write up and make decisions about publishing? These are old questions to
anthropologists, questions that have not outlived their relevance.

I believe that Malkki's call for anthropologists to consider the connections
between police work and fieldwork signals the need to think more critically
about the choices one makes as an anthropologist. What are the differences
between the anthropologist as investigator/inquisitor/police and the anthropologist as witness? Are there differences? Is our will to knowledge and our
methodologies (interviews, observations, and the archive, among others) so
fatally flawed, as Visweswaran and others suggest, that we cannot help but be
police? Of course, because I do critical work on the criminal justice system,
terms such as "police" and "witness" are not lighthearted words. It goes without
saying that the police and witnesses can produce evidence that can both condemn and exonerate. But when one works in a prison and listens to and
observes the sharp contrast between those who confine and those who are con-
fined, the line between the witness and the police is not philosophical. Being in
and of the world, as anthropologists are, should only heighten our awareness
that while police work involves police informants (who may act as witnesses)
and evidence, clues, and privileged information, police also employ suspicion,
fed by the larger discourse of criminalization, labeling, or racial profiling, and
ideologies of racism, sexism, homophobia, and classism. Indeed, as reports from

global human rights organizations such as Human Rights Watch and Amnesty International, as well as local human rights groups and social justice activists from all over the world have evidenced, much of police work relies on coercive measures that can be deadly, especially to the mentally ill, women, people of color, poor people, and immigrants.

Not All Fields are Created Equal; Neither Are Anthropologists

The moment I crossed the threshold between the "free world" and the world of confinement, I assumed that I was the one who chose between being an anthropologist who witnesses and one who polices. I did not know that the institution and its agents would quickly make that choice for me. Prior to my arrival at Rebibbia, I was a female researcher from a prestigious university in the United States. Over the phone, a friendly administrator from the prison director's office scheduled a morning meeting between us. After the meeting with the warden, I was to be introduced to the core staff (including social workers, health professionals, and senior prison guards), followed by a formal tour of the facility, where I could meet women and make arrangements to interview them according to their work schedules.

On a hot August morning in 1996, armed with a permission letter from Italy's minister of justice and a rather official-looking letter from my university, I announced myself to the guard manning the reception desk. I knew that he had seen me approach and I could tell that he was eyeing me with curiosity. As I slid my documents to him through the thick glass partition, I watched as he grew confused then suspicious. He eyed my passport and picked up the phone. I could not hear what he was saying, but I remember hoping that he would hurry up because I did not want to be late for my appointment. He was gesturing rapidly with my passport in his hands. He hung up the phone and turned back to the window. He called to another guard who I had not seen earlier. The two of them stood at the window reviewing my documents. I looked past them to the clock. "So you are an American?" the first guard asked. I dragged my eyes from the clock to him and back to the clock, trying to be obvious. "Yes." He leaned forward and I looked him in the eye. "Well, you don't speak [Italian] with an American accent." He pushed a button to his right and the large blue doors that separated the prison from the outside slowly opened up. "No," he said without missing a beat, "you have an Arabic accent." Knowing full well what his comment meant, I thanked him by saying that I agreed that American accents were awful in any language, including English. I walked through the prison doors and was greeted by the second guard, who informed me that I was allowed to bring in only a pen and paper. As I went through the metal detector the second guard called after me, "You are here to speak to the Nigerian girls?" "Yes," I replied. "Well tell your compatriots that they should stop bringing drugs into Italy." He added, "Maybe they will listen to you." By the time the guard and I arrived at the main office, my entire morning schedule had been revised. I no longer had a meeting with the warden, my staff introductions were going to be limited to a social worker and a guard who would be present at every interview and whose main duty would be to "escort" me everywhere—from the office where I did my interviews to the bathroom door. As I prepared to leave the prison that afternoon, I was told that I had to get official verification from the American embassy stating that I was truly a U.S. citizen.

It was clear from the start that as an "other" American who had an "other" name, that I was seen as being on the side of the inmates. As a Black woman, I apparently had nothing in common with those who ran the facility. Not that I minded, and nor was I shocked, at how easily my race and apparent difference put me squarely in the corner of the detained African women in the eyes of the administration. Although I had convinced myself that any good anthropologist would be wary of approaching her work with bias (in graduate school I had been trained to stay away from the stuff—of bias) but I knew long before entering the facility, long before touching down in Italy, that my affinities were and would be with the inmates. My bias was built on the knowledge that my status as an "other" American (who did not appear to be authentically from the United States) would greatly affect my experience.

In her essay "The Evidence of Experience," Joan Scott (1991) writes of the problems associated with accepting experience as evidence when analyzing social and historical processes. It seems true, as Begoña Aretxaga suggests, that by underscoring experience, "one runs the risk of leaving unquestioned the conditions that enable it" (1997: 8). Like Aretxaga, I heed the warning sounded by Scott, but I too think that there is political necessity to recognize experiences that are shaped both discursively and through the everyday. Importantly, however, these experiences are not evidence of truth but rather a disruption of a normative truth. It is an acknowledgment that experiences are one way to interpret how subjectivities are produced and understood.

Anthropologists are, of course, very big on experience. Whether we are writing about the experiences facing the communities with which we work or are evaluating our own experiences, it is clear that "experience," particularly that which is gained in the field, is what makes one an anthropologist. As Gupta and Ferguson note, "we would suggest that the single most significant factor determining whether a piece of research will be accepted as . . . 'anthropological' is the extent to which it depends on experience in the field" (1997: 1). Though they are mostly concerned with the strictures and practices of fieldwork and its valorized place within the discipline of anthropology in their essay, Gupta and Ferguson are referring to the widely known (yet unwritten) criterion that one must spend a significant amount of time in the field (a year or more). Wrapped innocently in their language is the profound question of who determines what is an anthropological experience. Beyond the question of length of time spent in the field and where in fact that field is, the issue of experience, it seems, is uncontroversial here.

The question is, why? Why is it that despite the numerous critical anthologies and self-reflective essays, we still reify "Experience" as if it is something that can be duplicated and universally understood? Is one really a good anthropologist because one has spent years in the field, speaks the language fluently, and crafts beautifully written ethnographies? Perhaps these are the trappings of a good anthropologist, but I reckon that if all of these traits were bundled in an ethnography that was counterintuitive to what the audience thinks they know (regardless of whether they have any "experience" in the area) the anthropologist in question may be deemed "unanthropological." Is there an assumption in anthropology that the amorphous space known as the field is necessarily level? Here I am encouraged to reflect upon the experience of France Winddance Twine, who sought guidance in how to address the murky waters of what her brown body signified for both Blacks and Whites in Brazil. In thinking about how she might prepare to deal with being an African American subject in the field, she turned to anthropology and sociology. What she found was little discussion about race and fieldwork. As she puts it: "After decades of self-reflexivity among ethnographers analyzing the practice of writing and conducting field research, the lack of sustained attention to racialized dilemmas is particularly note worthy, considering the degree to which other axes of power have been theorized" (Twine 2000: 5). For as long as there has been anthropology, the race, gender, age, and social position of the anthropologist has affected the ways in which they are received in the field and in the discipline, among their peers. What has long been clear but seldom discussed is that where one works and how one looks when conducting that work factors in significantly. It is an old story that one's race, gender, sexuality, and social position can (and do) determine what kind of information one might receive, and influence the kind of knowledge produced. At the risk of stating the obvious, and as Donna Haraway (1991) reminded us, knowledge, like experience, is situated.

Politics of Listening

The she that opens up this essay, the one who taught me about the politics of ethnographic production and challenged my easy ability to name myself and my work "activist" was an inmate at Rebibbia. Her name, which is not her name, was given to her by the anthropologist/author who hopes to protect her identity and her dignity. She, "Esther," is no longer imprisoned but it does not change the fact that she will always be considered a condemned woman, an exconvict. When telling her story through the transcription of events that combines her memory, my remembering of our meetings, and an untrustworthy pen and note

pad, I am often pushed by anthropologists (and other academics) to reveal more
and more about her life. Her story, particularly the story of her arrest is, yes, a
potholed windy road on a foggy night. Hers is like the story of Eros and Psyche,
of love under the cover of darkness, thrilling, naive, and full of burning questions. The contours of her life are an enigma, but the minutiae are as big as
everyday. The combination of elusiveness and vivid description feeds the pun-
gent imagination of the listener.

The potholes in Esther's story, the seemingly inconceivableness of her
experiences, created dilemmas for academics, scholars of all varieties, who have
listened to my rendition of her life as an African woman imprisoned in Italy.
Before she was incarcerated she had been a member of an elite family, most of
whom were killed in a massacre; she had been a refugee, a sex worker, and an
unwitting drug courier. Once, after I shared these details of Esther's story with a
group of academics, one woman asked me how I evaluated the veracity of it—
after all, the anthropologist added, "she is in prison."

Now I am not so naive that I thought that Esther's story would provoke collective soul-searching in the body politic. I was hoping, I admit, that this
woman, a fairly progressive individual by any standards, would be moved to dis-
belief because Esther had suffered more trauma than it would seem that anyone
should endure. I was hoping that she would be enraged at a world that could
accommodate this magnitude of human suffering. But no—for this woman and
several other anthropologists, Esther and all of the women that I worked with
were casualties of the contingencies of life. Furthermore, they were suspected
of not telling the truth, simply because they had been confirmed by the state
as criminals, regardless of the circumstance that brought them to prison. I am
reminded here of a similar discussion by Luana Ross, who works with incarcerated Native American women in Montana. She writes: "Because I was interested
in how racism and sexism function inside prison and affected imprisoned
women, I concentrated on the women's subjective experiences of prison. Some
critics of my work and of other qualitative research argue that prisoners do not
tell 'the truth'" (Ross 1998: 5). Indeed, academics tend to be an arrogant lot, and
we believe that the world is an open book that must be analyzed and judged by
the elite cadre known as "us."

I often wondered how people would respond to my research if I did not work
in prisons but, say, in a refugee camp or a shelter. Would there be the same concerns about truth telling? Would it be easier to accept the violence and the pain
that mark many of the women's lives if they had been in a shelter and not in a
prison? I am struck by the ways that "crime" still defines the criminal, to crudely
paraphrase Foucault. When I choose not to write about a woman's particular
crime, or if I flatly state that it is not my goal to confirm the veracity of a
woman's "testimony," which would require me to go through their court papers,
initial police reports, and lawyers' notes, I am often met with sideways glances

and questions about my methodology. According to the unwritten codes of anthropology, how much am I supposed to know? How much do you need to know? Perhaps the broader problem is, as Wendy Hui Kyong Chun suggests, is that "we assume that we know how to listen" (1999: 114).

To be sure, Esther's "story" is not a story but a testimony, and my story of her testimony is and was in some ways a small act of witnessing. But I wonder why my anthropology audience couldn't see that the listener enters into the contract of testimony (Laub 1992b). The problem is, of course, that we have developed "listening defenses," which Dori Laub describes as a "Foreclosure through facts, through an obsession with fact finding; an absorbing interest in the factual details of the account which serve to circumvent the human experience. Another version of the foreclosure, of this obsession with fact finding is a listener who already 'knows it all,' ahead of time, leaving little space for the survivor's story" (73). If we think we know it all before a word is uttered, then what does that say about our ability to receive the details of another person's experience or testimony? What does this say about the possibilities for ethical engagement (Chun 1999)? Can we be engaged scholars or activist intellectuals if we do not know how to listen or if we seek or even demand knowledge that confirms what we already think we know?

To be the receiver of testimony, as some anthropologists are, is to be, in part, a witness, but it is also to assist in that witnessing process. As Laub writes: "To a certain extent, the interviewer-listener takes on the responsibility for bearing witness that previously the narrator felt he bore alone, and therefore could not carry out. It is the encounter and the coming together between the survivor and the listener, which makes possible something like a repossession of the act of witnessing. This joint responsibility is the source of the reemerging truth" (1992b: 85). When I think through the practice of ethnography, I see that we have concerned ourselves with the authoritative act of what it means to witness. That authoritative act is the act of speaking, giving voice, reclaiming and reconstructing an event. Ironically, however, an anthropologist's job is supposedly based on the act of listening. Listening does not imply that the listener is an expert or an authority. I believe that there are valuable lessons to be learned if we open our ears to experiences that might not fit what we think we know. Critical reception might just lead to ethical engagement.

NOTES

1. See the work of Chesney-Lind 1986; Bhavnani and Davis 1997; Kurshan 1998; and Davis 1998.

2. I think here of two events, from which my reflections are drawn, that occurred when I first returned from Italy. The first event was a lecture that I gave to a group of anthropologists and the second event was a seminar with anthropologists, historians, and criminologists. The audiences were indeed very generous and lively. I learned much from these exchanges.

3. I will speculate that perhaps the answer lies, for Scheper-Hughes, in her assertion that the act of bearing witness has an "almost theological character." I am unclear what Scheper-Hughes means, but I will take her to mean theological virtue. If this is the case, the anthropologist as witness is by no means ecclesiastical, but is an individual process that underscores the importance of gathering information.

4. Of course there are notable exceptions, but this charge applies to most North American anthropologists who write about violence in Africa, Latin America, Asia, Eastern Europe, and urban centers in the United States, Part of the reality that we need to face as academics, in the United States, Europe, and Australia, including the Ph.D.-holding elites from the global south living and working in the United States or Europe, is that we are not only a privileged class but that often, in part because of funding constraints (few foundations are willing to support research that places individuals in dangerous locations), we are part of the collective of people who "witness" the aftermath of violence. There is promise in this, one that has the potential to recognize the tremendous responsibility we have.

REFERENCES

Agamben, Giorgio. 1998. *Quel che resta di Auschwitz: L'archivo e il testimone.* Torino: Bollati Boringhieri.

Aretxaga, Begoña. 1997. *Shattering Silence: Women, Nationalism, and Political Subjectivity in Northern Ireland.* Princeton: Princeton University Press.

Behar, Ruth. 1996. *The Vulnerable Observer: Anthropology That Breaks Your Heart.* Boston: Beacon.

Bhavnani, Kum-Kum, and Angela Davis. 1997. "Fighting for Her Future: Reflections on Human Rights and Women's Prisons in the Netherlands." *Social Identities* 3.1: 7–32.

Borofsky, Robert. n.d. http://www.publicanthropology.org/Bookseries/prospectus.htm.

Chesney-Lind, Mede. 1986. "Women and Crime: The Female Offender." *Signs* 12.1: 78–96.

Chun, Wendy Hui Kyong. 1999. "Unbearable Witness: Toward a Politics of Listening." *Differences: A Journal of Feminist Cultural Studies* 11.1: 112–149.

Clifford, James. 1983. "On Ethnographic Authority." *Representations*, 1.2: 118–146.

Davis, Angela. 1998. "Racialized Punishment and Prison Abolition." In *The Angela Y. Davis Reader*, edited by Joy James. Oxford: Blackwell Press.

Gordon, Edmund T. 1991. "Anthropology and Liberation." In *Decolonizing Anthropology: Moving Further toward an Anthropology for Liberation*, edited by Faye Harrison. Washington, D.C.: Association of Black Anthropologists, American Anthropological Association.

Gupta, Akhil, and James Ferguson. 1997. "Discipline and Practice: 'The Field' as Site, Method, and Location in Anthropology." In *Anthropological Locations: Boundaries and Grounds of a Field Science*. Berkeley: University of California Press.

Hale, Charles, and Edmund T. Gordon. n.d. "Concept Statement." http://www.utexas.edu/cola/depts/anthropology/activist/concept%20statement.html.

Haraway, Donna. 1991. "Situated Knowledges: The Science Question in Feminism and the Privilege of the Partial Perspective." In Hanaway, *Simians, Cyborgs, and Women.* New York: Routledge.

Harrison, Faye. 1991. *Decolonizing Anthropology: Moving Further toward an Anthropology for Liberation*, edited by Faye Harrison. Washington, D.C.: Association of Black Anthropologists, American Anthropological Association.

Hatley, James. 2000. *Suffering Witness: The Quandary of Responsibility after the Irreparable.* Albany: State University of New York Press.

Kurshan, Nancy. 1998. "Behind the Walls: The History and Current Reality of Women's Imprisonment." In *Women's Lives: Multicultural Perspectives*, edited by Gwyn Kirk and Margo Okazawa-Rey. Mountain View, Cal.: Mayfield.

Laub, Dori. 1992a. "Bearing Witness or the Vicissitudes of Listening." In *Testimony: Crises of Witnessing in Literature, Psychoanalysis, and History*, edited by Shoshana Felman and Dori Laub. New York: Routledge.

——. 1992b. "An Event without a Witness: Truth, Testimony and Survival." In *Testimony: Crises of Witnessing in Literature, Psychoanalysis, and History*, edited by Shoshana Felman and Dori Laub. New York: Routledge.

Malkki, Liisa. 1997. "News and Culture: Transitory Phenomena and the Fieldwork Tradition." In *Anthropological Locations*, edited by Akhil Gupta and James Ferguson. Berkeley: University of California Press.

Rosaldo, Rosaldo. 1987. "From the Door of His Tent: The Fieldworker and the Inquisitor." In *Writing Culture: The Poetics and Politics of Ethnography*, edited by James Clifford and George E. Marcus. Berkeley: University of California Press.

Ross, Luana. 1998. *Inventing the Savage: The Social Construction of Native American Criminality*. Austin: University of Texas Press.

Scott, Joan. 1991. "The Evidence of Experience." *Critical Inquiry* 17.4: 773–797.

Scheper-Hughes, Nancy. 1992. *Death without Weeping: The Violence of Everyday Life in Brazil*. Berkeley: University of California Press.

Twine, France Winddance. 2000. "Racial Ideologies and Racial Methodologies." In *Racing Research, Researching Race: Methodological Dilemmas in Critical Race Studies*, edited by France Winddance Twine and Jonathan Warren. New York: New York University Press.

Visweswaran, Kamala. 1994. *Fictions of Feminist Ethnography*. Minneapolis: University of Minnesota Press.

PART TWO

Lessons from Agents of Change

5

Moral Chronologies

Generation and Popular Memory in a Palestinian Refugee Camp

JOHN COLLINS

Scholars who work with oral sources when doing historical research most commonly solicit testimony either from individuals who have passed well into adulthood or, more often, from those who are even older and thus able to reflect on a full lifetime of accumulated experience.[1] If we begin, however, from Luisa Passerini's (1996: 23) simple but vital premise that "memory speaks from today," no matter who is doing the remembering, then we must recognize that even the relatively young are capable of developing and articulating an historical perspective on the events of their youth. In Palestine, where roughly half the population is under the age of eighteen, this realization opens up significant new avenues of research into a generations-long struggle for national liberation.

Prior to the first Palestinian *intifāda* (uprising) of the late 1980s and early 1990s (hereafter referred to simply as the "intifada"), scholars sympathetic to this struggle tended to use the stories of "ordinary" Palestinians primarily as evidence, as documents assumed to bear an unassailable truth-value deriving from a particular relationship to experienced events. Rarely were such narratives analyzed as narratives—that is, as creative constructions of the past told in particular circumstances for particular reasons that are not always self-evident, even to the teller. The documentary model remains strong today, but research on Palestine is increasingly being undertaken by scholars who, while retaining the ethical commitment to document the reality of Israeli repression, also insist on bringing critical perspectives (for example, those associated with cultural studies, literary theory, or critical ethnography) to bear on the Palestinian situation. In this respect, Ted Swedenburg's *Memories of Revolt* (Swedenburg 1995), steeped in critical theory and relying heavily on the notion of popular memory, was an important intervention that has influenced a great deal of work, including my own.

Popular memory research is an ideal tool for understanding the complexity of the discursive universe within which Palestinians tell their own stories. Unlike the concept of oral history, which often leaves one mired in unhelpful debates about the "accuracy" of oral sources, the popular memory approach (Collins 2004; Passerini 1987, 1996; Popular Memory Group 1982; Portelli 1991) insists that what matters is how people *produce the past* through a dynamic engagement with the present (and even the future). This production occurs in constant dialogue with a variety of discourses: official and popular, dominant and oppositional, individual and collective. When viewed from the perspective of popular memory, it is clear that the intifada is very much a living event to which Palestinians give meaning every day through the articulation of stories that explore the conflict between an idealized (albeit tragic) past and a deeply unsatisfying present.

I went to Palestine in 1996 to study the relationship between generation, narrative, and nationalism. I was particularly interested in talking with members of the "intifada generation" (*jīl al-intifāda*), those young people who experienced the first intifada as children and youth. For my research site I chose Balata Refugee Camp, the largest camp in the West Bank (pop. 22,000), whose original residents were displaced from the regions of Jaffa, Ramleh, and Lyyda in 1948, settling briefly in Nablus before the United Nations and the Jordanian government created the camp in 1950. An urban camp that enjoys a strong sense of collective identity, Balata has long been a center of militant activity against the Israeli occupation of the West Bank and Gaza that began in 1967.[2]

During the first half of 1997, I conducted approximately fifty open-ended interviews with a total of twenty-six Balata residents, the majority of whom (twenty one) were between the ages of eighteen and twenty-seven.[3] Initially I used what has been called the "snowball" method, trying as much as possible to follow existing networks of friendship and social affiliation in order to identify potential interviewees. Later on, in order to broaden the collective social and political profile of the larger group, I sought out suggestions concerning specific types of people (such as, someone a bit younger, or someone known to support Hamas). The ease with which I was able to do this work was a product of at least two factors: the relative calm that prevailed on the ground in early 1997, and the fact that, owing to the high concentration of researchers and journalists in the West Bank, so many camp residents were quite comfortable with the idea of speaking with outsiders about their lives.

In the formal interviews and in everyday conversations, I found that even as the intifada continued to animate the nation's political life—several days of intense clashes broke out shortly after my arrival—it was simultaneously slipping into the realm of "history." The simple passage of time, of course, is the most basic condition of possibility for popular memory research. In this case, however, the years between intifada events and their narration also took on an important generational meaning, for the members of the "intifada generation" had passed, in those years, from one stage of the life-course to another. Although the recognition of their "adult" status within the larger community was still an open question, the very fact of having completed secondary school, or having passed the age when it is typically completed, had a number of basic implications for these individuals: the growing need to make money, for themselves and/or to help support their larger family; the chance to extend their education at a university or vocational college; the possibility (or impossibility, depending on their political leanings) of working for the Palestine National Authority (PNA), which has presided over Palestinian political life in the West Bank and Gaza since 1994, subject to continuing Israeli domination; and the looming issue of marriage. Moreover, the major political events of the early 1990s—the first Gulf War, the end of the intifada, the Oslo accords,[4] the creation of the PNA—had all contributed to a gradual distancing of these young people, in many of their minds, from the position they had once occupied as activists with the ability to "make history." In other words, as the narrators themselves had changed, the world had also changed around them.

This article examines what happens to popular memory when mass mobilization yields to the logic of political negotiation and state building, and when the generational solidarities of "youth" give way to the economic and social pressures of "adulthood." In the early intifada stories of many of these young people, deeply felt notions of generational unity are clearly identifiable; generation, in other words, is one of the most important devices through which memories of that period are structured. As a result, discussions of subsequent events, primarily the gradual implosion of the intifada and the growing hegemony of the Israeli-Palestinian "peace process," stand in even sharper relief. Instead of excitement and pride, for example, these more contemporary narratives are tinged with regret and detachment, and in place of stories rooted in collective action, we find stories marked by a relative sense of personal isolation. In the following pages, I explore one of the most striking elements of these self-representations: the construction of "moral chronologies" through the operation of narrative contrasts for which the beginning of the intifada, increasingly distant and idealized, is a fundamental touchstone.

Moral Chronologies

Early 1997 was a time of profound uncertainty for Balata's young people. Given the disappointments of the "peace process," the continuing political detention of friends and relatives, and the seemingly perpetual economic instability facing the *mukhayyam* (camp), many found it difficult to speak confidently about the intifada; it was as if all of the cognitive pillars on which they had built their understanding of the uprising were shaking, if not crumbling altogether. It might seem strange, therefore, to find the same young people continuing to make strident moral judgments about the intifada. Yet it is possible to see this component of their narratives as arising from some of the very ambiguities and contradictions that crept into their memories in the years after the Oslo accords. Indeed, one of the most powerful and effective ways of dealing with such contradictions—for example, between remembered goals and observed results—is to integrate them into a new narrative whose tone is explicitly ethical and judgmental, thereby creating a frame of reference within which the contradictions "make sense."

The most dominant existing narrative of the intifada to which these young people have access is the "official" nationalist narrative of which the Palestine Liberation Organization (PLO)—the coalition that has led the Palestinian national liberation movement since the late 1960s—has traditionally been the custodian. In this narrative, the uprising appears as a crucial stage in the long but steady (and, as of this writing, still unfulfilled) ascent to statehood.[5] Many of the assumptions, categories, and collective longings embedded in this official narrative are indeed present in the stories examined here, particularly those articulated by young people who are sympathetic to Fateh (the secular nationalist faction that dominates the PLO) and the PNA. Thus Samer, a twenty five-year-old officer in the PNA's Preventive Security Force, firmly disputed the notion that the uprising was in any way a revolt against the "outside" leadership of the PLO.[6] Taken as a group, however, these personal narratives suggest what I call a "moral chronology" of the intifada that is rooted in a markedly different interpretive framework from the linear, triumphant story associated with official nationalism. The outlines of this alternative chronology emerged when interviewees employed the language of contrast to show how much the end of the uprising differed from its beginning. Generally eschewing precise, calendrical markers, these young people instead relied heavily on pairs of phrases such as *fil-bidāye ... w ba^cdēn* (in the beginning ... but afterward), and in the context of their self-representations, these discursive signals were as much evaluative as temporal. Particular events and processes identified in interviews, in other words, were invested with meaning less through their exact location in time than through their placement in a narrative universe built on the deliberate juxtaposition of opposing elements.

To say that any of these interviews contained a fully articulated chronology (in the strictest sense) of the intifada, then, would be both inaccurate and beside the point; as Portelli (1991: 63) notes, "Historians may be interested in reconstructing the past; narrators are interested in projecting an image." To the extent that such a moral chronology exists in the stories of these young Palestinians, it is undoubtedly a "national" narrative, but clearly not one steeped in nationalist teleology. Instead, the nation appears here as a community winding its way along a tortuous, often downward path from "the beginning" of the uprising through the "afterward" of decline, corruption, and loss of collective will.

This basic contrast can be mapped on a number of different axes, including shifts in personal motivation (from selfless to selfish), tactics of resistance (from stone throwing to suicide bombings), and figurative terminology used in the interviews (from the intifada as "outbreak" to the peace negotiations as "tranquilizer" or "abortion"). Despite individual differences in supporting detail, the young people I interviewed were remarkably consistent in terms of the kind of story they told: time and again I heard later developments contrasted sharply, and almost always negatively, with the early period in which one young man (Nabil), with deliberate emphasis, suggestively called "a *real* intifada" (*intifāda haqiqiyye*).

Equally important, this alternative chronology cannot be separated from the issue of generational identity, for all of the descriptive and normative elements included in the narratives are set against the backdrop of the narrators' own movement from youth to adulthood. It is significant, for example, that several interviewees defined *jīl al-intifāda* with specific reference to the beginning of the intifada, thereby linking their own political influence as youth with a particular stage of the uprising. In general, then, we might say that within the world of meaning constructed in this moral chronology, youth is identified with many of the earlier and more positive elements such as mass politics, purity of intention, active involvement in events, democratic forms of resistance, and local (or "inside") authenticity; becoming an adult, on the other hand, is linked with elite politics, selfishness, passive observation of events, specialized forms of resistance, and the relocation of political authenticity and authority in the hands of the formerly exiled ("outside") national leadership. A closer examination of four key themes in the interviews indicates some of the ways in which this discourse operates.

Disruptions: Money and "Outside Forces"

In many interviews, young people constructed moral chronologies when discussing the role of "money" (*masâri*) in the intifada, taking the offensive against questions (asked or implied) about economic issues by speaking of money not as a motivating factor for action (through its absence), but rather as a potentially divisive factor working against national unity. Here the role of the PLO, still headquartered in Tunis at the start of the uprising, emerged as a source of significant controversy, generating angry denunciations and awkward moments in the conversations. Samer, in keeping with his contention that tensions between the "inside" and the "outside" were minimal during the intifada, argued that the PLO played a thoroughly positive role in the movement through its ability to offer various kinds of "support" (*diᶜam*), including financial support, to those struggling on the "inside." In this view, however, he was in a small minority when compared with other young people in Balata, including several who identified themselves as PNA supporters. Nabil, a twenty-five-year-old soldier in the PNA army, claimed that the PLO "interfered" in the intifada after about six months by sending financial support into the West Bank and Gaza, leading to rumors that some activists were motivated by greed rather than patriotism. He was also careful to distance himself from these dynamics:

JOHN: You said that the PLO didn't really have a role in the uprising for the first six months, but after that, it started to influence it with money, is that [right]?

NABIL: It *supported* the intifada. Not influence—support.

JOHN: OK. And when you say support, you mean that they were providing money to people to help people get by because of the situation, because of the conditions?

NABIL: Right . . . the PLO would send money to the local leaders, and then the money was distributed, first of all to the poor people. And for intifada activities, to pay for uniforms, spray paint for graffiti, leaflets.

JOHN: All of this sounds to me like it was probably very important in helping to keep the uprising going, so why do you think it was a mistake?

NABIL: Well, let's say I am in the streets, facing the occupation. There were some people who used to say that this person, he is not throwing stones because of the nation. Because the most money went to the families that were the most active. . . . But I'm not fighting for the money—I'm doing it for my land, to get rid of the occupation.

JOHN: Did they also—did they specifically give money to families who had someone who was a martyr?

NABIL: There was some support for martyrs' families and for people who were wounded. But it was informal support, not official . . . not like a monthly salary. The support was under the table.

JOHN: But everyone in the camp was aware of who was getting money and who wasn't, for example—or was it not that clear?

NABIL: No, it wasn't well known . . . it was a very secretive process.

JOHN: [But] you also said that sometimes people would accuse other people of being active only because of the money. So they must've known who was getting money.

NABIL: At the end of the '80s, maybe around '90 or '92, there were special monthly salaries [for the martyrs' families].

JOHN: Official salaries?

NABIL: Official . . . you would go to Amman [to get the money].

JOHN: Did this affect your family?

NABIL: Yes, until now.

JOHN: Were there people who ever accused you, for example, of throwing stones for the money, because you had a brother who was martyred?

NABIL: Never—the ones who were accused were . . . the leaders on the inside. This is one of the negative sides of the intifada.

The insistence that "money" only entered the equation after a specified period of time (in this case, after six months) serves to reinforce the picture of the preceding period as a time when motives were less suspect, a time when any thought of personal gain was eclipsed by the ongoing process of collective struggle. The "mistake" of the PLO leadership, then, lay in its attempt to tinker with, or exert more influence over, a locally generated movement rooted in the uncorrupted spirit of "pure" national feeling.

Hussein, an eighteen-year-old Fateh supporter, echoed Nabil's reading of the situation but gave events a different twist, absolving the PLO of direct responsibility for the negative influence of money on the intifada. His testimony, nonetheless, creates a familiar moral chronology:

JOHN: What exactly do you think was the role of the PLO outside in the intifada?

HUSSEIN: Support.

JOHN: What kind of support?

HUSSEIN: Financial support, support for the families of martyrs, for people under curfew, all types [of support]. The PLO encouraged the continuation of the intifada. . . .

JOHN: OK, about the PLO and the support that they gave, the money that they gave, I've heard from other people that that caused some problems here, that some people were jealous or were upset about who was getting money. Is that something that you were aware of?

HUSSEIN: That's right. But this happened after the deportations, after Husam Khader and the other leaders were deported at the start of the intifada. . . . After that, others [That is, other leaders] came, and every one of them wanted something [for himself]. Of course the occupation had a lot to do with causing problems between people. All of the honorable people were in prison. So you had collaborators, people who were paid by the occupation, maybe people who were less honest, and when the support came in [from the outside], they would keep a share for themselves.

In this case the moral contrast has to do with both factional and generational identities: the man Hussein identifies by name as being more "honest" in his handling of financial matters, Husam Khader, was closely affiliated with Shabiba, the Fateh youth movement, before his deportation by Israeli authorities in

January 1988.[7] On the other end of his moral spectrum, Hussein remains vague as to the identity of the people who subsequently were put in charge of distributing PLO funds and others who contributed to the "decline" of the intifada, referring to them only generically as "collaborators" and "rude" people. When these people started to take control of the situation, he recalled, "it felt like we lost something very important."

Similar assessments appear in the self-representations of those who are not directly or ideologically affiliated with the PNA, but here the blame for the moral backsliding is laid even more directly at the doorstep of the PLO. Khaled, a disgruntled former Fateh activist, provided a quiet but sarcastic example of this sentiment when I asked him to define the PLO's role in the intifada. Laughing, he replied (in English), "Only financing!" The outside leadership, he said, "tried" to control the situation politically and financially, but was only partially successful because local leaders would often ignore the orders that came in from "outside." PLO attempts to influence the uprising, in other words, only managed to sow the seeds of disunity within the movement.

Hassan and Isam, former and current Popular Front for the Liberation of Palestine (PFLP, a leftist faction within the PLO, which has generally opposed the "peace process") supporters, respectively, identified some of the resulting internal social problems. Isam related an incident from the beginning of the intifada as a way of setting up his own moral chronology:

> At first, all of us were struggling together . . . and anytime someone would see the [Israeli] army, you would automatically try to do something. I remember one such event that just happened by chance: I was with a group of guys, and I had an apple in my hand. Automatically I looked on the ground, but there weren't any stones, so I took the apple and threw it at the patrol. What I mean to say is, there was something, some kind of motivation, that came from inside of us. But then money entered in a big way and came between people, and it caused people to look around them and think, about someone, "Why is he getting more than I am? Didn't I do as much as he did? Maybe I even did more than him." And this was the major internal factor that really troubled the intifada.

Hassan, a recent university graduate and one of the few non-Balata residents I interviewed (he grew up in a refugee family in Jenin), echoed the general thrust of Isam's story by offering his own version of a saying he attributed to Mao Zedong. "The revolution is started by the courageous, exploited by opportunists, and its fruits are harvested by cowards," he said. "If I'm speaking about the intifada, I can say that there are people who sacrificed, those who had real beliefs. And the opportunists, they are the ones who came along a bit later, who had their own interests, and they abused our sacrifices. And the cowards—we're seeing them today."

Unlike Hussein, both Isam and Hassan were quite willing to trace such developments back to the actions of the national leadership. "They don't have the ability to invest the intifada. . . . These kind of people, they never see a real budget. Most of them, they have companies—they are rich people," said Hassan, his chosen imagery perhaps a function of the accounting degree he had received at university. Isam argued that as time went by, the allowances the PLO had traditionally sent to help meet the expenses of full-time activists and young people who were on the run from the Israeli security forces began to find their way into the pockets of people who were not even involved in resisting the occupation.

Like so many of their age-mates, Hassan and Isam both spoke of "money" as having entered the equation from outside, bringing jealous feelings and selfish attitudes to the surface and leading, ultimately, to the growth of factional disputes that sometimes turned violent. The memory of such conflicts was particularly troubling for Leila, a twenty five-year-old hairdresser who said that she favored the "unity" of all political groupings. "Toward the end of the intifada in Gaza, there was something between Hamas [the Islamic Resistance Movement, founded just after the start of the intifada as an Islamist alternative to the secular nationalists] and Fateh, a clash between them," she recalled. "But I think it was caused by outside forces (*harakāt kharijiyye*). . . . [T]here were people shooting at each other. Those who wanted to cause this trouble succeeded."[8] Once again we find that the identification of external factors serves both to reinforce notions of local authenticity, and to posit a moral chronology in which the interference of "outside forces" functions as a turning point.

Suicide Operations: Revenge and Stages of Resistance

For many young people in Balata, the mention of suicide operations (*^camaliyyāt intihariyye*)—some of which occurred during the months when I was conducting the interviews—elicited noticeably ambivalent reactions that rarely took the form of outright condemnation or unmitigated support. Of all the interviewees who spoke about suicide attacks, for example, only two offered straightforward defenses of those attacks as logical steps in a process of escalating resistance. "At the beginning of the intifada, the people weren't prepared to arm themselves, so they were obliged to use whatever was available to them, and the thing that was most abundantly available to them at that time was . . . the stone," said Majid, a Hamas supporter. When asked to comment on the specific role of suicide operations in the intifada, he stressed that "no suicide operation ever happened except as revenge for Israeli attacks on civilians . . . especially the massacre at the Ibrahimi mosque.[9] After that, people decided that they had to respond."

Similarly Ashraf, a political independent, argued for the importance of viewing the intifada as marked by a series of "stages," and emphasized Israel's role in provoking the most violent Palestinian actions. "The Palestinian people are launching a revolution (*thawra*). They are not playing with the Israelis—they are aiming at *liberation* from the Israelis," he insisted. "And the Israelis, they used too many men in the mass intifada demonstrations—they used rock-launchers, hot water, live bullets, economic sieges. They killed children. . . . As I said, we are in a revolution, not a football match." This last contention was an implicit critique of outside observers (like myself) to whom he imputed a willingness to support certain types of resistance but not others.

One may suspect that this is one of those situations that Jean-Paul Sartre had in mind when he wrote about "the moment of the boomerang" in his famous preface to Frantz Fanon's *The Wretched of the Earth*.[10] Indeed, both Majid and Ashraf discussed *ᶜamaliyyāt intihariyye* in a way that suggests a Fanonian reading of the political situation in which Palestinians, as a colonized people, have found themselves. In this respect, two major points emerge from their testimony: the absolute necessity of violence as a response to the violence of the colonizer/occupier, and the idea that liberation struggles are animated by a particular historical logic that plays itself out in definite, successive stages.

Both of these narrative building blocks are also available to other Palestinians whose personal view of these attacks may be somewhat less unqualified. For these individuals, invoking the notion of "stages" or speaking about revenge provided a way to smooth out their own ambivalence and to downplay the existence of disagreements within the national community over the strategic use of violence. Nabil, for example, suggested that the bombings should be viewed as a tactic of political or military resistance differing only in method or degree from other tactics used in the uprising, but his endorsement of the more violent actions was less than wholehearted in tone:

NABIL: In the beginning it was big, mass actions. . . . The first stage was the period of stones, and the second stage was the period of incendiary bottles. And the third stage, of course, was the suicide operations.

JOHN: How do you feel about those changes?

NABIL: Well, they led to what we have now.

JOHN: The intifada led to the peace process—do you consider it to be a success, the intifada?

NABIL: I didn't say that [the intifada] ended—it shrank. But it led to the peace process . . . and after the defeat of Iraq, we have no option but the peace process.[11]

On the level of narrative strategies, we might say that Nabil was dealing from both ends of the deck in this conversation, giving the bombings a new meaning by integrating them into a more generally accepted story of national liberation even as he hid those events within the same story, and invoking the "party line" even as he undermined it by saying that Palestinians had "no option" but to negotiate.

The notion of "revenge" (*intiqâm*) reappears in the narratives of two other interviewees who seemed to share Nabil's cautious reading of suicide attacks. Ayman, a strong Fateh and PNA supporter, diplomatically softened his own apparent disagreement with such attacks by arguing that we must take into account not only the religious convictions of Islamic activists who carry them out but also the violence to which they are responding. He specifically referenced two historical examples: the 1948 massacre by Zionist forces of Palestinian villagers at Deir Yassin; and the 1982 Israeli invasion of Lebanon, which culminated in the massacre of Palestinian refugees in the Sabra and Shatila camps by members of a Lebanese Phalangist militia closely allied with Israel.

Hatem was more explicit in his criticism of suicide operations, but he also picked up on the idea of revenge. "They made it clear to the Israelis that anytime they commit a massacre, like the Hebron massacre, they will find these operations as a response," he said. "On the negative side, there is the pressure that it puts on our workers [that is, those who work in Israel], because economically we are very dependent on Israel. . . . And also the tourism side . . . this affects the economy of the towns, the tourist towns like Jerusalem and Bethlehem, and this has a negative impact on us."

These comments suggest that for individuals who may have personal reservations about the use of suicide attacks, drawing on the idea of revenge enables them to smooth out their own ambivalence by shifting the terms of debate, foregrounding Israeli actions as both prior to and infinitely less justified than the Palestinian response, in the cyclical process of "terror, counter-terror, violence, counter-violence" (Fanon 1963: 89). Revenge discourse, to put it another way, serves as a kind of reassurance that even when the bombings are called into question on moral grounds, or in terms of their negative effects (in Hatem's view, exclusively economic effects) on Palestinians, it is ultimately the Israelis who must bear the responsibility.

These discussions of ʿamaliyyāt intihariyye also suggest the operation of another moral chronology with respect to the intifada's development over time. Ironically, embedded within this chronology we find an implicit critique of the very notion of progressive stages that so many of the narrators advance. Whether viewed as a "natural" process or as a response to Israeli violence, the shift in tactics from stone throwing to suicide attacks is nonetheless a shift in which each "stage" moves further away from mass actions and closer to highly specialized forms of resistance. This shift is reflected in both the structures and the articulation of memory: the more specialized the action, the more removed it is from the actual experience of the narrator, such that the difference between mass actions at the beginning of the intifada on the one hand, and suicide actions at the end of the intifada on the other, is the difference between events experienced and events observed. Ambivalent feelings, in other words, may derive from the conviction that the later actions are less "democratic" than the earlier ones.

Endings: Natural Causes or Political "Abortion"?

The arrival of PLO Chairman Yasser Arafat in Gaza in July 1994 after decades spent in exile signaled not only a new phase in the "peace process" but also a reassertion of authority by the *jīl al-nakba* (the generation formed by the first Palestinian experience of dispossession in 1948), following a period in which national politics had been temporarily dominated by an emerging generation born and raised under occupation. Arafat put his personal stamp on the passing of the intifada when he exhorted residents to join him in moving from resistance to nation building.

From the perspective of "official" nationalism, however, the intifada had clearly ended even before the PNA's creation. Arafat had already followed the signing of the initial Oslo accords in 1993 with a speech in which he called for a "return to ordinary life" in the West Bank and Gaza, effectively calling for the "abandonment of any strategy of nationalist mobilization or resistance" (Usher 1995: 15). Thus we can say that the various Oslo agreements, which provided for the establishment of the PNA, required the narrative cessation of the intifada; there could be no overlap, in a chronological sense, between the uprising and the PNA's arrival. Yet the intifada had no "official" ending: the accords refer ostensibly to a larger historical conflict to which the PLO is the relevant party from the Palestinian side. The intifada, however, had its own leadership which, while not unrelated to the PLO, nonetheless constituted a distinct body with a narrower constituency. The Israeli government, in other words, never sat down to negotiate with the leadership of the intifada as such; consequently, the field was left open for the PLO, initially working through a number of prominent political figures from the Occupied Territories, to join a negotiation process in which the end of the intifada would be an undeclared fait accompli.

Viewed in this light, the "end" of the intifada had little in common with the classic moment of decolonization, where the withdrawal of the colonial power coincides with the granting (or taking, depending on one's political persuasion) of formal independence. This has become all too clear in subsequent years as the machinery of the Israeli occupation has continued to create "facts on the ground." Indeed, the post-Oslo years have seen the emergence of a highly sophisticated legal-spatial "matrix of control" (Halper 2000) which, when combined with the use of brute force—most notably in Ariel Sharon's 2002 reinvasion of the West Bank, dubbed "Operation Defensive Shield"—allows the Israeli state to continue dominating the lives of Palestinians throughout the occupied territories.

In my 1997 interviews, I found that Balata residents were hardly inclined to smooth over the contradictions of the post-Oslo period, partly because these contradictions were a visible aspect of their everyday lives. In December 1995, when Israeli forces finally pulled out of newly "autonomous" Nablus, residents suddenly saw uniformed Palestinian police patrolling streets peppered with national flags and pictures of Arafat. When I began my interviews in the *mukhayyam* just over a year later, however, there were days when you could still see Israeli tanks stationed just outside the borders of the city. Residents told me that during periods of political escalation in 1996–1997, they were convinced that the Israeli troops were going to enter the "autonomous" area in full force and invade the camp (as, in fact, they have repeatedly done since the start of the second intifada in 2000).

This state of perpetual uncertainty opens up a range of narrative possibilities in terms of how to interpret the end of the intifada. During a visit to Nablus and Balata on August 31, 1996, for example, Arafat criticized the intransigence of the right-wing Netanyahu government in Israel and suggested that the intifada could be resumed. "One of our options is to return to the intifada," he told an audience at a Nablus girls' school; "We are the ones who waged the longest uprising in the twentieth century," he declared in Balata. "I don't have a magic wand, but I have the children of the uprising" (Immanuel 1996). On the one hand, by invoking the possibility of the intifada's "return," he confirmed that the uprising had indeed ended, or at least that it had been put on hold. At the same time, by carefully figuring the nation as a unified community ("*we* are the ones who waged . . .") under his leadership and control ("*I* have the children of the uprising"), he implied that the suspension/ending of the intifada had also been a decision of the national leadership, not a function of internal or external factors beyond its control.

In terms of personal narratives, the absence of formal closure in the intifada's political trajectory enables at least three distinct interpretations, the first of which is that the intifada is not over at all. With Hamas as the main focus of opposition to the PNA and the "peace process," it is not surprising that Majid took such a position. "The intifada won't end until we have a just solution for the Palestinian people," he told me. "Maybe it will shrink, but will it end completely? No." In this way he refigured the Oslo agreements, conventionally viewed as signaling the replacement of mass mobilization by political negotiation, as *unsuccessful* attempts to short-circuit an inevitable historical process—recall the "stages" discussed above—of which Hamas is the vanguard.

A second, more common interpretation offered only by Fateh supporters is that the intifada ended, appropriately and "naturally," as a direct result of the "peace process." As noted above, however, this kind of interpretation does not necessarily constitute a deliberate, unambiguous replication of the official story. Samer, for example, argued that the "fruits" (*thimār*) of the post-intifada period have not materialized for most Palestinians, and his explanation for this failure—that the Israeli side is not committed to peace—raises the unspoken question of whether the intifada could or should have continued. Given that his identity was so closely bound up with the PNA, his support for the PNA's diplomatic path came across as a surprisingly lukewarm endorsement rooted in the conviction that the intifada's conclusion was imposed rather than freely chosen.

Significantly, the only interviewees who articulated a relatively uncritical endorsement of the official position were two eighteen-year-olds, Ayman and Hussein. Relative age is a significant factor here: although both remembered the events of late 1987, neither became seriously involved in political activities until somewhat later, making them less invested in the initial period of mass mobilization than many others in the group, and therefore less likely to construct a moral chronology in which the beginning of the intifada serves as an idealized benchmark.

For older individuals who are more detached from political action, the passing of the intifada into history is anything but an unproblematic occurrence; on the contrary, it is a tragic, even catastrophic shift that requires a lengthy and often highly emotional explanation. Typical of this group is Salim, a twenty-three-year-old restaurant employee and amateur actor, who insisted angrily that the uprising was ended by what he called the "peace drama," in which the PLO distracted its people with diplomatic posturing and speechmaking while it abandoned long-standing national principles. Adding another powerful image, Salim concluded that the effect of the Oslo accords was equivalent to a "tranquilizer injection" through which the people—metaphorically drugged as well as entertained by the "drama" (*masrahīya*)—were manipulated into forgetting their past and believing that negotiations with Israel were the only viable course of action.

Ashraf, who has a fondness for offering political opinions couched in a semidetached, analytical style, used a different metaphor. "Let's take pregnancy," he said. "It goes for nine months, and then the child [comes]. Well, the intifada didn't make it from beginning to its conclusion. . . . It was an abortion." For him, the intifada ended not by accident, and not because Israel succeeded in subduing it, but rather because the PLO deliberately terminated the "pregnancy" (*il-hamel*). On one level, he was activating the symbolic link between biology (or "generation") and nationalism, or between biography and national identity, with the intifada representing the (tragically unfinished) birth pangs of the nation. On another level, the figurative language of pregnancy and abortion allowed Ashraf to distance himself, as analyst and critic, from the processes about which he was speaking. Yet he is also implicated, as a member of the "intifada generation," by this very language, for what he described as the uprising's "natural" growth parallels his own generation's journey to maturity. In this context, the "abortion" (*ijhād*) of the intifada is a doubly powerful act, not only killing a political struggle but also effecting a widespread arrest in the proper development of the *jīl al-intifāda*.

As I have argued elsewhere (Collins 2004), Isam articulated most explicitly this notion of generational failure, although he maintained that it was the process of political action itself, rather than its eclipse in favor of the "peace process," that left members of the *jīl al-intifāda* unable to complete their transition to adulthood. Nonetheless, on the issue of the intifada's conclusion, Isam joined Salim and Ashraf in formulating a clear moral chronology. In direct contrast to his statement, quoted above, that the initial mass participation in the intifada was motivated by "something from *inside* of us" (emphasis added), he posited an "outside," international dimension to the uprising's demise, seeing the "peace process" as part of a larger Pax Americana imposed on the entire Middle East with the complicity of many Arab leaders. "There are a number of reasons for [the breakdown of the intifada], not just one, but in my view it started with the Gulf War, with the defeat of Iraq, and the Arab countries turning [on us]," he argued. "And we didn't expect this—even though it's well-known that the Arab regimes suppress their own people, we didn't expect that it would be like this." The triumph of U.S. imperialism, as it functions in Isam's narrative, effectively completes a process that began with the apple he threw at the Israeli patrol: from this action, the ultimate example of individual resourcefulness and locally generated resistance tactics, initiative gradually moved outward until, in the end, a deeply unsatisfying outcome was imposed by the most global and alien of political forces.

Generation and Class: "The Harvest Is Always for the Rich"

The issue of economic inequality provides a fourth clue to understanding the larger moral chronologies I have examined here. As a group, the narratives speak to a deep dissatisfaction not with nationalism or nationality per se, but rather with the fact that the *narrative* of nationalism—with its references to progress, justice, and victory—has been derailed, rendered unrealizable by events that the narrators themselves have witnessed. For many, the question concerns a very familiar problem in the history of decolonization: the failure of the nationalist movement to deliver on specific political promises that are assumed to have material analogues in the lives of ordinary people.

One is reminded of Fanon's (1963: 74–75) description of postindependence disillusion as a situation in which "the masses by a sort of (if we may say so) child-like process of reasoning convince themselves that they have been robbed" of their just rewards. Fanon's entire analysis of the dynamics of national liberation, of course, is animated by his conviction that the moment of national independence is only the beginning of the struggle for the "masses." Given the general thrust of his argument, which operates on the assumption that national liberation programs can never deliver all that they promise, his description of popular dissatisfaction as "child-like" is strangely dismissive. His choice of imagery, however, is also suggestive if read against the grain, precisely because it raises the possibility of a link between generational identity and critical energy. The post-Oslo dilemma of the "intifada generation" indicates that young people are in a particularly suitable structural position to sense, and react to, the failures of national liberation—not because they are burdened by a "child-like process of reasoning," but because they have the highest national expectations *and* the highest personal expectations.

Thus Khaled summed up his feelings about the growing inequalities around him by telling me, with an air of resignation, that "the harvest is always for the rich" (*il-hasād dayman lil-aghniya*). His metaphor is, in an important sense, a generational one that recalls Ashraf's description of the intifada as having been "aborted" by the national leadership. Yet whereas the latter image calls to mind only unnatural death—the premature stoppage of the growth process—Khaled's choice of words suggests an even more troubling possibility, namely, that the process really did continue to its logical conclusion. To speak of the current period as a "harvest for the rich" implies that there are "fruits" to be picked, but that these fruits are not being given to those who deserve them.[12] Similarly Intissar, a student and political independent, described the plight of refugees like herself in dire terms: "The camps are saying, what is this peace? What has it done for us? Nothing! It hasn't done anything. We're all alone."

Intissar's critique of the "peace process" encapsulates a fear that is deeply rooted in the experience and consciousness of an entire generation of camp dwellers: the realization that while they may not always be young, they may always be refugees, and the suspicion that because of this, they may always be poor. Such concerns, while partially aimed at illuminating the differential impact of "peace" within Palestinian society, also suggest that despite the claims of the national leadership, Palestine is not undergoing a process of decolonization at all. Hatem, an erstwhile PNA supporter, spoke of quitting his position in the army after he discovered that soldiers and officers who had come from "outside" (that is, those who did not fight in the intifada) were being given preferential treatment, and that his superiors seemed to be abandoning the principles of the intifada.[13] "Everything I believed in, I found out they were against," he said. "Their first priority is the security of Israel."

Conclusion

In his work on popular memory, Alessandro Portelli (1991) invites us to consider the ways in which self-representations are inevitably colored by the struggles of individuals to maintain a sense of self that is at once changing and unchanging, a self that continues to reflect the influence of foundational events and principles even as it adapts to ever-shifting historical circumstances. "Narrators thus establish that they are both the same person they always were, and a different person, too," he writes. "At what time in the life cycle the story is told is, however, a crucial factor in its shape." The latter observation reminds us that such individual struggles are always informed, to a greater or lesser extent, by the generational identity of the teller. Age, in this sense, is a central component of the historical constellation that shapes popular memory.

The intifada generation is defined by its unique location in the history of the Palestinian liberation struggle. With the uprising serving as the "drama of their youth" (Mannheim 1952), these young people have already lived a set of deep contradictions between the promises of the intifada and the realities of the post-Oslo period. The "moral chronologies" discussed in this article are the products of precisely these contradictions, filtered through the lens of the passage from youth to adulthood. The mid-1990s were a time when the two elements that converge to produce generational solidarity—age and history—were both undergoing important transitions that were fundamentally unfinished. This conjuncture, and the frustrations it created in the lives of Balata's young people, go a long way toward explaining why their self-representations are also unfinished, lacking in narrative closure.

Subsequent events, of course, have only confirmed the apparent permanence of the Palestinian state of emergency (Collins 2004), leaving Palestinians with little option but to focus solely on the question of survival. It is not for nothing that the second intifada has seen high numbers of Palestinians facing Israeli soldiers not only in the streets but also in their houses and in their fields, under their trees. The Israeli "matrix of control" has effectively criminalized the stuff of everyday life, making even habitation an act of resistance. This new reality is undoubtedly producing narratives with a new inflection, narratives with no beginning and no imagined end—only the emergency of the present. With this in mind, the moral chronologies of the intifada generation emerge as documents of a transitional moment when the historical, political, and narrative logic of national liberation started to give way to a new logic that is considerably less optimistic.

NOTES

1. I would like to thank Asale Angel-Ajani, Danielle Egan, Bruce Lincoln, Victoria Sanford, two anonymous reviewers, and the members of the Denison University Global Studies Seminar for their helpful feedback on earlier versions of this chapter.

2. For more information on the history of Balata camp, its social structure, and its political role in the anti-occupation struggle, see Collins (2004: 24–30).

3. I am tremendously indebted to Abdul-Jabbar al-Khalili, Mohammed Odeh, and Mona Shikaki for their able assistance as translators for the interviews. The research was also aided by a grant from the Joint Committee on the Near and Middle East of the Social Science Research Council and the American Council of Learned Societies with funds provided by the U.S. Information Agency; and by additional support from the

MacArthur Program on Peace and International Cooperation at the University of
Minnesota.

4. In 1993, after a largely secret process facilitated by Norwegian mediators, Israel and
    the PLO signed a series of agreements that provided for the creation of the PNA and
    the gradual withdrawal of Israeli forces from certain parts of the West Bank and Gaza.
    Critics who pointed out the flaws in the accords—that they did not require a complete
    cessation of Israel's illegal occupation, and that they created what was, in essence, a
    "native police force" to control the Palestinian population—have been proven correct
    in subsequent years.

5. As Benedict Anderson (1991) and others have argued, national narratives are neces-
    sarily characterized by a retroactive impulse: history is written teleologically—or, in
    Anderson's words, "up time" (that is, projecting backward from the present)—such
    that past events are meaningful only insofar as they can be viewed as contributing to
    the taking of state power, which constitutes the ultimate triumph of the nation.

6. More than anyone else I spoke with, Samer clearly saw himself as performing a defen-
    sive function in relation to critiques of the official nationalist movement. When I first
    met him, I had already conducted the bulk of my interviews in the camp, and I suspect
    that as a well-connected political operative (and an employee of the intelligence serv-
    ice), he had already learned a great deal about me and about the lines of questioning
    I had been pursuing with others.

7. After his return, Khader was one of three Balata residents elected to the first Palestinian
    Legislative Council in early 1996. A widely popular figure in the camp, he has become a
    vocal critic of the PNA and a forceful advocate for the rights of refugees in the years
    since his election. Given his credentials as a lifelong Fateh organizer, Khader's antago-
    nistic relationship with the Fateh-dominated Authority is significant and speaks to a
    wider rift that has developed between younger, "inside" activists—those who "paid their
    dues" in the streets and the interrogation cells during the intifada—and the older, "out-
    side" leadership that returned from exile in the wake of the uprising.

8. The incident to which Leila was referring—a November 1994 shoot-out between PNA
    police and Hamas activists that left at least twelve people dead and roughly two hun-
    dred wounded—provoked a great deal of shock and anxious discussion throughout
    the West Bank and Gaza, briefly raising fears of a Palestinian civil war. Significantly,
    Leila said nothing about the PNA's role in the battle, preferring to label it a case of fac-
    tional infighting exacerbated by unnamed "outside forces." Although it is theoreti-
    cally possible that her use of this term was a veiled reference to the PNA, a more likely
    explanation is that she was misremembering the timing of the event (placing it before
    the PNA's arrival) and accusing Israel or Iran (via its backing of Hamas) of fomenting
    tension in Gaza. It is significant to note in this context that in the aftermath of the
    clash, the notion of "outside forces" proved equally useful for supporters and critics of
    the PNA's actions. In a statement issued the day after the battle, the Fateh movement
    implicitly invoked the specter of Iranian support for Hamas when it warned Palestini-
    ans against taking part in "conspiratorial plans on behalf of foreign parties," while
    other observers, such as one young Gazan quoted in the New York Times, suggested a
    different conspiracy: "This was all done on the orders of [then-Israeli prime minister]
    Rabin and [U.S. president] Clinton" (Haberman 1994).

9. On February 24, 1994, Baruch Goldstein, an American-born settler and member of the
    far-right Kach movement, opened fire on worshipers at Hebron's Ibrahimi mosque—
    located in one of the most bitterly contested religious sites in Palestine, the "Tomb of

the Patriarchs"—before he was beaten to death by survivors. Most accounts list the death toll at twenty nine individuals, a number of whom were killed by soldiers while attempting to flee the area.

10. "It is the moment of the boomerang . . . it comes back on us, it strikes us, and we do not realize any more than we did the other times that it's we who have launched it," writes Sartre. "The Left at home is embarrassed; they know the true situation of the natives, the merciless oppression they are submitted to; they do not condemn their revolt, knowing full well that we have done everything to provoke it. But, all the same, they think to themselves, there are limits; these guerrillas should be bent on showing that they are chivalrous; that would be the best way of showing they are men. Sometimes the Left scolds them. . . . 'You're going too far; we won't support you any more.' The natives don't give a damn about their support; for all the good it does them they might as well stuff it up their backsides" (Fanon 1963: 20–21).

11. PLO support for Saddam Hussein during the first Gulf War left the Palestinians diplomatically isolated in the "new world order" famously proclaimed by U.S. President George H. W. Bush. Most observers have viewed the Oslo process as a product of the new reality ushered in by the war, with the Palestinians, weakened by Israel's repression of the intifada, pressured into signing agreements that fell well short of giving them their full rights under international law. The parallels with the situation that has prevailed since the second U.S. invasion of Iraq in 2003 are striking.

12. The arrival of the PNA—the major entry point for international assistance coming into the West Bank and Gaza—represented a crucial turning point in this context, for the new Authority had the power to create jobs and, more generally, to distribute political and economic "rewards." That it has done so in a highly selective manner is not unexpected, especially given Arafat's history of maintaining power through the careful use of political patronage. Although Balata has never been a classless community, the particular kind of relative privilege and deprivation that has emerged under the PNA does not sit well with camp residents who tend to remember the past, including the intifada, in terms of circumstances that were shared rather than fought over. Part of what is at issue here is the shifting political meaning attached to labor. In the past, when jobs in Israel were widely available, working on the "other side" could only be justified if the work were divorced from its political context. Such a feat is more difficult under the PNA: not only are many appointments transparently political, but the work itself is also seen as *national* work—one is building the nation, defending the nation, or (in the eyes of some) betraying the nation. The self-representations of young people reveal complicated, sometimes contradictory attempts to come to grips with this new reality. On the one hand, many are reluctant to find fault with individuals (especially friends and neighbors) who are benefiting from the PNA's presence; on the other hand, for those who are not benefiting, discussions of the issue often provoke bitter denunciations and reassessments. For a sensitive discussion of post-Oslo class dynamics in Balata and in the wider Nablus community, see Bucaille (2004).

13. The history of the Palestinian security forces created since 1994 provides a fascinating glimpse into the social, political, and economic divisions that continue to shape Palestinian society. See Usher (1995) and Bucaille (2004).

REFERENCES

Anderson, Benedict. 1991. *Imagined Communities: Reflections on the Origin and Spread of Nationalism*. Rev. ed. London: Verso.

Bucaille, Laetitia. 2004. *Growing up Palestinian: Israeli Occupation and the Intifada Generation.* Translated by Anthony Roberts. Princeton: Princeton University Press.

Collins, John. 2004. *Occupied by Memory: The Intifada Generation and the Palestinian State of Emergency.* New York: New York University Press.

Fanon, Frantz. 1963. *The Wretched of the Earth.* Translated by Constance Farrington. New York: Grove Press.

Haberman, Clyde. 1994. "12 Die as Arafat's Police Fire on Palestinian Militants." *New York Times*, November 19.

Halper, Jeff. 2000. "The 94 Percent Solution: A Matrix of Control." *Middle East Report* 216 (Fall): 1–19.

Immanuel, Jon. 1996. "Arafat Hints at Renewal of Intifada." *Jerusalem Post*, September 1.

Mannheim, Karl. 1952. "The Problem of Generation." In *Essays on the Sociology of Knowledge.* London: Routledge & Kegan Paul.

Passerini, Luisa. 1987. *Fascism in Popular Memory: The Cultural Experience of the Turin Working Class.* Translated by Robert Lumley and Jude Bloomfield. Cambridge: Cambridge University Press.

——. 1996. *Autobiography of a Generation: Italy, 1968.* Hanover, N.H.: University Press of New England.

Popular Memory Group. 1982. "Popular Memory: Theory, Politics, Method." In *Making Histories*, edited by Richard Johnson et al. Minneapolis: University of Minnesota Press.

Portelli, Alessandro. 1991. *The Death of Luigi Trastulli and Other Stories.* Albany: State University of New York Press.

Swedenburg, Ted. 1995. *Memories of Revolt: The 1936–39 Rebellion and the Palestinian National Past.* Minneapolis: University of Minnesota Press.

Usher, Graham. 1995. *Palestine in Crisis: The Struggle for Peace and Political Independence after Oslo.* London: Pluto Press.

6

"In Our Beds and Our Graves"

Revealing the Politics of Pleasure and
Pain in the Time of AIDS

MICHAEL J. BOSIA

We stood facing each other across the kitchen island in his apartment as he recounted his story.[1] I had known him for eight years, and I was in town for a conference when he told me his news. He had tested positive for HIV. Like many gay men of our generation, we had never known a time without AIDS and free of condoms. This scene was not unfamiliar to me. In the course of my research, people touched by HIV told me about their lives and the fear, pain, and loss they had suffered. Across from me in their living rooms, they recounted how they came to be HIV positive and what they had done about it. I had been to meetings on safer sex, where men talked about why they had taken risks, had read letters from those who had died, and had examined court transcripts where people with HIV talked about the injustices they faced. Each testimony was as difficult as that night. Some easily talk of their experience, of course. Others feel isolated and are afraid of being judged. My friend was among the latter. He gradually revealed to me more details, but only after I was able to reassure him, repeatedly, that I would not judge the choices he had made.

Becoming HIV positive was no accident, the result of a broken condom. He did not blame it on ignorance, or the failure of government to adequately fund education. For him and many young men like him, it was an intentional act, called "barebacking." Increasingly common in gay communities around the world, barebacking is a decision to forego the prevailing rules of safer sex. But it also reflects a profound exhaustion with the rules themselves. Today, gay men negotiate the once concrete regulations that have governed same-sex encounters since the early 1980s. A growing number of men report intercourse without condoms, and Web sites dedicated to unprotected sex or personal ads soliciting "barebacking" are increasingly common, while estimates suggest that the rate of HIV infection is increasing and STDs are being seen more and more among gay men from Australia to France.[2] In San Francisco particularly, such experiences are occurring in a city with the most effective gay and lesbian organizations, the most extensive network of AIDS-related services, and the most accepted gay and lesbian community. Gay men are choosing intercourse without condoms, sometimes as part of a loving, long-term relationship, perhaps during an anonymous encounter during which HIV status is not discussed, or as part of an intentional decision to transmit or receive HIV. This all happened before and after former San Francisco supervisor and current State Assembly member Mark Leno in 2000 was the only elected official in the country to argue against AIDS-related federal policies that effectively deny gay men a right to donate blood.

These juxtapositions of "safe" and "unsafe" sex, "clean" and "unclean" blood, of experiences and rights, are at the heart of a crisis in AIDS politics. Officially, AIDS has changed from a source of pain and death. It only rarely inspires the anger and outrage of the die-in or the political funeral. HIV has survived political action, accusations of genocide, scientific research, and medical intervention to become its representations within a system of scientific knowledge and through rules known as "safer sex." For many, AIDS activism has overcome death, and new silences about the disease often close off the pain of AIDS.

I will argue in this chapter that this overcoming (of death and the physical) is incomplete, and I do so in an effort to return physical experience to the center of our research. Just as the official representation of AIDS removes physical experience from sexual identity and HIV, much social science and even ethnographic research submerges physical experiences within systems of representation and knowledge, as advocates and scholars can be trapped in a worldview outside the body. However, this is not an ethnography. It is a wake-up call. Drawing from my own experience with fieldwork, as a gay man, and as an activist and friend, I will touch on a variety of testimonies—essays, disclosures at public forums, and personal accounts—to advocate an empathetic turn in research, giving priority to the lived experiences of our research subjects as witnesses. Listening to their stories of physicality can provide a solution to the crisis in AIDS politics, and so affirm that empathy for physical experience gives meaning to our studies of social action.

Knowing AIDS

My object is not to analyze the discourse through which AIDS is understood, but to begin with discursive analysis and then to refocus method on the physical experience as presented by the witness, with the phenomenon of barebacking as an example that dramatically introduces the necessity for socially relevant and revealing research. Poststructuralist approaches offer valuable insights into the formation of human nature through discourse and knowledge, and we must begin with this perspective in understanding the nature of subjectivity, agency, and action. The tendency to assume this approach in the field as if it is always a step forward, however, can produce two steps back. I mean this metaphorically and in a literal way. For example, when Judith Butler discusses drag and performativity in *Bodies That Matter*, she unlocks such discourses through an analysis of the film *Paris Is Burning*, discussing at times the "gaze" of the film's creator, but never actually engaging the participants themselves. In effect, she is two steps removed from the action.

This is neither to "deconstruct" or discount Butler and others, who do not claim fieldwork, nor simply to take a side in the debate over the value of experience in social analysis. Scott, for example, argues that a focus on experience, by failing to move outside the discursive system to interrogate the historical processes that make identity and experience, actually solidifies and cannot contest the categories of identity. But she also notes that discursive systems are never closed, cohesive, or uncontested (Scott 1992). In her debate with Scott, Downs seeks to locate something "real" in experience, but she also returns to a "tension" in the relationship between discourse and experience (Downs 1993).

I begin from Scott's admonition within this debate: interdisciplinary approaches are a "difficult and risky business" (Scott 1993: 438). I suggest that the application of poststructural analysis without regard to experience, of those narratives of discursive domination that do not consider the narratives of physical experience offered by the dominated, end up constraining our methodology and limiting our understanding. In the question at hand—AIDS, sex, and barebacking—I locate the limits of this approach in the ways poststructuralist accounts can be used to dismiss physical and bodily experiences as mere artifacts. In doing so, I move beyond Downs's argument about social experience and Scott's concern about the conservative nature of experience to locate the body and its physicality as a contested site within a discursive system.

Indeed, much of the stuff that links the articles in this volume can be found in the result of social action on the flesh, and in the organization of a reaction to or through physical experiences. Each delves into, drawing on Butler's terminology, the "strategies of erasure" which produce abject subjectivities. These, of course, can be discursive erasures, as they are when strategies of safer sex veil the practice of barebacking in silence and—only when necessary—shame. But strategies of erasure are also physical and violent. They can produce pain and death by intent or neglect, such as the initial silence surrounding AIDS that produced death among gay men and those who received HIV-contaminated blood, and the physical erasure of Maya communities through genocide in Guatemala. In striking ways, it is not relevant to the victims of erasure that their physical experiences are only realized through a given form of knowledge and a specific subjectivity. What is instead revealed in their testimony is the sense of the physical as meaningful, a sensitivity to the body as the location of pain and pleasure, as the origin of social and political ostracism or action. This, I believe, is just one way our fieldwork can demonstrate through actual experiences how, as Foucault explains, "deployments of power are directly connected to the body" (Foucault 1990: 151) and, as Sanford asks, "how silent are silences?" (Sanford 2000: 15).

But there is also an often unstated assumption in poststructuralist approaches as they disentangle the power of erasure or abjegation to control and discipline the subject. What goes unstated is the question of the efficacy of erasure. What is it about the subject that compels conformity to a given identity as part of a community? What is it that compels nonconformity through the occupation of transgressive identities that also take the form of kinship or community? Again, fieldwork requires that we answer these questions through testimony, through the lived experiences of participants as they negotiate the very discourses that are often the subject of analysis. In this way, we can focus through discourse on the individual within a given discursive network—and find the ways individuals articulate community or kinship through the flesh.

I will argue that fieldwork requires us, while understanding subjectivity, to shift from subjectivity to distinctions between the body and the soul, the material and the discursive, to the relationship of these within the subject. This tentative engagement between self as performance and self as substance should be the guiding narrative of an empathetic methodology that engages the witness as a vital—but not the only—voice in his or her experience. This is how we must refocus, and I would say return, social activity and its meanings to an understanding of actions and intentions, not as simple texts that we can read but as life experiences, as real, to the participants.[3]

From the beginning, AIDS has had at its core a tension between its representations and its physical experiences (Haver 1996).[4] Today, this tension has reached a crisis because, in order to grasp what is happening in bathhouses, bedrooms, parks, and back rooms around the world, we need to reincorporate the individual physical experience as an influence in the process of knowing, understanding, and acting. Applying theory to practice with regard to AIDS, such an approach requires us to value the physicality of AIDS, bodily experiences that are true to the participant, and in the process expose an underlying tension that exists between the discourses of AIDS, on one hand, and pain or pleasure in the flesh, on the other. Certainly, it is not possible for a witness to conceptualize and later describe the pain or pleasure surrounding AIDS without a referent, outside a system of knowledge, or beyond the structures of desire. But it is analytically necessary for us to examine how the physical experiences of AIDS have informed action through knowledge, and how some experiences are simply incompatible with the forms of knowledge available for their understanding.

Disentombed and Disembodied

The public story of AIDS—easily available and familiar—is its purposeful representations within the social and political fields. For example, not long ago in

San Francisco, the leaders of AIDS-related organizations created the National AIDS Memorial Grove in Golden Gate Park.[5] I was away at graduate school for four years, and had never seen the Grove until I happened upon it one rare sunny day the summer before I left for field work in France. Like many other San Franciscans, I was taking advantage of the unusual weather for a morning run. Moving through the park, I was lost in thought, in the list of things I needed to accomplish before I moved to Paris. As I ran, the air became colder, the path became a hard surface. I saw a large boulder, a creamy clean stone not spoiled by moss or dust. Words were cut into its surface: "L'Chaim—To Life!"

I stopped. I caught my breath. I was confused by this "toast," in Hebrew, chiseled in stone. I entered a small sanctuary walled in by trees. The paved surface of the site was covered with names. More boulders marked its limits, and there were others in the distance down the path, also engraved with names. On each such marker, a small collection of stones appeared to have been placed by mourners who had come to say *kaddish*. The paving formed a circle, like the heart of a small domed temple.

I realized that I had found the National AIDS Memorial Grove, and revisited it time and again over the next weeks. I was surprised to find it intensely unnatural, so clearly outside of experience, a queer hybrid of iconographies; indeed, a stylized cemetery, in part evoking a church transept where ancient bishops were once buried, in part a memorial of names that evokes a comparison with the Vietnam War Memorial. But this site is purely representation, without the bodily markers that hold in place a cemetery, a church, or a memorial to the dead. It was not a cemetery. The tombstones did not mark the burial of bodies, but instead often noted the financial backers, and the small stones that mourners had placed on the boulders were quickly cleared away, as they disrupted the design of the site. It was neither a sanctuary nor a memorial to the dead. The names on the paving confused those who had died with the donors who funded construction, obscuring the distinction between life and death. Indeed, the "recognition" of donors, or, more accurately, the sale of space for the donor's name, would be shocking if this were truly a memorial dedicated to victims.[6] However, in this case, the names not only link the living and the dead but also those who fought for access to drugs with the pharmaceutical industry that profits from their sale and continues to deny a fair price, for example, to people with AIDS in Africa. Called a place of remembrance, meant for contemplation and memorial services, this was a memorial in disguise, a memorial that sealed a community around a theme of celebration. The fullness of disease—the all-too-real face of death—was veiled, the struggle for justice and care was silenced, the bodies of the dead would not disturb the visitor, mortality itself was eliminated in favor of a transcendent life. What should have divided the names in stone—profit or health care, living or dead—was used instead to bring all together. "L'Chaim—to Life."

The representation of AIDS as life is a result of the success of AIDS politics. Activists have entered the corridors of power, granted an unheard-of access not available to people with other diseases. They sit on government advisory panels, they work alongside researchers, they negotiate with pharmaceutical companies. Activists speak the languages of virology, biochemistry, law, social programs, and profit. Activists who once created street theater have become educators well versed in a particular knowledge that they share at forums in every major city. Safer sex has been transformed from a necessity during a time of war—a war against disease—into a lifestyle, a set of defining rules and norms that create the contemporary gay male. Faced with an unbearable death toll, AIDS activism has created of itself a new community that includes the living, the doctors, the researchers, the elected officials, and corporate entities. Death has been silenced.

But what has been required for this success?

Earlier in 2000, a San Francisco local elected official joined with a regional blood bank to demand that the Food and Drug Administration change their regulations, which prohibit blood donations from men who had sex with men after 1977. The current policy was adopted in 1985, after much controversy. For several years before, federal health regulators, gay rights advocates, and blood bank administrators had all debated the various methods of donor screening, surrogate testing, and finally HIV testing. With each proposal, some argued civil rights, others argued economic necessity, but by 1983 when the industry was first advised to implement donor screening, the CDC believed it had ample evidence to demonstrate that AIDS was caused by a blood-born pathogen transmitted similarly to Hepatitis B. While the debate continued and various screening methods were proposed or recommended before testing and the exclusion were adopted, many of the estimated 10,000 hemophiliacs who live with or have died from HIV were infected (Bayer 1989, 1999).

That year's double call against the current policy holds a striking similarity to that earlier debate, but moves beyond it in a critical way. I will focus on one similarity as it relates to the priority of knowledge and representation over physical experience. San Francisco supervisor Mark Leno followed gay rights advocates from fifteen years before to argue that the current policy is discriminatory in that it isolates gay men as a group. "The guidelines should ask about sexual behavior, not sexual orientation," he has said (Curiel, 2000). He focused his attention on the category "men who have had sex with other men" and sought to move from there—from the body in pleasure—to the idea of sexual orientation.

Leno is arguing that sexual orientation as identity represents a protected category of citizen, a state of abstract belonging and representation, removed from the physical. The key to his understanding is the way his words slide from the originals in the policy—"men who have sex with men"—to "sexual orientation" through the juxtaposition of orientation with behavior. What Leno is suggesting is that the pleasures of the body are not an identity. Instead, the rules that govern sexual expression—the guidelines of safe sex—constitute gay orientation. His distinction with regard to behavior is not simply a distinction between the act of sex and the conception of an abstract category. He intends a specific orientation beyond the question of with whom you have sex. Leno argues that those who practice "safer sex" should be allowed to donate blood. This constitutes his gay community, and makes it constituent of a large whole. The opponents of blood screening in the 1980s formed "gay" out of sexual acts, but Leno takes the rules of sex as his defining principle. In this context, civil rights and participation in commodity politics (blood is a commodity) follow from the acceptance of the specific abstract norms.

As a result, Leno's representation of gay identity after AIDS is based on knowledge and control, or in more explicit terms, a Foucaultian system of power/knowledge where "A soul inhabits him and brings him to existence, which is itself a factor in the mastery that power exercises over the body" (Foucault 1991: 30). Sex in the age of AIDS has moved beyond the regulation of physical desire. The question of sexuality is removed from physical experience, gay is removed from sexual pleasure, and orientation is transformed into the very norms of safe sex where sexual citizenship controls pleasure. Safe sex arrives through a series of dangers in the body—from sex, sperm, and HIV—and it prohibits their exchange in order to find an identity beyond the simple interplay of two bodies in an act of physical pleasure. "Sexuality" as a category of citizenship and community in the era of AIDS becomes the rules of safe sex.

This AIDS—the AIDS of knowledge, of rights and identity, self-control and victory, of the representation instead of the experience—is the AIDS that one should expect in what Anne Norton calls a *Republic of Signs*. Norton argues that the American character is one written in text. It is a character that is self-represented, a process of overcoming "flesh" by making "flesh" into text. This desire to overcome is, according to Norton, a reaction to our material limits. She carefully selects the term "transubstantiation" to describe the movement from individual body to representation in text, from the physical to an abstract belonging. In Catholic ritual, transubstantiation is the act wherein the priest transforms, through "the word," a simple wafer and chalice of wine into the divine body and blood of Christ. In communion with Christ's body, made possible by "the word," the communicant joins the abstract body of the Church. Norton argues that our secular process of abstraction also transcends the limits of the individual. We build community in the body politic as our bodies become text. "In authoring this new, ideal being, they overcome the isolation and incompletion of their corporeal individuality" (Norton 1993: 125).

Norton makes clear that she is speaking not only of America but also of any community that defines itself through text. It is the "constitution" of the whole in text, of "America" or "La Republique" (1993: 124). It follows, then, that we can understand the notion of AIDS as text and the defining of sexuality as rules through this desire to move outside our physical limits and craft an identity that is timeless, that transcends disease, that is written, now and everlasting, in the words carved into stone. Confronting AIDS, with suffering and pain all around, with the ravaged bodies of the dying, we found survival in the rules of science, certainly rules that have been modified by activists, but text nonetheless. Facing the mortality that arrived through sexual pleasure, we made sex into text, carefully crafting a set of rules that is fixed and timeless, that abstract the physical experience. Glorious in our final victory over death, in the overcoming of AIDS through science and practice, a new community was crafted in stone in a grove in Golden Gate Park. It is a community in text, a living community that celebrates AIDS as transubstantiation, ultimately as a denial of physical limits through a new life that is timeless.

If officially AIDS and death are being vanquished through knowledge, how then do we understand those who excommunicate themselves through their own actions, their very denial through physical experience of an abstract community? How can we even begin to address such issues if we lack the ability to empathize with such experiences?

Pleasure in the Time of AIDS

Shortly after my arrival in Paris, I woke one morning to find an exposition on *le retour du risque* from HIV in the journal *Libération*. In a series of articles, the newspaper explored the ways that gay men in France were redeploying their sexual bodies outside the rules of citizenship defined by safer sex, and in its coverage *Libé* ended any silence about barebacking and unprotected sex within the Paris gay community. Back rooms, "hedonism," and barebacking are all on the rise, denying safer sex and replacing this knowledge with a return to the flesh. As one activist noted, what has emerged/returned is a *culte du sperme*. In the United States, such phenomena remain silenced, despite occasional visibility in the gay media, on the Internet, and in the debates among activists. Where the response in the American gay community has been not to speak, the reportage in *Libé* launched a public debate within the gay community between AIDS activists and proponents of barebacking. The French response, however, has been organized in relation to prevalent attitudes through which American homosexuality, and not that in France, is considered to be irresponsible. Sexuality in France is a private affair, unless its practice challenges basic national values. *Libé* even illustrated these stories with a photograph from an American sex club.

This debate has unveiled the incomprehension of many AIDS activists, officials, and journalists who have incorporated and enforced the representations of AIDS. They cannot understand why men would risk death when the text enables its overcoming. The initial articles were followed by a series of editorials by AIDS activists and those who promote barebacking. Act Up Paris, which is still a vibrant force in AIDS politics and one of the most respected organizations on the left in France, called an assemblée générale de pédés (loosely, *pédé* is the French equivalent of "queer") to take place during the organization's regular weekly meeting. Four hundred queer men, a few women, government officials, and the media gathered in a crowded hall for a debate and discussion—and often a war of words—that lasted three hours.

On one side, activists and officials argued a form of diminished capacity. Unprotected sex occurred because young people are ill-informed, in many situations individuals are unable to make reasonable decisions, or condoms are not immediately available in all areas of back rooms and sex clubs. In calling for "testimony" from those who had barebacked, relapsed, or who from time to time ignored safe sex rules, the vast majority of the attendees applauded those testimonies that reenforced this perception. One young man, Laurent, recounted his history, a single act of unprotected anal sex during a visit to New York. Among the young, he said, "there is an ignorance about condoms." He expressed regret, anguish, and guilt, though he could not fully articulate why he did it. "I found myself in a situation where I did not reflect," he explained. For many, his confession of sexual misconduct in an American city was sufficient. The physical act itself was silenced in favor of its overcoming, in the story of diminished capacity, of ignorance, rehabilitation, and reintegration, that transformed his body into part of an abstract community. Many began to blame seropositive gay men, narrowing the possibility of gayness much as Leno had done in the United States, by making it virtually impossible for "tainted" bodies to join an abstract community founded on the rules of safe sex. One veteran activist clearly felt his exclusion, later telling me, "It was an *assemblée générale de seronegatives!*"

Those who advocate barebacking attacked the very foundations of safe sex. "Act Up is under a delirium of hygiene and morality," exclaimed the writer Guillaume Dustan during the meeting. He has become well known to those assembled as a proponent of barebacking. Elsewhere, Dustan wrote that "the condom has never existed" (Dustan 2000: 8). These advocates testify that the condom is not a means of protection against HIV but rather a protection against pleasure, a sign of shame and self-hate promoted by those who fear their sexuality and the physical nature of sex. For barebackers, the solution to AIDS is not the removal of sexuality and physical pleasure but the celebration of the physical, of intimate contact flesh to flesh, that is the basis of their sense of community. "We take off the condom because we feel nothing. That is the reason the condom is not, has not been, and never will be used except in exceptional circumstances, and is not, has not been, and can never be the rule in matters of human sexuality" (ibid.).

My friend, in his kitchen, cautiously revealed his story by bridging these two explanations for risk. At first, he confessed much like the young man at the Act Up meeting. But there was something he was not saying, and he seemed to both relish the silence that suppressed his truth and longing to say more. As I reassured him, he fleshed out his story. Tired of condoms, he said he could no longer imagine a time when he would be able to feel a physical connection with another person. He had given up hope—for a cure and for a partner with whom he could safely abandon condoms. The rules that kept him safe also inhibited real contact, flesh to flesh. So he took greater and greater risks, in silent encounters, in an effort to touch another person.

These phenomena of unprotected sex themselves, both barebacking and the relapse, can be seen as a response to the discourse that has defined AIDS, as a denial of that text. Frequent, anonymous encounters, increasing the number of sexual partners, and pushing the limits of what is considered "safe" result from the silences that veil physical experience today—pleasure, pain, the process of HIV in the body—within the representations of AIDS, and subsequently within a disembodied sexual identity. It has been a quiet and anonymous revolt in back rooms, saunas, parks, and tea rooms, where gay men are using their bodies to experience and know sexuality. This reaction reaches its fullest with barebacking, which is a *culte du sperme* in which seropositive and seronegative men celebrate HIV through unprotected anal sex. Barebacking embraces the knowledge of HIV but reverses the process to return from the text to flesh. It celebrates the mingling of material life and the building of community through flesh, denying one that is abstract in favor of another community felt as real.

AIDS and the Politics of the Physical

This rebirth of unprotected sex, in its embrace of physical experiences that bring pleasure and pain, has a genealogy that connects to the emergence of Act Up and other forms of militancy that used the flesh as the source of identity and protest. These earlier activists chose to make the experience of HIV a weapon, forcing a physical process of disease onto the public space. Death was marked with political funerals. They refused a citizenship of silence where rights are granted regardless of HIV status and instead broadly acknowledged the disease in their flesh. Government officials were accused of "murder" and "genocide" because so many were dead and dying. In one particularly striking moment, activists interrupted Mass at St. Patrick's Cathedral in New York, trampling the Eucharist, which is the veritable object of transubstantiation. But activists demanded more than an acknowledgement of the physical nature of AIDS as disease. They insisted on the new "queer" sexuality that celebrated sex despite the existence of AIDS, and used explicit, physical imagery and language to make their point.

This is the heart of crisis among gay men in AIDS politics today. We have one discourse that has removed physical experience from the nature of the disease, making of it only a representation. Officially, AIDS has become its knowledge, its forms of control and regulation, its transformation of sexual identity, its treatment and prevention. It is the realm of the doctor and the researcher, the informed activist. It is a cemetery without bodies, a memorial that is uncomfortable with the dead. On the other hand, we have these physical experiences of unprotected sex, pleasure, disease, and pain. In them, AIDS has a meaning in the flesh. It is a real presence, a truth that through pleasure can bring pain. This AIDS is in the body, in its fluids, in the bedroom, in the back room. This AIDS also unites, as community, through the physical nature of HIV in the body.

It is my argument that no form of knowledge, no text or assembled abstraction of citizenship, ever overcomes what Norton claims is our mortal, "corporeal individuality." Yes, forms of modern knowledge and power bring to life identities, abstract and transcendent, which we inhabit by exercising discipline over our selves. These are the questions of subjectivity and control addressed by Butler, Foucault, and Norton. Where Foucault sees the result as hypercontrol, a disciplined society, Norton and Butler locate acts of rebellion. The individual is constantly negotiating the text—the representations of self—enabled, in Norton for example, by the commodification of culture and the increase of public space at the expense of private life. But in so doing, Norton argues that the individual remains within the frame of a transubstantiation that moves from flesh to new text and still negates the flesh.

However, the abstracted self is only half an answer. Instead, we perform, to borrow a phrase, a "double movement" through which we address our mortality.[7] The transcendent, abstract citizen is one solution to our understanding of the mortal body, and, indeed, an insufficient one at that. Against whatever desire we might have to overcome our material limits, arising naturally within the self or as a creation of modern knowledge, is the force of the flesh. Pain, pleasure, sensation are all manifestly physical experiences. We remain physical beings, constantly reminded of this physicality in sex, in intimate touch, in disease, in pain, in aging. Granted, our understanding of all physical experience is only possible through forms of knowledge—through speech and discourse—that imagine our bodies and identities. We cannot articulate the experience for ourselves or others without representation. But without the flesh, there is no experience to articulate, and it is these physical experiences that drive our most intimate sense of belonging and community.[8]

This physicality, though limited by our inability to understand without a field of knowledge, is an experience that begins in the body. And the rules of bodily engagement do not negate the fact that intimate touch and pleasure, for example, are physical experiences. Indeed, where Norton can solve our mortal dilemma only through an abstract community, unprotected sex responds to mortality with the pleasures of bodies engaged together. Such experiences of the flesh represent a moment when the overcoming is sought through tangible and not abstract solutions.

Physicality is central to my understanding of the crisis in AIDS politics today. How can we explain the complex and often contradictory responses to AIDS except by reinserting the physical alongside the abstract? The body in action is at the core of AIDS as disease, and it is evidence of the inability to comprehend the abstraction of AIDS. The flesh is a reply to the very idea of sexual identity as a series of rules so carefully defined, a response to a traumatic disease made into a form of knowledge, a medical record, a series of medicinal doses, statistics and averages, or legal rights and citizenship. Unprotected sex is an answer to the mortality that has been removed from AIDS, a more physical manifestation of our desire to overcome through contact with another.

This means that AIDS is a story of both life and death, and at both moments is text and flesh. It is sensual, at one time the process of infection, ravages of a disease on the body, of the need to monitor and know bodily functions, of the torments produced by treatment. AIDS cannot be overcome by text, for it remains physical, irreducible to a singular representative experience. It arrives in physical acts, indeed the very act of penetrating the body. It marks the flesh. As historian William Haver argues so persuasively, AIDS is both its text and its physical experiences. "In the first instance, I think we must work toward thinking of the impossible object that is called AIDS as a multiplicity" (Haver 1996: 3). In flesh and in text, AIDS exists. Just as it is manifest in many physical forms, it is also the forms of knowledge we use to comprehend and control it. By marking as both physical and abstract, it is always mediated by an understanding of what it is, by its essence in flesh, by the physical limits of a discourse that give it name and rules.

(Re)locating Pleasure and Pain

Didier Lestrade, founder of Act Up Paris a journalist at the national gay news-magazine *Têtu*, and a leading partisan of a kind of moral safer sex, offered a surprising *témoignage* or testimony in the magazine that reveals the multiplicity of AIDS and reinserts a narrative of physical experience in crafting community. He is writing in full knowledge of the emergence of unprotected sex, and of course of the priority that has been placed on medical knowledge and legal rights. As a result, his effort can be seen as a reinsertion of physical experience as a locus of knowledge and the source of community, as well as the recognition of the difficult relationship between the text and the physical. It is a response to both the abstraction of rules and the denial of risk during what he calls "a war." Lestrade seeks a physical community, one founded on life and death and on the immediacy of physical touch.

He is recounting the story of his friend Alain, who died this year, suddenly, after the onset of AIDS. For Lestrade, who has lost many friends and comrades to the fight against AIDS, it was a rare occurrence in this age of HIV testing and treatment. Lestrade tells us about his last visit to the hospital. "I pushed open the door to his chamber and saw Alain in bed. The room was in shadows, the window open, a warm breeze ruffled the curtains. Alain was alone, and I saw quickly that he was not conscious. He had nonetheless a good appearance, a little feverish, which you could see in his disheveled hair and in the sweat that covered his arms. But he did not have the appearance of one destroyed by a great epidemic" (Lestrade 2000b: 111).

Alain, we find, is not alone. He has a husband and a family, friends, who all arrive at the hospital for his final days. Lestrade takes on the role of comforting Alain's partner when he needs rest. "I accompanied him to bed, I caressed his uncommonly beautiful hair that I had admired for many years. I placed myself next to him, he cried but I soon felt him relaxing, so that he fell into a deep sleep. I remained there a while, in the shadows, so that I wouldn't wake him. He is a handsome man. I thought it stupid to know that we were brought together like this. I had kissed him the summer before, on the beach, but it was a kind of pact and not a sexual or amorous act" (ibid.: 111–112). Lestrade's selection of *pacte* to describe this relationship, a pact made real through a simple physical act, calls to mind another pact, the French civil union law, granting rights similar those of to marriage to gay and lesbian couples. Called the Pacte Civile de Solidarité, it is popularly known as PaCS. Lestrade seems to indicate that there are many *pactes* among gay men, some legal and some physical, some sexual and some in other ways physically intimate.

Such testimonies were not unusual in the early days of AIDS, when dying bodies left behind grieving ones, and we became acquainted with the gaunt and blemished face of AIDS, the use of bodies and blood as political action, and the self-branding of HIV status. But with the discovery of treatment and the opening up to activists of participation in scientific and market protocols, in the laboratories and the board rooms of pharmaceutical companies, this insertion of death and mourning lost its place. By returning physical sensations to the narrative of AIDS, Lestrade recognizes the importance of acting and knowing socially through the flesh. Care and comfort, for example, arise from touch, from the sense of another's pain through this touch, from the comfort that can flow through the palm of the hand as it gently strokes another's hair, and from the memory of a pact sealed with a kiss. He is building community through such experiences— the tender moment on the beach and the commitment from it. In an era when knowledge has gained a premium over such tangible expressions, even as a necessity in avoiding the dangers associated with sex, Lestrade instead derives the need for knowledge from these real moments. He again calls for coming out and recoming out of those with HIV, returning to the knowledge of a physical experience—the experience of the virus in the body—as a foundation for community. "I no longer want to be in denial," he tells a friend. "I know you are positive" (ibid.: 112). These living bodies, feeling life, are in contrast to the body that is dying in the shadows but which remains at the heart of his recounting until the end. "Alain's body passed before us wrapped in a black plastic bag" (ibid).

Unfortunately, Lestrade's testimony fails in its attempt to overcome the incommensurability that divides those who have accepted AIDS as its representations and those who practice unprotected sex, between the text and the flesh. While he arranges bodies with HIV in front of us—his own, that of the dying Alain, Alain's husband, and their friend who must go on living with HIV—he remains unable to reconcile his social experience with a "safe sex" that is devoid of the physicality of sex. He frames his story about AIDS, much as earlier activists had, through the experiences of his flesh and his memory of these experiences, told with an intense sense of the physical. Lestrade's argument emphasizes the tangible coupled with knowledge and a return to the injection of HIV status into public spaces. This is a reflection of both the manifestation of the body and the limits of its own articulation outside of discourse. Lestrade situates the physical body, the expressions of the body in death and in caring, within his narrative, yet he remains unable to imagine the sexual body outside the official narrative about safe sex.

Nevertheless, Lestrade's attempt is as important for academics as it is for activists. If AIDS is its representations, then scholarly and social research on AIDS can be twice removed, merely a representation of the representations in search of a reality. Haver argues that the multiplicity of AIDS requires a rethinking of method. We cannot entirely explain the complexity of phenomena, the forms of disease and of the physical, through the rules and knowledges that are our traditional tools. What tools do we use, then, if we are to expose the tension in AIDS politics and other similar conflicts that take form in the flesh? It is my contention that these issues can be best addressed through testimony and ethnography. We must avoid theories and sciences that search for the general, simply deconstruct the social, take knowledge for granted, find in the body only the location of subjectivity and thus isolate social action as primarily a creation of social forms. These approaches ignore the very individual physical experience that we need to examine, what Foucault points to as "bodies and pleasures" (Foucault 1990: 157).

Conclusion: Knowledge and the Physical

Making sense of bodily acts and experiences requires us to recognize agency and intentionality, which itself requires us to listen to the agent—not ask them our questions. To do this, we first must share a frame of reference. This places a premium on our analysis of discourse if we are to fit in the skin of the participants, in their experiences in the past, and in their memories of them as they are reported to us. Our understanding of such discursive environments should provide a picture that approaches the one that our participants once had and the one they hold today, their very subjectivity and their reactions to the social world. Indeed, in many ways we must be more knowing partners with them. Their world, their knowledge, and their stories must take on a reality for us, but one through which we move, both inside and outside, feeling like the participant but always aware of being the observer. Our goal is a position that allows us to see the tension between the body and the subject, enabling a comprehension of the participant that remains critical.

This is one way we can heed Paul Rabinow's call for a critical cosmopolitanism: "Understanding is its second value, but an understanding suspicious of its own imperial tendencies" (Rabinow 1986: 258). When we deconstruct culture and meaning, we can risk a new danger built on our fear of Taylor's "incorrigibility thesis" by being overly critical and purposefully unengaged, taking on the imperial tendencies of science but under the guise of understanding. To be good cosmopolitans, I would argue, is to move inside and outside the understandings of the social worlds we study. We cannot even begin to develop adequate theories if we cannot empathize, as good friends do, with the pains and pleasures and the infinite ways physical experiences are central to action. This is the move beyond subjectivity to the identification of the bodily experiences that refract against social positions.

Testimony about such experiences of course is a limited resource. It is encumbered by the inability to frame physical experience without the interference of knowledge. Testimony is offered in words and gestures and expressions that are mere articulations, abstract and limited as a source of truth. It most often comes in narrative form, giving a social if not moral meaning to the agent's actions (Polkinghorne 1988; MacIntyre 1984; Polletta 2002). Testimony can be further specialized by its purpose: in a court of law, for example, as part of a newspaper story, in fiction or in an essay, during an interview, a heated debate, a casual conversation. Yet, testimony and observation are the only vehicles we have to understand the experiences of the flesh. If we listen without our analytical or moral judgments, the physical emerges as a truth-claim beyond the words and the expressions. It arrives in the deliberate way a story is told, in the site of its telling, in the willingness or inability to give words to bodily experience, in reluctance and enthusiasm as participants, in a subtle and unconscious nod, in the things the participants feels are important to relate—the items of experience they want to explain. Physical experiences begin to take shape and we can understand their meaning in the body politic. Testimony can reveal both the need for a tangible physical community—a community of intimates—and the desire to overcome the pain, the limits of material existence.

I awoke my first morning in Paris with another friend living with HIV. He is a long-time AIDS activist, and he has experienced the physical effects of disease, could not work, watched friends die. He is much better now. Like many Parisians, he works long hours and is making a little more money. And he enjoys sex and the intimacy of flesh against flesh. That morning, we had to get up early because he had a doctor's appointment. It was a Saturday, but because of his busy schedule, the doctor had become only another item on the list of household chores he needed to complete during the weekend. In many ways, just another item. We went out into a beautiful fall day. He talked about the results of treatment, the side-effects that, despite his general wellness, still caused problems. Sometimes he can't eat. He tires easily, and he has frequent headaches. His body is a constant source of concern, in one way or another, and also a constant negotiation between how he experiences it and the forms of knowledge required to manage HIV. He said he fights with his doctor because he wants to take a holiday from the drugs. Treatment has brought him such benefits, but his body needs a break. It is inserting itself into the doctor's office, into the subjectivities of a gay HIV patient. But his doctor won't let him. She is worried that the virus might return in a stronger form. She has not seen enough proof that a holiday can be beneficial. During this visit, she wins again. Knowledge prevails, though the flesh will continue to inject itself into experience.

NOTES

1. I would like to thank Victoria Sanford and Asale Angel-Ajani for their consistent engagement with my work and long-standing support, as well as the energy and vision in crafting this volume; Northwestern University Comparative Politics and Political Theory Faculty who have encouraged and informed my research and methods; the Fulbright program and Northwestern's Center for International and Comparative Studies and the French Interdisciplinary Group, as well as the Political Science Department, for providing financial support for my research.

2. A survey of sexual activity among gay men in 1998 found that 37 percent reported at least one incident of unsafe anal sex in the previous six months ("Barebacking Now Reported by 37 percent of Gay Men in a Recent ACT UP Golden Gate Survey," press release from ACT UP Golden Gate by Don Howard, April 16, 1998). In Australia, a recent survey found that 24 percent of seronegative men and 45 percent of those who are seropositive reported unsafe sex with men who were not their primary partners; and a CDC national survey found that the rate of unprotected anal sex in the United States has increased from 29 percent in 1995–1996 to 38 percent in 1997–1998 ("Enjeux de la prévention chez les homosexuels et les bisexuels masculine au Sud et au Nord," by Michael Bochow, *Journal du sida*, numéro special, fall 2000, 58–62). Statistics available in France from government and private studies show a similar increase in unsafe sex and increases in transmission of STDs, including a doubling of the number of cases of gonorrhea among gay men in the Paris region ("Sida, le retour?" by Christophe Martet, *Têtu*, October 2000, 110–111; "Les chiffres de 'relapse'," by Christophe Martet and Joël Métreau, *Têtu*, April 2001, 106–110).

3. I think a return to Charles Taylor's critique of the "science of verification" can refresh our understanding of meaning as tentative and real; Taylor, (1985).

4. Haver's argument is complex and hesitant, by his own admission, and thus an original and invaluable discussion of the multiplicity of AIDS, the limits of our comprehension in the face of its complexity, and the relationship between AIDS, death, and the erotic.

5. The National AIDS Memorial Grove received Congressional designation, establishing it on par with, for example, the Vietnam War Memorial.

6. In "Don't Box Me In: Gifts That Don't Need Wrapping," the December 2000 issue of *In Style*, offers shopping advice "for the person that has everything, or never seems to love anything. . . . Have a name engraved at the National AIDS Memorial Grove."

7. Karl Polanyi uses the term "double movement" to describe another "interior/exterior" relationship, wherein the state both engages itself in global markets and protects itself from them; Polanyi (1944).

8. In addition to my fieldwork and the works of Haver, Butler, and Norton, my understanding of the relationship between flesh, text, citizenship, and community is informed by a variety of works on liberal and modern polities that treat these issues directly or discuss similar tensions, including: Giorgio Agamben, *Homo Sacer: Sovereign Power and Bare Life,* (Stanford: Stanford University Press, 1998); Teresa Brennan and Carole Patemen, "Mere Auxiliaries to the Commonwealth: Women and the Origins of Liberalism," *Political Studies* 27. 2(1979): 183–200; Michael Rogin, *Ronald Reagan: The Movie*, (Berkeley: University of California Press, 1987); Michael J. Sandel, *Democracy's Discontents*, New York: Cambridge University Press, 1998); Seyla Benhabib, *Situating the Self: Gender, Community and Postmodernism in Contemporary Ethics* (New York: Routledge, 1992); Michael Warner, *The Trouble with Normal: Sex, Politics and the Ethics of Queer Life* (New York: Free Press, 1999); Robyn Wiegman, *American Anatomies: Theorizing Race and Gender* (Durham: Duke University Press, 1995).

REFERENCES

Act Up Paris, 2000. "AG de pédés." *Action*, December 6–7.
Bayer, Ronald. 1989. *Private Acts, Social Consequences.* New York: Collier Macmillan.
———. 1999. "Blood and AIDS in America: Science, Politics, and the Making of an Iatrogenic Catastrophe." In *Blood Feuds*, edited by Ronald Bayer and Eric A. Feldman. New York: Oxford University Press, 1999.
Benhabib, Seyla. 1992. *Situating the Self: Gender, Community and Postmodernism in Contemporary Ethics.* New York: Routledge.
Benkimoun, Paul. 2000. "L'épidemie de sida ne régresse plus que faiblement en France."*Le Monde*, November 21, 10.
Blanchine, Sandrine. 2000. "Je ne sais pas pourquoi, j'accepte parfois le 'no capote'."*Le Monde*, November 21, 10.
Butler, Judith. 1993. *Bodies That Matter.* New York: Routledge.
Curiel, Jonathan. 2000. "Gay Male Blood Donor Ban Called unfair." *San francisco Chronicle*, January 7, A21.
Joseph E. Davis. 2002. "Narrative and Social Movements: The Power of Stories." In, *Stories of Change: Narrative and Social Movements*, edited by Joseph E. Davis. Albany: State University of New York Press.
Downs, Laura Lee. 1993. If "Woman" is Just an Empty Category, Then Why Am I Afraid to Walk Alone at Night? Identity Politics Meets the Postmodern Subject. *"Comparative Studies in Society and History* 35.2 (April): 414–437.
Dustan, Guillaume. 2000. "La capote n'a jamais existé." *Libération*, October 21–22, 8.
Epstein, Steven. 1996. *Impure Science, AIDS, Activism and the Politics of Knowledge.* Berkeley: University of California Press.
Ewick, Patricia, and Susan S. Silbey. 1995. "Subversive Stories and Hegemonic Tales: Toward a Sociology of Narrative." *Law & Society Review* 29.2: 197–226.

Favereau, Eric, et al. 2000. "Ritour du risque, Homos: la capote n'a plus la cote; Paris, la capitale des backrooms." *Libération*, October 11, 2–5.

Foucault, Michel, 1990. *The History of Sex: Introduction*. New York: Vintage Books.

———. 1991. *Discipline and Punish/The Birth of the Prison*. New York: Vintage Books.

Haver, William. 1996. *The Body of This Death*. Stanford: Stanford University Press.

Heredia, Christopher. 2000a. "Gay Blood Donations Ban May Be Lifted." *San Francisco Chronicle*, September 12, 1 and 15.

———. 2000b. "Panel Upholds Ban on Gays Giving Blood." *San Francisco Chronicle,* September 15, 1 and 20.

Lestrade, Didier. 2000a. *Act Up: une histoire*. Paris: Éditions Denoël.

———. 2000b. "Mort en l'an 2000." *Têtu*, October, 110–112.

Lisandre, Hubert. 2000. " 'Gui-gnol! Gui-gnol!'" *Combat Face au Sida"* 12 (December): 36.

MacIntyre, Alasdair. 1984. *After Virtue*. Notre Dame: University of Notre Dame Press.

Martet, Christophe. 1993. *Les combattants du sida*. Paris: Flammarion.

———. 2000. "Édito. L'agenda de Têtu." Têtu, December, 3.

Norton, Anne. 1993. *Republic of Signs*. Chicago: University of Chicago Press.

Polanyi, Kal. 1944. *The Great Transformation*. Boston: Beacon.

Polkinghorne, Donald E. 1988. *Narrative Knowing and the Human Sciences*. Albany: State University of New York Press.

Polletta, Francisca. 2002. "Mobilizing Stories in the 1960's Student Sitins." In *Stories of change: Narrative & Social Movements*, edited by Joseph E. Davis. Albany: State University of New York Press.

Rabinow, Paul. 1986. "Representations are Social Facts: Modernity and Post-Modernity in Anthropology." In *Writing Culture: The Poetics and Politics of Ethnography*, edited by James Clifford and George E. Marcus. Berkeley: University of California Press.

Sanford, Victoria. 2000. *Buried Secrets: Truth and Human Rights in Guatemala*. Ph.D. dissertation, Department of Anthropology, Stanford University.

San Francisco Chronicle. 2000. "Change Blood Donation Rules." September 14, A22.

Scott, Joan W. 1992. "Experience." In *Feminists Theorize the Political*, edited by Judith Butler and Joan Scott. New York: Routledge.

———. 1993. "The Tip of the Volcano." *Comparative Studies in Society and History* 35.2 (April), 438–451.

Taylor, Charles. 1985. *Philosophy and the Human Sciences.* Cambridge: Cambridge University Press.

———. 1992. *Sources of the Self: The Making of Modern Identity*. Cambridge: Harvard University Press.

7

Portrait of a Paramilitary

Putting a Human Face on the Colombian Conflict

ALDO CIVICO

During a trip to Italy, I was sitting in an Internet café in Rome at the bottom of the much-celebrated Federico Fellini Via Veneto, performing the daily technological ritual of checking e-mails.[1] That morning, the headline of a message forwarded by a friend and colleague provoked my heart to beat more rapidly, and anxiety rose in my body. The news, copied and pasted from the *New York Times*, reported the killing of a Colombian paramilitary leader whose life was ended by a single bullet guided by a mysterious hand that emerged from the shadows. His name was Álvaro, and I had met him several times.[2] I perceived his death as a consequence, almost an obvious one, of a pattern of violence he had chosen to pursue during his life. And yet, at the same time, I was enveloped in sorrow. Calling a friend to share the news, I found myself with a knot gripping my throat. I was overwhelmed by emotion, and also surprised by my reaction, unexpected and unforeseen. That morning in Rome the magic of La Dolce Vita was gone.

Questions surged and occupied my thoughts during the following days. Over time, who did Álvaro represent for me? Was he only an informant, or did he turn into something else or something more? Did he become a sort of "friend?" And if so, is it possible as an anthropologist not only to become acquainted but also to develop a friendship with someone who ordered and carried out massacres, killings, and gross human rights violations? Is it possible to have benevolent feelings for someone whose ideas and deeds I not only disapprove but whom I also despise and abhor forcefully? Moreover, who was I for him? Was I just an anthropologist interested in investigating and comprehending the complex dynamics of Colombian violence? Or did I, over time, represent for Álvaro something else or something more? At times he would write me an e-mail addressing me as *estimado amigo*, that is, "dear friend." I always felt awkward when he defined me as a pal, but now I am wondering if perhaps he really meant it. More generally, what does my experience with Álvaro and even with other members of the paramilitary and guerrilla groups in Colombia tell me about the relationship between anthropologist and informant? Though motivated by professional reasons, and in my case by academic interest, the relationship is nevertheless one between persons. How does this relationship affect the collection of data, its analysis and interpretation? How did these relationships allow me to understand what is going on in Colombia? Why was it possible to develop trust and confidence with Álvaro and my other informants? If trust and confidence is possible, what is the common ground where I and my interlocutors meet? Moreover, is a relationship built on mutual trust a trigger for change for people like Álvaro?

In this chapter I reflect and translate in writing my own experience with commanders and pawns of paramilitary organizations involved in a chess game in which violence is both the means and the end of a power scheme. I intend to compose a portrait of the Colombian paramilitary, and their deeds, their way of life, their vision of the world. To put it in just one question: why is it that someone ends up enveloped in violence that he or she contributes to perpetuating? It will be an edited portrait, of course, since it will necessarily (and purposefully) rely on my own experience and my perception of people who kill and massacre for a living. Vincent Crapanzano warns us that we "must assume knowledge not only of the Other as an external actor—a soulless marionette—but as an experiencing individual with whom we are in association." In other words, this chapter will mirror the synthesis I have made thus far in my own mind about my experience in Colombia.[3] It will reflect the complexity of life itself, and the intricacy of its motivations, which are never black and white. And I will suggest that at times the anthropologist can find himself in situations where he unintentionally becomes an agent of change.

Bodies as Political Messengers

From the very outset of my time in Colombia, I encountered the bloody and horrifying actions the paramilitaries carried out.[4] Looking at power where it takes place has always been my academic interest. The testimonies I collected from dozens of victims, most of them living in the periphery of Medellín, recounted the cruelty and the excess of violence employed by gangs, death squads, and paramilitary groups. Walking through desperately poor neighborhoods at the margins of Medellín, for example, one observes people in a permanent state of numbness, traumatized by violence both witnessed and experienced. Their hearts cease to feel emotions, their eyes are dry and mute, and joyful smiles are erased from their lips. Laughs, when erupting at all, are nervous and sad. Life has been suspended, and theirs is the voice of a trauma "emerging from the wound itself." For a loving mother, it is a torture no longer to be able to sense and externalize the pain for a son slaughtered by the paramilitary.

This is today's reality for the people of Puerto Valencia, for instance, a remote village in the Colombian countryside I visited, and who are now displaced in

Medellín after being threatened and persecuted by Álvaro's group. Accused of living in a *pueblo guerrillero*—that is, in a village occupied and controlled by an insurgent guerrilla group—they were forced to abandon their homes, their few possessions, their community, and their own roots, in exchange for life. They lost the little that they owned, and today they live—I should say, they "survive"—in miserable shelters, segregated in wretched barrios, often still controlled by right-wing paramilitaries and their affiliated and subjugated gangs.[5] "We might live just on bread and water, but at least we don't fear anymore for our lives and those of our families," admitted more than one displaced person.

By employing violence, armed groups in Colombia inscribe their own sentence in the victims' bodies.[6] The victims' death or displacement carry a political message, and mark the borders of that social space where one or the another armed group exercises its hegemony. The disputes have been going on for decades. The line between "us" and "them"—that is, between "friend" and "enemy"—is often marked by blood and killings, and that border shifts back and forth as violence is applied. As noted by Carl Schmitt, "the distinction of friend and enemy denotes the utmost degree of intensity of a union or separation, of an association or dissociation."

Moreover, this line divides the social space between pure and impure, and those who are caught in the interface, are sentenced to death or are displaced.[7] The almost three million displaced persons are to everyone reminders of the extension of power exercised by particular armed groups. In other words, anybody who is displaced is at the junction of a power net that captures space and excludes any possibility of otherness. There is little room for redemption, and death is often the only way one is allowed to move from the impure to the pure. There is a sense of divine almighty power in those who carry out violence to assure or to restore—in the armed groups' view—justice.

It is thus not by chance that paramilitaries in Colombia speak of the need to *limpiar* an area that is infested by the guerrillas. Limpiar means to clean, to wash, to clean out, to cleanse, to polish, or to wipe out.[8] "This is a cleansed area," sneered a self-satisfied young paramilitary from Álvaro's group that wiped out the guerrillas of that particular area of Colombia where we were meeting. While I am writing, I have in mind the pale face of Angela, a seventeen-year-old young woman, holding her swollen belly. She was expecting a child from a husband who had been burned alive by the paramilitaries because he was suspected of siding with the guerrillas. She was at once embodying both life and death, the tragedy of the present, and the uncertainty of the future. Angela, too, no longer had tears.

Testimonies of paramilitary violence I recorded in Medellín and in other parts of Colombia describe the paramilitaries as merciless, cruel, and blood-thirsty assassins. Their accounts are confirmed by the testimonies of the same paramilitaries. Lucas, a paramilitary, told me once how a buddy tortured and killed a victim. My question had been what was the most horrifying deed he had witnessed: "The most critical [act] I saw was when a buddy lost it because there was a guy living in the barrio, at the time the militias still existed, who mugged my colleague many times when he was still a kid, insulted him and also killed some of his relatives. Therefore when we sized that territory, this guy was captured and the one who got him was my companion. He was very angry with him, thus he at first killed him very slowly and later he dragged him with a horse through the entire barrio. To see someone dragged by a horse left a great impression on me."

Power from the Shadows

Later I had the opportunity to meet with a group of paramilitary commanders. The appointment with one of their spokespersons was at a McDonald's in a Colombian city. I arrived a couple of minutes early. I spotted two young men sitting at a table and looking at me. While I was ordering a beverage, my cell phone rang. I put my hand in my jacket pocket to get the phone, but when I held it to my ear the connection suddenly died. I knew I had been identified. I turned, and following their invitation to come closer, I walked toward the two men. I sat down. I introduced myself—explaining my academic interest in knowing more about their paramilitary group. Only one of the two men, Miguel, talked to me while the other sat in silence, without offering even the slightest smile in greeting. "You will meet with our commanders and you will be able to ask them questions," offered my interlocutor, catching me by surprise. We then stood up and I followed them to a parking lot where a van was waiting for us. I had no idea where we were going. I felt like a small fish pretending to be comfortable in an aquarium. My heart was now beating fast.

After a few miles we met a police unit on a motorbike. I was hit by the quick interrogative look of one of the policemen. A few minutes later, we were stopped and surrounded by police heavily armed with revolvers and machine guns. I had never been before surrounded by so many guns. "Sons of a bitch," growled Miguel who was sitting right next to me. He got out of the van, and showed his ID. "I am working for the president's office," I heard him explaining. As a matter of fact, his paramilitary group was among those who had agreed in July 2003 to open peace talks with the Colombian government.[9] The driver and the other man accompanying Miguel slipped from below the shirts their guns and unloaded the cylinders, handing them to a policeman together with their permit. Miguel tried to smooth things over by giving the police some notebooks and colored pencils he took from a box in the van's truck. The message he wanted to convey was clear: we are not criminals, but nice people doing social activities with children in the poor barrios of the city. Some laughs were exchanged between the police and the paramilitaries, and after documents and guns were returned, we were allowed to leave. "They are good people," Miguel told me as he got back in the van.

Later, when one of the commanders explained to me that "we are not against the state, but neither are we with the government,"[10] I could better understand and read the friendly exchange between the policemen and the paramilitaries I had just witnessed. Paramilitaries, as Michael Taussig defines them, are like ghosts flitting between bare life and order. They arise, grow, and develop in the shadows, that is, a gray area where the borders between order and disorder, clarity and obscurity, light and darkness, legality and illegality are blurred and confused. It is in the shadows that links are built and sustained by paramilitaries with military commanders, mayors of villages and towns, congress representatives, and entrepreneurs in a malevolent reciprocity that is holding Colombia's democracy (and ultimately peace and security) in check.

Though the paramilitaries are considered illegal groups, it is not uncommon to see members conversing affably with soldiers and police officers. After all, in their common fight against the insurgents, they are buddies and allies. In Puerto Valencia I saw a paramilitary commander chatting openly with two soldiers on a main road and another paramilitary sitting next to a group of four soldiers in a tavern while eating his lunch undisturbed. I also observed two paramilitaries on a motorbike driving through the main square, drawing no attention from the many patrolling soldiers and police. In another village at the border between Eastern Antioquia and Middle Magdalena, while driving in a car with a paramilitary, he gave a friendly greeting to an army patrol searching a bus. In Colombia many times the presence of the paramilitary coincides with the presence of the state; they work in synergy as two faces of the same coin. Over the years, like the tentacles of an octopus, the paramilitary have increasingly gained control over Colombia's economic and political life. In the gray area, according to dynamics resembling those of Cosa Nostra—the Sicilian Mafia—ballots and political power are exchanged for impunity.[11]

Experiencing the Power of Fear

I followed Miguel up to the second floor of a house, and I suddenly found myself in a small room with five paramilitary commanders. Their boss, a former guerrilla leader converted to the right-wing armed group, was sitting behind a desk busy with a laptop and several cell phones. Hostile looks pierced me. I felt under the meticulous scrutiny of a microscope, like an unknown and therefore suspected bacterium. Every word and the slightest movement of my body was scanned and evaluated. I tried to control every tiny contraction of my muscles, trying to appear at ease in their company. I remember many times consciously fighting the instinct to cross my legs, and having on purpose left the upper buttons of my shirt unlaced, so that my neck could be seen—all signs of openness in the effort to ease communication. I had never before felt so physically uncomfortable in the same room with other people. For two hours the boss did most of the talking, giving me a synopsis of the principal events in Medellín's history in the previous two decades, and giving coherence to his group's violence. The others were just staring at me with their cold looks, and at times laughing at the boss's jokes. After meeting with them for two hours, I felt very relieved when I got into a taxi to head home.

That afternoon I experienced fear and its paralyzing power of keeping in check thoughts and movements. In that little room there was no display of weapons, nor was I physically or verbally threatened. And yet what I sensed was an environment filled with violence. Violence was shown in the inscrutable looks of the paramilitaries. It was present in the cynical and, at times, sarcastic words chosen by the *jefe*, the boss, who did most of the talking. It was displayed in the very presence of my interlocutors. It was part of their role. It could be measured by the commanders' deferential silence before their boss. It emanated from their power to condition my thoughts, my imagination, and my movements. That afternoon, my skin absorbed some of the fear millions of Colombians feel daily while journeying through an often uncertain life.

Meeting Commander Álvaro

Harshness is what I was expecting with commander Álvaro, as well. In fact, I knew he was among those who planned the occupation of the municipality of Puerto Valencia and ordered the massacre, where about twenty people were furiously and randomly killed, guilty only of having been in the wrong place at the wrong time on a Friday morning. Even the elderly and children fell under the fire of Álvaro's men, many of them shot in the back while running away from terror and looking for safety. For commander Álvaro, I had one simple question: why?

The day of our appointment, on a Sunday morning, in the company of a friend, I drove out of Medellín for about five hours until I reached a tiny and isolated village lost in a Colombian mountain range. Three young men surrounded the car I parked at the agreed-upon meeting point, the church square. After having checked my identity, one of the paramilitaries in his mid-twenties got into my car, and we left the village riding on a bumpy and narrow road. We stopped before a humble house, where a woman was mopping the porch. Though we parked on her property without asking permission, she showed neither impatience nor disappointment. Apparently indifferent to our presence, she continued her task as if we were not there. People riding horses passed by, throwing furtive and curious looks at us.

About half an hour passed, and Álvaro arrived in a four-wheel drive vehicle escorted by two men and a dog. The commander and his men were in military uniforms, and Álvaro wore dark sunglasses that made it impossible to measure his gaze. They were all heavily armed, each carrying a rifle with a telescope as well as a gun in their belts. I and my friend were invited to go into their van. I sat in the front, next to Álvaro, who was driving. He put his rifle between my legs. The cold metal pressed my left thigh. "How many times have you been to Colombia?" Álvaro asked me. "This is the fourth time. I almost feel Colombian at this point," I responded. With that, the commander burst into a spontaneous and open laughter.

After about twenty minutes we reached an abandoned cottage overlooking a wide and green valley. The beauty and the gentleness of the landscape contrasted with the roughness and the stiffness of violence and war. We sat on a porch ready to start our conversation. Álvaro finally took off his glasses, revealing a look that was anything but cruel, cold, or malign. Looking his big dark eyes I remained puzzled. They were quiet different from what I had expected. I remember thinking that instead of hiding in the mountains and killing guerrillas, Álvaro could have been a good father conducting a decent life with his wife and his kids, who—he later told me—he was able to meet clandestinely and only very rarely. My interest in why he chose this paramilitary life only increased.

Álvaro was born into a world of privilege, and he joined the military after finishing high school. To be a soldier was his dream and his passion. He found himself fighting against the guerrillas in the Boyacá region at the side of the Colombian central chain of mountains, the Cordillera Central. In the same region, at the beginning of the 1980s, land and mine owners organized paramilitary self-defense groups to protect their interests and their possessions from guerrilla raids. From the very outset, the self-defense paramilitary groups were created and supported with the complicity of the armed forces, and were subsidized by the emerging narco traffickers. When Álvaro was dismissed from the military and after he applied for law school, he had the opportunity to join the AUC paramilitary group led by the brothers Fidel and Carlos Castaño. More than anything, for him this was a chance to do what he liked, and what he knew best: to fight. "There were men . . . who lived for perpetual war, the production of death," observes Barbara Ehrenreich writing about the members of the German Freikorps.

For years, Álvaro would fight in the mountains and in urban centers against the guerrillas. He would wage war, but he would also find himself in regions of Cordoba collaborating with Fidel Castaño in introducing development and social projects as added components of the overall paramilitary strategy. "If it wasn't for the assassination of his father," Álvaro once told me, "Fidel would have sided with the guerrillas." As a matter of fact, in the 1990s there was an effort by some paramilitary leaders to add some drops of ideology to their violent deeds. Actions of war justified by ideology might make violence look better and, to perpetrators, even justified.

In general terms, their tactics followed a simple plan: the paramilitaries would occupy a territory with violence and massacres; they would eliminate the guerrilla units and those believed to be their informants and collaborators; they would displace campesinos, and would occupy, or buy at a very cheap price, the land of the displaced; and finally they would introduce some sort of agrarian reform—granting parcels of land to poor farmers. At the beginning of the 1990s,

Fidel Castaño—who disappeared in 1994 and is believed to have been killed—created a foundation called Fundpazcor (Foundation for Peace in Cordoba).[12]

That Sunday with Álvaro we had a long conversation about his own experience and the nature of the paramilitaries. We continued our dialogue on other occasions but, at times, it was interrupted by events that forced him to disappear into the shadows, from where he would suddenly reemerge. The last time there was a blackout in our ongoing conversation was during the weeks following the attack against Carlos Castaño and his subsequent disappearance.[13] Álvaro wrote to me: "What happened with Castaño distracted me quite a bit, because I cannot deny that all of this directly affects myself and my family. Now let's resume our conversation."[14]

"I Lived in a Bubble"

What follows are excerpts of our conversations, summarizing chapters of Álvaro's life, and offering his own comments:

> I come from an upper-middle-class family, and as a child I was living as if in an artificial bubble, unaware of what was going on around us. We had everything we needed and all we wanted. We had clothes, food, transportation, good schools, books, professors, and an entire educational infrastructure at our disposal. More than anything, we had a sense of security and stability. I and my companions had no worries at all, and we didn't think about those who had social problems. What we knew is that there were poor people and that we had to do acts of charity for them. This is what we learned from the priests. But life outside the bubble gets real. At that time, it was the life of children who got up at three o'clock in the morning to go to work in order to get something to eat. There were people who had only two changes of clothes for a whole year.
>
> But destiny provides the circumstances to remove one from the bubble. When, because of insufficient academic performance, my brothers were forced to move from a private high school to one in a popular barrio, I met the reality outside the bubble. I noticed the difference. My friends were part of the political and economic elite, and were vacationing in Miami and traveling to Disney World. They all had a project for their lives already defined by their parents from the very outset. Those living in the reality, instead, experienced the uncertainty of not having a project at all. It is not that the life within the bubble was false, but once you encounter the reality outside the bubble, you realized you were living a deception.

"To Become a Soldier Was My Passion and My Obsession"

Once out of high school, Álvaro decided to join the armed forces. He was very attracted to the army, experiencing it as a sort of vocation. He enlisted in the years when President Belisario Betancurt was offering a peace process to the FARC and the M–19 guerrillas; an initiative which within the context of the Cold War was viewed with suspicion from the right. "In the context of a Prussian militarism mingled with American [democratic security] doctrine," explained Álvaro, "the president was considered to have been infiltrated by Marxists who intended, little by little, and with subtlety, to debilitate the institutions and empower the communist guerrilla, as it happened." He continued:

> I could say that I carried within me [a passion for] the army. I felt like an interior power was calling me. It was a real passion. Over time it became like an obsession. Everything which had to do with [the military] was highly interesting to me. The weapons, the uniforms, the military discipline, the mystique, the patriotism, and the fighting—everything which had to do with martial life excited me. To be a soldier was like a great desire. Some want to become lawyers, others economists or whatever. I wanted to become a soldier even if this job was not well paid. . . .
>
> The change from civil to military life is traumatic. . . . The first difference in the armed forces is the absolute loss of liberty. In the process I am describing to you now, they take out from you even the freedom to move and of physiological needs. For the smallest move you needed to solicit and obtain an authorization. It was like instructing someone that he didn't exist any more as individual, but that he was part of a great machine and that he needed to be in the right gear so that the machine worked. Even dreams were controlled by the superiors. . . . It was a process of mental subjugation in which the desired outcome is that a person finally thinks like the institution. As one progressed in his formation and absorbed the institutional thinking, he could gain more freedom, which was relative because at that point you already thought the way the institution wanted. . . .
>
> [We were instructed] that the military was the fundamental pillar sustaining the democratic system and the individual liberties; that all of this was threatened by both external and internal enemies of the democratic system; that democracy was an imperfect system . . . but that it was the best one existing if compared with the totalitarian option of communism; that we had first and foremost to defend democracy; that in some circumstances we had temporarily to set aside and ignore regulations prescribed by the system itself, and that this was only necessary in order to preserve our system . . . ; that the fortress for the defense of the democratic regime was the armed forces. . . .

We were preparing for a horrible war, without support, and without resources. [We were training] to defend democracy, to die for her, without anyone acknowledging it or being grateful for it.

"Killing Time. Killing Guerrilleros"

Alvaro fought for several years against the guerrillas in the Colombian mountains. He was aware of the relationship between commanders of the armed forces and the Middle Magdalena paramilitary groups. But only when he was dismissed from the military did he have the opportunity to meet with the paramilitaries and join their forces. The contact happened while he was applying for law school:

> In those days, a retired army major offered to me the opportunity of getting in touch with friends of his, who were of a special kind: civilians fighting against the guerrillas. I thought I could help them and advise them in military tactics. I had been out of the army for about a month, and I liked the idea, so I agreed to get in touch with them. The university had not started yet, and I thought that this was a way for me to kill time. Thus, I was planning to help them while studying at the university. I thought I could alternate the two things, that is, I could continue studying while at the same time striking against the guerrillas. This was nothing new to me. It was a way to follow my ideas to help the people living in the countryside, by becoming free from the bondage to which they were subjugated by the guerrillas.

"Back with the Paramilitary I Felt at Home"

At one point, tired of fighting, he left the paramilitary organization and worked as a security officer for a major company in the Urabá region. Feeling mistreated and humiliated, he preferred to return to fighting. Within the paramilitaries, he felt he was someone, that he could make a difference, and that he could live up to his ideals and values. In the world of legality, instead, he was just one of many:

> I'm going to tell you in great honesty something that characterizes me. Working for a private company was something that affected me a lot.... Among the things that impressed me was the fact that I met with several people who were my classmates during the years I called "the bubble." I thought that having shared those years with those people was going to at least provide some sort of acceptance or acknowledgment on their part. But it wasn't like that. They acted as if we had never met before. There was an invisible barrier separating us. It was a class barrier. They considered all people working for general services as in servitude, as inferior beings. I was like a butler to an English lord. Then, for about a month, I served as a bodyguard to the boss. I was with him from the early hours of the morning until late at night. During all this time, he never addressed me directly. When he had something to tell me, he would do it through a servile employee.... Therefore when Fidel [Castaño], who was a simple person and worked

shoulder-to-shoulder with his workers, who ate and behaved like one of them, invited me to go back to working with him in his social project, I didn't think twice and I agreed. I was only making a third of what I was earning with the private firm, but I felt happy. In fact, I felt like I was at home, like I was in a family, and free from people who didn't give any value to those they considered of an inferior class.

"That Massacre Was a Mistake"

During our first meeting in the mountains, I asked Álvaro about the massacre in Puerto Valencia. The several testimonies I had collected unanimously confirmed that paramilitaries had entered the village and randomly killed whoever they ran into. Alvaro's version was at first slightly different:

ÁLVARO: [One of our commanders] entered with a patrol and a confrontation took place with the police. They truly killed some militias [guerrillas], but also several people were victims of crossfire who didn't have anything to do with it. So this was really . . . I would say that it was a mistake. This is what happened. How many people died?

CIVICO: Nineteen.

ÁLVARO: Yes, that's what happened. This was not the plan.

When Álvaro admitted to me that the action carried out by one of his men in Puerto Valencia was a mistake, for the first time during our conversations he diverted his gaze away from me. His face shifted from secure to sad. It was just a moment, a few seconds in which I detected in Álvaro a spark of humanity, of shame and regret. It was in those moments that I perceived that beneath the skin of a tough commander there was a person who needed to be discovered, in order to understand the chain of choices that were more and more wrapped up in violence, until a bullet in his head stopped all the absurdity.

The first time we met, Álvaro had the attitude of a teacher, sketching dates and maps on a notepad. He enjoyed explaining how things were in Colombia to an outsider who traveled from the United States to meet with him in the middle of nowhere. Over time, he lost that attitude, and more and more it was as if he was talking more to himself than to me. I became little more than a mirror. Today I wonder if he had the perception that those could have been the last weeks of his life.

To be sure, Álvaro never conceded that behind his ideas communicated with noble words, and his intentions masked with honorable values, there was an unacceptable life of violence and of death. The more I asked him about his experience and his motives, the more he struggled to make sense of his choices. Maybe he was trying to convince himself that his life had meaning or purpose.

That all that happened with his life was for the well-being of Colombia, a country Álvaro always defined to me as "so beautiful." One day, during a conversation, he suddenly stopped me and asked: "What do you think about all of this? What is the interest of your work? I would like to know more about your work. For me so far, it has been useful [to talk to you] and a form of self-analysis." Thus, one day we spoke about fear, life and death. He told me:

> Fear is something you continuously sense, like a conscious phenomenon. It is a part of human self-preservation mechanisms. One was trained to dominate fear, and to control it so as not to be dominated by it. But fear is always present and doesn't go away. You experience fear in different degrees. Sometimes it is uncertainty about the future. Sometimes it is perceived in a more direct way, like when one goes into combat and leaves the shelter of several days that gave an impression of security. In some moments, you feel great fear: fear of not coming back, fear of not seeing your loved ones any more, fear of not seeing again what your eyes can see right now. This, always, I experienced when I set out for combat. It is a fear you are conscious of, and you think, "who among us will be the one who will have his appointment with death? Is my appointment with death today?"
>
> The other kind of fear you experience as a self-preservation mechanism; it is the one during the fighting. One feels immensely vulnerable.
>
> Fear is something that I as a person should not perceive, since I received a special training so that fear can be controlled and doesn't turn into terror. Paradoxically I never understood the use of the word "terror" and its psychological implications in people's minds, until last year I had to confront the psychological terror of [groups I was confronting].
>
> Death, for someone like me who has met more dead than living people, is an appointment that each one of us has with our own destiny. To me no one dies young, or old, early or late. Simply, one dies at the first opportunity given to him after he has accomplished his mission in this life. Death and how it happens can be the climax of his mission. No one's death is meaningless.
>
> I have always wondered how it will be for me. Will I have the chance of a conscious death and be able to stay calm, having the possibility of keeping my thoughts? Will I have, in that moment, the opportunity to be lucid and serene? To die is something normal in life, just like birth. But somehow both moments are traumatic.

Conclusions

In this chapter I have tried to put in writing the experience of an anthropologist discovering the human dimension of a paramilitary leader who in Colombia terrorized barrios and villages. It is not the experience of a relationship with a poor farmer displaced by violence, nor one with a paramilitary or a guerrilla pawn who enrolled with an armed group, as often happens, because of economic hardship, or as a response to a previously suffered trauma (Sanford, forthcoming). It is a relationship with someone who grew up in a well-to-do family, who received a good education, and was gifted with a vivid and sophisticated intellect. It is the experience of a relationship with someone who, during his lifetime, repeatedly chose a pattern of violence to the point that he remained wrapped in it, ultimately determining his own destiny and death.

If it is true that anthropologists have a tendency to offer sympathetic readings of the people they study, it might also be his or her task to put a human face to the dynamics of power and the strategies of terror. State, war, violence, power, terror, and pain cease to be an abstraction in our imagination when they acquire a face, a story, an experience, a feeling, an emotion, or a struggle. As noted by Philippe Bourgois, "we become intimately involved with the people we study," and when someone does fieldwork in a context of conflict and war, over time, one necessarily befriends paramilitaries, guerrillas, narco-traffickers, police officers, soldiers, and especially victims. In fact, ethnography is, as sustained also by Crapanzano, "a very human experience."

Carolyn Nordstrom in her study on shadow powers suggests that gems, arms, and drugs do not circulate in a void, but pass from hand to hand. She encourages us to record and to study the different stories behind those hands. After all, participant-observation is not possible without being physically present and personally involved.

Over time, the ethnographer gains the confidence of the people he or she interviews, becoming a sort of attentive mirror, where his or her interlocutors reflect their lives, their thoughts, and their choices. Maybe those are moments of truce. And truce is probably the most that people like Álvaro can hope for. There is a sense of reciprocity in this dynamic of sharing and listening in which the character of a story might seize the opportunity to order ideas, incidents, and images. I believe this is what happened with Álvaro, and why he decided to share with me observations of his own life's chapters. It happened with this paramilitary commander and it happens again and again in many other ethnographic encounters.

I recall Lucas, a former paramilitary of the Bloque Cacique Nutibara, which demobilized in Medellín on December 2003. I met him in the Peace and Reconciliation Program's office of the city hall, in a moment of despair, because he had been left without a job and without shelter. When I asked him about his family, he broke down in disconsolate tears. I was not ready to see a paramilitary weeping, overwhelmed by anguish. "I miss my mom," he sobbed at one point. I could not help but put away my pen and my notepad, and invite Lucas to stay for some days at my place. He then shared with me, for hours, his tough life, and how he had moved from disaster to disaster. For him it was like freeing his chest from a heavy weight. It was a moment of truce. One morning, during breakfast, he told me: "Life would have been different if many of us would have found someone like you, ready to listen and able to give some good guidance." He stood in silence for a moment, and then added: "They [the paramilitaries] offered me to go back to fight in Urabá. I don't want to go. I am sick of it."

Because of experiences like this, I sometimes wonder if, in certain circumstances, anthropologists involuntarily (or unknowingly) become agents of change. And I mean it as an unintended consequence. As a matter of fact, my encounters with Álvaro and Lucas represent the coming together of different worlds, generating a mutuality of otherness where an exchange and a reciprocal contamination of views and experiences occur. A simple smile, an act of courtesy, of attention, or a sincere and deep listening, might involuntarily represent for the anthropologist's interlocutors the encounter and the discovery of a different set of values and worldviews.

When I meet people like Álvaro or Lucas, I am not only an anthropologist but also a citizen, and it is this attitude which, at times, might elicit the human dimension that I believe is buried in the worst and most bloodthirsty killer.

When this occurs, then a common ground is found and a bond is established between the anthropologist and his or her interlocutor. In the end, anthropologists care about the people they study, and this may be particularly true of places charged with pain, violence, and war. This is what Álvaro, Lucas, and many of the people I encountered in Colombia taught me: that to care about the other—that is, to love—matters, and it can make all the difference between peace and war.

NOTES

1. I would like to thank Victoria Sanford for inviting me to write a chapter for this book. She provided me with a great opportunity to reflect on my field experience in Colombia in a critical moment of my research, due the assassination of one of my interlocutors. I would like to extend my gratitude to Open Society, the Conflict Resolution Network at Columbia University, and the International and Transcultural Studies Department at Teachers College for providing the grants that sustained the data collection presented in the this essay between June 2003 and August 2004.

2. Names of individuals and places have been altered for the protections of the people involved.

3. I have been traveling to Colombia since 2001, conducting research on internally displaced people, and since summer 2003 on the demobilization of the paramilitary.

4. In Colombia an internal conflict has been going on for more than forty years. There are multiple illegal armed groups waging war among which the leftist Fuerzas Armadas de Colombia (FARC), the Ejército de Liberación Nacional (ELN), and numerous right-wing self-defense groups, some of them organized in a federation called Autodefensas Unidas de Colombia (AUC). According to a 2002 study of the army and the National Planning Department, in Colombia there are approximately 40,000 illegal combatants.

The American NGO Human Rights Watch, in a 2003 report, calculated that about 11,000 combatants are children.

5. According to statistics provided by the mayor's office in spring 2003, in the city of Medellín there are a total of 211 gangs operating, with about 6,030 members.

6. Echoing Foucault, in *Formations of Violence*, Feldman observes that "political power increasingly becomes a matter of regimenting the circulation of bodies in time and space in a manner analogous to the circulation of things" (1991: 8).

7. Building on Boal and Murray, Allen Feldman defines the interface as "a spatial construct preeminently linked to the performance of violence" (1991: 28).

8. Michael Taussig observes that the word *limpieza* is marked by ambiguity: "Sure, limpieza, as 'cleansing' now means to wipe out and kill defenseless people, much the same as 'purge' of the unclean. But . . . it is also used—and has a far older history—in healing a person or a home from malignity due to spirit attack or sorcery. Such healing not only neutralizes deadly force, but enhances a sense of self in place and time" (Taussig 2003: xiii).

9. On July 15, 2003, an accord was signed between the Colombian government and the AUC for the demobilization but not disarmament of the AUC by December 31, 2005. In December 2003 a reported 868 paramilitary belonging to the Bloque Cacique Nutibara demobilized in the city of Medellín. It is now known as Cooperation Democracia, a legal and recognized NGO. Starting in July 2004, the ten most senior AUC leaders with their bodyguards, about four hundred persons in all, will be concentrated for a period of six months in San Ralito, an area of 142 square miles, extendable upon agreement by the parties.

10. In his diary of a limpieza in Colombia, Michael Taussig writes: "There is no outside anymore, just as there is no clear boundary between the paras and the state, which is, I believe, the most crucial characteristic of the war machine. The paras are part of the state. But at the same time, they are separate and even opposed to it" (23).

11. At the beginning of the 1990s I worked as a freelance journalist on Sicilian Mafia-related issues. In my observations in Sicily, as in Colombia, I found similar patterns between the Sicilian Mafia, and the Colombian paramilitaries. Both are at the same time outside and within the state. Both are at the same time against and with the state.

12. According to Álvaro, Fidel Castaño was killed during a battle with the FARC on January 6, 1994.

13. Carlos Castaño was the best-known senior leader of the AUC, and the one who in July 2003 announced the unilateral ceasefire of his paramilitary group. On April 16, 2004 he was attacked, and as of this writing his whereabouts remain unknown. As time passes by, the general sense is that he was killed in a conspiracy planed by other paramilitary commanders.

14. E-mail, May 2, 2004.

REFERENCES

Bourgois, Philippe I. 2003. *In Search of Respect: Selling Crack in El Barrio*. Cambridge: Cambridge University Press.

Crapanzano, Vincent. 1980. *Tuhami: Portrait of a Moroccan*. Chicago: University of Chicago Press.

Ehrenreich, Barbara. 1987. "Foreword." In *Male Fantasies*, edited by K. Theweleit. Vol. 1: ix–xvii. Minneapolis: University of Minnesota Press.

Feldman, Allen. 1991. *Formations of Violence: The Narrative of the Body and Political Terror in Northern Ireland.* Chicago: University of Chicago Press.

Foucault, Michel. 1995. *Discipline and Punish: The Birth of the Prison.* New York: Vintage Books.

Human Rights watch. 2003. "You'll Learn Not To Cry: Child Combatants in Colombia." New York, September.

LaCapra, Dominick. 2001. *Writing History, Writing Trauma.* Baltimore: Johns Hopkins University Press.

Medina Gallego, Carlos. 1990. "Autodefensas, paramilitares y narcotráfico en Colombia: origen, desarrollo y consolidación: el caso 'Puerto Boyacá.'" Bogota: Editorial Documentos Periodísticos.

Nordstrom, Carolyn. 2000. "Shadows and Sovereigns." *Theory, Culture & Society* 17.4: 35–54.

———. 2004. *Shadows of War: Violence, Power, and International Profiteering in the Twenty-First Century.* Berkeley: University of California Press.

Pintacuda, Ennio, and Aldo Civico. 1993. *La Scelta.* Casale Monferrato, Ala.: Piemme.

Richani, Nazih. 2002. *Systems of Violence: The Political Economy of War and Peace in Colombia.* Albany: State University of New York Press.

Romero, Mauricio. 2003. *Paramilitares y autodefensas 1982–2003.* Bogota: IEPRI.

Sanford, Victoria. 2003. "Learning to Kill by Proxy: Colombian Paramilitaries and the Legacy of Central American Death Squads, Contras and Civil Patrols." *Journal of Social Justice* 30. 3 (2003): 1–19.

———. 2006. "The Moral Imagination of Survival: Displacement and Child Soldiers in Colombia and Guatemala." In *Troublemakers or Peacemakers? Youth and Post-Accord Peace Building,* edited by Siobhan McEvoy. Notre Dame: University of Notre Dame Press.

Schmitt, Carl. 1996. *The Concept of the Political.* Chicago: University of Chicago Press.

Schneider, Jane, and Peter T. Schneider. 2003. *Reversible Destiny: Mafia, Antimafia, and the Struggle for Palermo.* Berkeley: University of California Press.

Taussig, Michael T. 2003. *Law in a Lawless Land: Diary of a Limpieza.* New York: New Press.

PART THREE

Trauma, Violence, and Women's Resistance in Everyday Life

8

Fratricidal War or Ethnocidal Strategy?

Women's Experience with Political Violence in Chiapas

R. AÍDA HERNÁNDEZ CASTILLO
TRANSLATED BY MARÍA VINÓS

On January 1, 1994, a guerrilla movement of Mayan peasants in the southeast of Mexico rose up in arms against the Mexican state. This indigenous movement, known as the Ejército Zapatista de Liberación Nacional (EZLN) (Zapatista National Liberation Army) violently rejected the neoliberal policies promoted by the government of President Carlos Salinas de Gortari (1988–1994).[1] On the same day that the North American Free Trade Agreement (NAFTA) came into effect, the indigenous peoples of Chiapas called the world's attention to the failings of the new economic model.[2] The political discourse of the Zapatistas, spelled out in the EZLN charter, identified as the immediate cause of the uprising the negative effects of neoliberal policies on the lives of thousands of indigenous peasants in Mexico.[3] At the same time, they linked their struggle to the five-hundred-year-old resistance movement of indigenous peoples against colonial and postcolonial racism and economic oppression. The Zapatistas also took up the demands of other groups in Mexican society, and became the first guerrilla movement in Latin America to advocate and prioritize gender demands within their own political agenda. Zapatista women became some of the most important advocates of indigenous women's rights, through the Zapatista's Women's Revolutionary Law. This charter has been of great symbolic importance for thousands of indigenous women who are members of peasant, political, and cooperative organizations. Since then, women from different regions have voiced their support for the demands of their partners and the collective interests of their communities, while simultaneously pressing for greater respect for their specific rights as women. But the intense participation by indigenous and mestiza women in the political mobilizations in support of the Zapatistas demands has been met with violence from a militarized state. Political violence has become a weapon of repression used by official security forces and by paramilitary groups.

Violence is being used as a method of controlling a women's movement that has begun to question official state nationalism and the neoliberal economic project that exclude their peoples. Although the military confrontation between the Zapatistas and the Mexican Army only lasted a few weeks and there have been several attempts to reach some peace accords, the indigenous peoples of Chiapas have been living in a context of militarization and paramilitarization for more than a decade.[4] Characterized by human rights groups as a low-intensity war (see Olivera 2001), the majority of deaths in this war have occurred after this twelve-day conflict as a result of the ongoing violence, and from 1994 to the present has given rise to a total of 21,000 refugees. Human Rights groups have denounced the paramilitary groups that have substituted for the national army in the confrontation of dissidents.[5]

In this chapter I address the specific experience of indigenous women in the context of militarization and political violence.

How Can We Analyze This Gendered Violence?

For those of us who have lived in an unrecognized war since 1994, to reflect on the violence in Chiapas is something of a challenge, since we have not only analyzed this reality but have also become social subjects affected by it on a day-to-day basis. How can it be analyzed without making it trivial? How can we attempt to transmit the daily pain, without reifying it through our own texts?

When writing on violence from an academic point of view, a double challenge has to be faced: finding its analytical explanations while understanding on an experiential level what it represents for social subjects. Rescuing the pain and the subjectivity of those who experience violence in their lives is just as important a task as understanding the social processes that give rise to it and replicate it.

The Chicano anthropologist Renato Rosaldo, in a critique of the objectivism that pervades classical ethnographical texts on violence and death, points out that "eliminating intense emotions not only distorts their descriptions, but also discards some variables which are key to their explanation" (Rosaldo 1991: 59). With this in mind, I set out to weave this chapter using several voices: academic ones, among them my own, which try to find rational explanations for the irrationality being experienced in Chiapas in the last decade, and the voices of those who have personally known the violence, the terror, and the demobilization that it has engendered.

The principal sources of violence have been the paramilitary groups that began to form in 1994 in various regions of Chiapas. Targets of aggression are Zapatista sympathizers, supporters of the leftist Democratic Revolution Party

(PRD, Partido de la Revolución Democrática), organized peasants, or anyone who refuses to join or cooperate with the paramilitary gangs.

The fact that most of the members of the ten paramilitary groups active in Chiapas since the Zapatista uprising belong to Indian ethnic populations has influenced public opinion and caused talk of the development of a "fratricidal war." The Acteal massacre of December 22, 1997, was the most violent and most widely condemned paramilitary action.[6] The fact that forty-five Tzotzil community members were murdered has been repeatedly construed by government officials and the media to mean that this has been a conflict between brothers, which was aggravated by the Zapatista uprising. Explanations that have placed the origin of the massacre in "interfamilial disputes" imply that Indians tend to solve their disagreements through violence. This naturalization of violence has been used in several contexts as an intellectual strategy to "orientalize" indigenous people; furthermore, it masks a racist perspective which continues to view these societies as "violent and irrational."[7]

These arguments are not new. They have been used to explain the so-called "intertribal" wars in Africa, and more recently the interethnic conflicts in the Balkans. Behind the distinction of so-called conventional wars and interethnic or intertribal wars lies an evolutionary perspective of societies which still sees the West as linked to democracy and rationality, and the so-called non-Western societies as irrational and violent. The U.S. bombardment of Iraq, or the NATO intervention in Kosovo, are described as "rational" military actions, justified in the name of democracy, whereas wars between Hutus and Tutsis, Serbs and Croats, Israelis and Palestinians are called tribal or ethnic conflicts, and are made to appear as unchangeable historical elements. However, a look at their history shows that in the case of the African countries many of the current intertribal conflicts arise more or less directly from the mark left on these societies by Western colonial administrations. Nor is it possible to explain the conflicts in the Middle East or in Eastern Europe without taking into account the regional geopolitics or the influence major powers have had in the creation of new nation-states, the establishment of national borders, and whether dictatorships have been legitimized or not. In the same way, it is not possible to understand fully how intercommunitary differences have arisen and deepened in the Chiapas highlands without analyzing them in the wider context of the historical relations between indigenous people and the nation-state.

If the historical perspective allows us to denaturalize violence and place it in the context of wider processes affecting the region and the nation, the gender perspective allows us to understand the specific forms assumed by violence under a militarized state, in the framework of a low-intensity war. It is not a coincidence that rape is being used as a weapon of repression by both the federal army and paramilitary groups, nor that the majority of the dead in the Acteal massacre were women. Political participation of indigenous women is becoming a threat, as much to community power structures as to the national hegemonic project that has been built ignoring the indigenous population (see Hernández Castillo 2002 and Speed in this volume).

The Paramilitarization of Society in Chiapas

Since 1994, Chiapas society has undergone two processes that affect the daily lives of the indigenous community: militarization and paramilitarization. On one hand, thirty new large-scale centers concentrating military forces have been established in the region, housing over sixty thousand federal army troops. In 2004 there were ninety-one military bases in the region, covering military operations in thirty municipalities of Chiapas: Acala (1), Altamirano (2), Amatenango del Valle (1), Benemérito de Las Américas (5), Berriozábal (1), Bochil (1), Catazajá (1), Chenalhó (12), Chiapa de Corzo (1), Chicoasén (1), Chilón (3), Comitán (2), El Bosque (2), Frontera Comalapa (1), Las Margaritas (7), Maravilla Tenejapa (5), Marqués de Comillas (3), Ocosingo (22), Palenque (1), Pantelhó (1), Sabanilla (1), Salto de Agua (1), San Andrés Larráinzar (2), San Cristóbal de Las Casas (4), Simojovel (1), Tenosique (1), Tila (5), Trinitaria (1), Tuxtla Gutiérrez (2) and Yajalón (1) (see *Nuestra América* May 9, 2005, www.pacificar.com). On the other hand, national and international organizations have denounced the existence of no fewer than thirty-one paramilitary groups operating freely in zones of Zapatista influence. The existing paramilitary groups are a new version of the so-called white guards (*guardias blancas*), which for decades have defended the interests of landowners in Chiapas. During several historical periods, the existence of armed civilians in the service of local power groups has even been legalized by state governments. From 1952 to 1958, the government of Efraín Arana Osorio authorized the creation of an Auxiliary Livestock Police Corps (Cuerpos de Policía Auxiliar Ganadera). In the sixties, Samuel León Brindis issued the Livestock Act (Ley de Ganadería), supporting the existence of an Honorary Livestock Police (Policía Honararia Ganadera) financed by land-owners' associations. These armed groups have kept themselves updated under new modalities, serving the interests of cattle- and landowners, or traditional Indian bosses (*caciques*), or responding to alliances between the two, depending on the region, helping them to keep their control over land and natural resources.[8]

The strategy of setting Indians against Indians was implemented as part of the counterinsurgent war in Guatemala with the formation of Civil Self-Defense Patrols (PAC, Patrullas de Autodefensa Civil), where all males over the age of fifteen were forced to join. The unraveling of the social fabric that this strategy caused is one of the high costs of war still being paid in Guatemala (see Lebot 1995 and Sanford 2003). In contrast to the PACs, paramilitary groups in Chiapas are not openly financed by the government, but their links to the official party and local power groups have been denounced by human rights organizations (see Centro de Derechos Humanos Fray Barolomé de las Casas 1996, Human Rights Watch 1997). The best documented case is that of representative Samuel Sánchez Sánchez, deputy of the official Institutional Revolutionary Party (PRI, Partido Revolucionario Institucional) and promoter of the paramilitary group Peace and Justice (Paz y Justicia) that since 1995 has spread terror among PRD supporters and Zapatista sympathizers in the Chol region.

Two important factors have contributed to the paramilitarization of the Chiapas society. First, there is a large number of young Indians without jobs, land, or expectations in their own communities who have found in the paramilitary groups both economic support and power. Also, indigenous cacique leaders, linked to local power groups, who see their power threatened by the Zapatista uprising have decided to ally themselves with the most conservative sectors of the official party. These cacicazgos originated in the postrevolutionary period, with the establishment of a new relationship between the Mexican state and the indigenous population. During the thirties, moving away from the segregationist policies of the Porfiriato decades, the government of Lázaro Cárdenas (1934–1940) promoted the organization of peasants and Indians into cooperatives through the National Revolutionary Party (PNR, Partido Nacional Revolucionario), which was the political party that emerged from the revolution, the PRI's forerunner.[9]

In 1938, with President Cárdenas's support, the National Peasant Confederation (CNC, Confederación Nacional Campesina) was formed, linked to the PNR, to assist with agrarian transactions and offer credit to those affiliated to the official party. At that time, in the Chiapas highlands the official party began to back political bosses who assumed a religious role within the traditional Cargo system (sistema de Cargos). Bilingual young people, many of them trained in the new Indian boarding schools set up under Cárdenas, managed to fuse political, economic, and ritual power into one single power structure, legitimized and supported by the state (see Morquecho 1992, Rus 1994, Robledo 1987, Garza and Hernández Castillo 1998). These new cacicazgos assumed control of liquor, bottled soda, and transportation, benefiting directly from ritual consumption of alcohol.

During the 1950s, the Tzotzil-Tzetzal Indigenous Coordination Center (Centro Coordinator Indigenista Tzotzil-Tzeltal) was founded in San Cristóbal de las Casas by the National Indigenist Institute (INI) to promote the acculturation of the Indian population, with the goal of integrating it into "the nation's development plan." Bilingual health and education advocates were trained as a result of indigenist efforts, and were considered "bridges between two cultures." Many of these advocates later assumed political control of their communities, using their links to regional power groups. In the 1960s this new power structure began to be questioned by a sector of the population, those who found in Protestantism a space to live their religion without onerous ritual expenditures. Converts refused to participate in religious organization and rejected alcohol consumption.

In San Juan Chamula, seeing their power threatened by new religious ideology, the caciques began in the 1970s to expel Protestants and Catholics who questioned or rejected their political and religious control, in the name of respect for "culture and tradition." At the same time, the local caciques were confronted for the first time with emerging nonreligious spaces, such as opposition political parties and peasant, indigenous, and teachers' organizations that offered new generations of young Indians the possibility of organizing outside of the official party.

The Zapatista movement was echoed in these new political spaces, where a local restructuring of power was being attempted. It is not by chance that some of the earliest responses in support of Zapatismo were the takeovers of local governments and the establishment of resistance governments, which in time have assumed the structure of autonomous governments. Beginning in 1996, thirty eight autonomous municipalities were created in zones under Zapatista influence, later combining into autonomous regions with the aim of regaining political and territorial control over the indigenous regions, and of establishing new, more democratic forms of government, independent of local cacicazgos. The repression of the inhabitants of autonomous regions has run from imprisonment of some of their members (as in the case of the Autonomous Municipalities Ricardo Flores Magón and Tierra y Libertad) to more violent actions of paramilitary groups, as in the case of the Acteal community, in the Autonomous Municipality of Pohló.

Besides affecting the economic interests of cattle- and landowners, the creation of this new political structure endangers the survival of the indigenous cacicazgos. This overlapping of interests has led to alliances between the indigenous PRI supporters, the mestizo landowners, and the more conservative sectors of state government who resort to paramilitary groups, the federal army, and the law-enforcement apparatus in an attempt to dismantle the autonomous regions.[10]

Women are among the most affected by the militarization of society and the paramilitary actions against the autonomous regions. Daily life has been upset by the establishment of military bases and roadblocks on community lands, and prostitution and sales of drugs and alcohol have been denounced as corollaries of the army's presence in the indigenous communities. On March 8, 1996, five thousand women from all over the state marched in San Cristóbal de las Casas, asking the army to leave their communities. One of the speakers said: "We want the army to leave. Our houses are used as brothels. The few classrooms we have for our children are occupied by soldiers, the sports fields are full of tanks and helicopters and armored cars of this *mal gobierno* (evil government)" (*La Jornada*, April 9, 1996: 12). Paramilitary groups have also employed rape as a tool of repression and intimidation against communities trying to set up autonomous governments, or any considered close to the EZLN.

Violence against organized women is at once a "punishment" for their political participation and a message to the men of their families or organizations. To understand the way in which gender defines the specific forms that violence assumes in Chiapas, it is important to approach the symbolic and political role played by women in recent struggles for democracy and autonomy.

Structural Violence: An Ethnic Extermination Strategy?

On December 19, 1997, María Ruiz Oyalté awoke with terrible bleeding; the blood was running between her legs and she did not know what to do.[11] The smallest of her seven children was looking at her with the fear reflected in his eyes. She had been bleeding for several days, since her family had come to take refuge in Acteal, but that day the bleeding was worse. Her husband went to look for Juan, the health promoter, in Xoyeb, where he was looking after the refugees. It would take him nearly two hours to get there and back. Finally her husband arrived with the promoter; he examined her with great care and, using the language learned in his reproductive health care classes, declared: "prolapse of the uterus." No one understood the term, but it seemed to be something serious, so she would have to be taken to San Cristóbal. The promoter explained to her, "Your womb has collapsed from having so many children and working so hard. We will have to take you to the hospital to be operated on." It was a difficult job convincing her to be taken to the city: who would mind the children? Who would make the food? And if the Priistas (adherents of the PRI) came when she was away, who would protect the kids? And what if the armies stopped them on the road and she never came back again? There were too many accumulated fears to make such a difficult decision. The promoter spoke to her with the tenderness that had won him so many friends among civil society, the Zapatistas, and even among some of the Priistas. His work on health, his solidarity, and his dedication to community work surrounded him with a halo of trust, which helped him to convince María and to overcome her fears.

At the hospital, Juan had to confront the health system once more. Hours of waiting for someone to see her, the nurses' scornful attitude toward María's bloodied garments, the burning in his stomach after a day in the city without eating, and worrying that María had not eaten. But if he went out to look for food, the doctor might come, and they would miss the chance to be seen. There was nothing to be done but fill himself with patience and wait. Finally the doctor arrived, and after a routine check announced that Juan had been right, "prolapse of the uterus," they would have to operate, but at the moment there was no anesthesiologist on duty and they would have to find a blood donor. They would have to continue waiting, sitting there in the waiting room, because the beds were full. "Don't be so obstinate, I'm telling you we will look for an anesthesiologist. Don't you understand it's the holidays?" the nurse said to him coldly.

María was despairing; she did not understand much of what Juan was discussing with the nurses, but from the tone of their voices it did not sound like they were helping. She was hungry and thinking about her children, alone in Acteal, about the bullets that nights ago had whistled over the rooftops, about the Priistas' threats that they would finish off everyone, Zapatistas and non-Zapatistas alike. They were neutral, they had put a white flag at the entrance to their village, but that did not count, either you supported the Priistas or they immediately considered you an enemy. She began to remember how Acteal had slowly filled with people; they arrived from various directions, fleeing from the Priistas who were harassing them. She and her family had joined another seventy or seventy-five families who sought refuge in this community. Although the majority came from nearby places, it took them a long time to get there because they had to make many detours. Many left by night, carrying the children, with nothing other than some bedding or just the diapers.

The majority of people in Acteal were from Las Abejas, from civil society which was not with the Zapatistas but also not against them.[12] For months the Priistas had been harassing them, they wanted them to take up arms and rob, burn houses, and kill Zapatistas. But as Catholics they knew that they must not kill their brothers, so it was better to flee because they could see death was near. Some men returned to mind the houses, others went farther away to hide, and for this reason there were more women and children than men in Acteal. The people from Las Abejas in Acteal had been good to them, giving them blankets. Some of them had family there, but the majority did not. They helped them to build roofs of sticks and banana leaves among the coffee trees to protect themselves from the cold and the rain. It was difficult to live huddled up, afraid, waiting.

María did not understand what was happening. How did the hatred start and why did the neighbors from Los Chorros start arming themselves? Where did they get those gigantic rifles they could hardly carry? How did Agustín, who was hardly a man, come by that black uniform, and become so rude to the elders? All these ideas were going through her mind as she waited with an empty stomach for Juan to find someone who would give her blood for the operation. Filled with nostalgia, she thought about the good times when the Priistas, Zapatistas, Cardenists, Presbyterians, and Catholics all lived together with mutual respect, and, of course, with arguments and drunken fights, but without such hatred. She did not really know what was going on, but little by little she had lost faith in almost everyone; she preferred not to talk much, not to speak her mind and instead to ask God to stop the war.

In addition to her sadness in leaving her house, her cooking pots, her animals, and her cornfield, now there was this sickness and this bleeding that never stopped. Juan had never warned her that she would have to spend the night sitting in this cold hall, she was afraid, and she wanted to go back to Acteal. Juan was losing hopes, he had called on various people he knew but the town seemed empty, the doctors on shift came and went, and none of them had an answer. The anesthesiologist never appeared. After waiting for two days, at dawn on December 22,

María decided to go home. Juan had no option but to go with her. The shame and the anger were plain to be seen in the face of the promoter. What effort it had cost him to convince the women that their health was important, that traveling to the city—despite the risks that this implied—was important in order to get better treatment. How would he tell María's husband that the trip had been for naught, that María was the same or worse. At nine in the morning they arrived in Acteal. The atmosphere was tense, rumors of a Priista attack continued. The women were praying in the church and a catechist was calming them, telling them that God would protect them. The promoter spoke to the family. There were no reproaches; they were used to being cheated by the *caxlanes*, the white outsiders.[13] Juan was too innocent and persisted in thinking that the doctors were different. María thought: There is nothing left to do but pray that the blood stops, that which is running from my body and that which is being spilled between brothers, friends, neighbors. She went to the church with the other women.

María Ruiz Oyalté's name appeared in the national newspapers December 23, along with forty-four other names in the list of victims of the Acteal massacre.

The last days of María Ruiz Oyalté's life were reconstructed on the basis of testimonials collected among family and friends, refugees in the Xo'yeb community, belonging to the San Pedro Chenalhó municipality. Her experience tells us about the structural violence that Indian women experience day to day, an integral part of the same system that is now using physical and symbolic violence to spread terror and demobilization among organized Indians.

Graciela Freyermuth, who has investigated maternity death in San Pedro Chenalhó for years, has written about what she defines as a silent genocide in the Chiapas highlands (see Freyermuth 2001). Her work documents the health-care sector's guilt by omission in the deaths of hundreds of Indian men and women.

In the case of Indian women, the indiscriminate sale and use of oxytocin compounds, which have been made available to practically anyone, are pointed out as a relevant cause in the increase of maternal death, contributing to a high frequency of rupture of the uterus and fetal death in San Cristóbal hospitals.[14]

At the same time, she reports on the aggressive birth control campaigns that have been implemented in Chiapas highlands, substituting birth control pills for the distribution of basic medicines. Freyermuth complains that hospitals provide transportation services for women asking for their tubes to be tied, but will not do so for patients who face serious complications. Testimonials she collected from medical personnel in Chenalhó point out to a wider strategy, appearing to combine high rates of death by omission with low birth rates caused by direct intervention:[15]

It seems to me that this "Chiapas Mission" was really genocide because the aim was for women to have no more children.[16] Government health officials showed up here to swamp us with contraception devices and pills. The people want to be cured, cured of diarrhea, bronchitis, pneumonia, and you have to tell them, "You know what? Well, we don't have penicillin, nor do we have anything to take away diarrhea, but we do have something so that you don't have any more children." It seems absurd to me, but this is the reality lived here in Chenalhó, in Chiapas. It's tough—I mean, there are no cures, nothing to save you, but there's a ton of birth control. You ask for it and they give you whatever you want, even condoms, I can't take it anymore. It is my obligation to offer contraceptives to every woman who walks through this door, and if I convince all of them, better. Personally, I find the situation to be quite unnerving. Here I am offering contraception options to a sixteen-year-old girl. For me it is logical that if you lower mortality rates, birth rates will automatically come down as well. But if you lower birth rates and mortality rates stay high, you're going to end up without a population. (Freyermuth 2001: 79)

The mortality causes reported by this researcher are now increased by violent deaths that result from paramilitary actions. Some jurists claim, in the face of government indifference and total impunity for both structural and paramilitary violence, that there is a genocide strategy directed against the Indian people of Chiapas. These accusations are founded on the Genocide Convention approved in 1948, which points out a definition (Article II): "It is to be understood as genocide any of the following actions, committed with the intention of destroying wholly or partially a national, ethnic, racial, or religious group: a) slaying members of the group; b) inflicting serious bodily or mental damage to group members; c) deliberately inflicting life conditions calculated to produce complete or partial physical destruction of the group; d) imposing measures directed to prevent birth within the group, and e) forcing the transfer of children from one group to another" (Osomañczyk 1976: 585–586).

After analyzing the wider context of violence in which the Acteal massacre happened, Martha Figueroa, a legal adviser to families of the victims, argues:

We must think about what happened on December 22, 1997, about the events leading to the armed uprising of 1994, and about responses of state and federal Governments in order to "pacify" the insurgents; implementing counter-insurgency plans, militarizing the entire country and clearly initiating a low intensity war, not only in the "conflict" zone but in all zones, regions, and entities where there is a significant presence of indigenous peoples. It is valid to affirm that there exists at a high level in the government hierarchy a "coordinated plan of different actions aimed at the destruction of the essential basis for the life of national groups" and that therefore the Government itself is guilty of the crime of genocide. (Figueroa Mier 2001: 109)

Upon reviewing the Acteal file and analyzing human rights reports over the last four years, law experts form the Center for Justice and International Law and from Human Rights Watch have framed these facts as a "punitive genocide hypothesis" (*La Jornada*, February 26, 1998: 8).

Although the feminist lawyer Martha Figueroa, the Center for Justice and International Law, and Human Rights Watch have characterized the massacre of Acteal as genocide since 1997, it was not until February 2005 that the Centro de Derechos Fray Bartolomé de Las Casas filed a complaint with the Inter-American Commission of Human Rights, accusing the Mexican army and the state and federal governments of implementing the "politics of a state of genocide and crimes against humanity" in the case of Acteal.[17] On the basis of the testimony of a former commander of the paramilitary group Paz y Justicia, the human rights organization states that using the definition of the

> crimes against humanity from the Nuremberg Trial, President Ernesto Zedillo (1994–2000), General Enrique Cervantes Aguirre (Secretary of national defense, 1994–2000), and General Mario Renan Castillo (commander of the 7th Military Region 1995–1997) . . . are responsible for committing generalized and systematic attacks against the civilian population, with knowledge of such attacks, such as assassinations, forced relocation of a population . . . serious deprivation of physical liberty, torture, persecution of a self-identified collective founded for political, ethnic, and religious reasons, and the forced disappearance of persons.

According to the report, these instances of violence reflect "clearly and forcefully" the existence of a strategy in which "diverse paramilitary groups, linked with the municipal, state and federal authorities, including the Mexican army, have been the instrument used in an attempt to bring an end to what the army itself, in its "campaign plan," calls the "organization of the masses." The report states that, up to that point, no government officials have been investigated for these crimes. Ex-president Zedillo is current head (2005) of the Yale Center for the Study of Globalization.

From an academic, standpoint, it is difficult to prove that there is a political intent behind the structural and paramilitary violence affecting the daily life of indigenous people in Chiapas, but it is possible to evaluate and analyze its effects. The "complete or partial physical destruction of a national or ethnic group" has not been achieved, but serious damage has been done not only physically but also culturally. The low-intensity war has left in its wake internal divisions in communities, destruction of the social fabric, and a destructuring of organizational spaces.

From the cultural identity perspective, those who have analyzed the effects of violence in Indian communities in Chiapas point out that "from the cultural and emotional point of view, the Low Intensity War affects daily life, traditional customs, Rooted in birthplaces where ancestors live together with protecting gods, and the cyclical hopes of having enough to eat. This strategy affects not only bodily health, but also that of emotions and feelings; it attempts to introduce doubts regarding the political project, it demobilizes people; in summary, it completely disrupts life and culture, deeply affecting indigenous and gender identities" (Olivera 2001: 116).

The indigenous peoples in Chiapas have not been passive victims of these strategies, but have developed resistance mechanisms against this type of violence, from the restructuring of organizational and cultural spaces in new settlements of displaced people to inventing new traditions that allow a confrontation with the delegitimized rule systems of Indian cacicazgos. It is difficult therefore to speak of a consummated genocide, and I would rather talk about ethnocidal strategies, which not only imply the physical destruction of a sector of the population but in a wider sense are an attempt to destroy its cultural integrity. Any genocide implies ethnocide, but the latter also includes other government practices and policies that are often justified for the sake of "acculturation," "modernization," or "pacification" of the people.

At the end of the 1960s, the term *ethnocide* was reintroduced into academic and political debates by the French anthropologist Robert Jaulin, in order to extend the meaning of the term *genocide* beyond physical violence, to include the cultural impact that colonial and postcolonial administrations have had on the indigenous population of the Americas. In an attempt to establish responsibilities of nation-states in the specific case of the indigenous people of the Amazon basin, Robert Jaulin found there was great resistance to accepting the term *ethnocide*. In regard to this, years later he wrote: "In all probability, the term must have been known or invented on repeated occasions for some time, but rejected or forgotten because of the absence of a context which would authorize its usage. Of course, this lack of 'context' is not recent. In the West, for centuries, or even millennia, popular or public, and specially official explanations of the ethnocide problem have been forbidden, made impossible, or reduced to anecdotal accounts" (Jaulin 1973: 10). Once again, we face an absence of the context that would allow the use of the term ethnocide in academic or legal practice in reference to what is happening in Chiapas. Social sciences play an important role in the building of such intellectual context.

The Terror: December 22, 1997

Micaela is eleven, but she has been helping her mother make tortillas and carry her little brother around for years.[18] She is a big girl now, as they say in the community, meaning that she is becoming a woman. She is very afraid; since seven a.m. she has been in the church with her mother, half praying, half playing with her brother and sister so that they do not make a fuss. They do not know what is happening; from time to time they ask for their daddy, who went into hiding the day before because they say that if the Priistas come in they will kill the men or take them away and make them kill Zapatistas. The women stayed; they do not want the children to be in the mountains and cold, again. They prefer to pray, asking for the war to stop. They believe that the killers will not touch women and children.

The warning was brought by some people from Las Abejas who had been forced to work for the Priistas in Los Chorros; they had escaped and brought the news. They had arrived just the day before. They told them that the Priistas were planning their attacks and had told them: "You are Las Abejas, if we win tomorrow, you will provide the food and the tortillas . . . when we have finished the fighting with the Zapatistas you will kill two pigs and we will have a feast." That is what the man who arrived yesterday had told them. That is why they were fasting, to stop the killing.

At about eleven o'clock they began to hear the shooting; nobody moved, it was not the first time shots had been fired. The catechist tried to calm them; Micaela tried to quiet her brother and sister, who had started to cry. Men and women were kneeling, some stopped and began to run, others were hit by the bullets there in the church. The shots came from above. Someone shouted that they were being surrounded. Micaela's mother finally decided to run, carrying the two little ones and pulling her along by the hand and running. By now the men were outside the church; Micaela managed to recognize the faces of some men form Los Chorros under their red bandannas. They are Priistas and Cardenistas, her mother said. The only way out was the steep bed of the stream; they ran there and they were followed to the stream. The bullet hit her mother in the back; the children's crying gave her away. First they shot her mother and then the little ones. Micaela lay under their bodies, which is what saved her; she kept quiet, she could feel the weight of her mother's warm body; she did not know if she was dead. She was afraid, very afraid.

From where she lay, Micaela saw them, recognized Diego, Antonio, Pedro: "There were many of them, more than fifty, from Los Chorros, Pequichiquil, La Esperanza, and from Acteal as well. They came dressed in black, with balaclavas, they were real paramilitaries; the others, the leaders, were dressed like soldiers," she would say later in her testimony to the human rights people. She saw them killing the catechist and shooting women and children in the back.

When the men left, Micaela went to hide on the bank of the stream. From there she saw how the same men come back with more men and they all had machetes in their hands. They were whooping and laughing and talking among themselves, "We have to get rid of the seed," they were saying. They stripped the dead women and cut off their breasts, they put a stick between the legs of one woman and they opened the bellies of the pregnant women and took out their babies and played ball with them, hacking them from machete to machete. After that they left.

In the afternoon people began to come out of their hiding places. The public security police were there and took them to a hall. There she met some relatives. Micaela saw her father's brother, but she also realized that many had not appeared. It was there that she had found out that her mother, her sister, and her little brother were dead. She had thought as much when she had seen them full of blood, but while she had been waiting in hiding she had prayed to God that they might only be wounded. She did not know if they had killed her father and her grandfather, too, both of whom had gone to hide in Pantelhó. Her uncle Antonio took her by the hand and they went to look for her cousins or other people who might be wounded or alive among the dead, as she had been. "We saved two little ones who were at the side of their dead mother, the boy had one leg totally destroyed; another girl had her head smashed, she was bleeding a lot and tossing around trying to hang onto life. The wounds of the living and the dead were terrifying because the weapons were very high caliber. The police took us away, some of us went to Polhó, others to San Cristóbal. Many people have been displaced, there is a lot of terror everywhere," her uncle told the Interior Ministry officials some days later.

After the burial Acteal was silent with death. Only the police, the ones who arrived later, are there, apparently in case the murderers come back. Micaela is living with her uncle and aunt. She misses her mother; every night she dreams that her warm body is protecting her and then that stops and she and her brother go to look for her daddy in Pantelhó.

Micaela is a pseudonym I have used to write about the story of one of the survivors at Acteal. Her experience was reconstructed based on statements she made to the Centro de Derechos Humanos Fray Bartolomé de las Casas. After the media told about the cruelty toward the pregnant women in the massacre, a rumor spread saying that it was an exaggeration made up by the humans rights organizations and the media. When speaking to reporters, some local Red Cross employees denied that the bodies had been mutilated. Even in academic circles, the rumor spread saying that the facts were exaggerated. The magazine *Proceso* took on these arguments and denied the existence of corporal mutilations.

In a war context, rumors become an important weapon that causes demobilization and misinformation. Regardless of the fact that I had read the testimonials presented by the survivors at the Centro Fray Bartolomé, and even though I had written a more extensive version of the chronicle that I am presenting here, the rumors made me doubt, too. What if the nervous shock of the survivors had made them exaggerate? And what if the bodies hadn't been mutilated? Nevertheless, I was able to confirm in the autopsies what had been described in the testimonials. These documents are the best proof to face the rumors with.

Denial tends to be a response to occurrences that are overwhelming and give us doubts about the human condition, but sometimes it is also a strategy used by the forces in power to hide violence. Those who have studied the social effects of violence and terror have pointed out the difficulties implied in analyzing and "explaining" these occurrences from the point of view of academic discourse.

The Australian anthropologist Michael Taussig has written about colonial strategies of control, in terms of what he calls the "culture of terror." Taussig describes the life of the Putamayo Indians of the Colombian rubber plantations at the beginning of this century, where even though violence was not cost-effective for the plantation owners because it debilitated their work force, torture, corporal mutilations, and massive murders were part of daily life on the plantation. Taussig remarks on this contradiction by saying that the stories of violence and terror confronted him with an interpretation problem until he realized that the problem of interpretation is essential for the reproduction of terror; it not only makes it very difficult to create an effective counterdiscourse but it also empowers the terrifying aspects of death squadrons, disappearances, and torture, because it causes immobility and limits people's capacity to resist. Since terror depends so much on interpretation and sense, it ends up feeding on itself by destroying any evidence of sense and rationality (see Taussig 1987).

In a similar fashion, the extreme violence with which the Acteal victims were treated caused the double effect of immobility and awakening skepticism, making the elaboration of a counterdiscourse very difficult. How can the viciousness and violence of Acteal be explained? The National Commission on Human Rights turned to local university specialists in an attempt to "explain the physical mutilations of the Acteal massacre" by exploring the San Pedro Tzotziles's cultural practices. The local anthropologists rejected the NCHR's request and have remained silent. Developing a counterdiscourse has limited possibilities in a war context, in the face of the efficiency of terror.

In today's context, it has become a priority to develop an effective counterdiscourse against rumors, practices, and discourses of terror. The academic milieu has much to contribute to the demystification of the "cultural practices" of violence among the Indian people. Graciela Freyermuth, who during the last five years has been analyzing deaths in Chenalhó, points out that before the appearance of paramilitary groups, violence was not a major cause of death among pedranos.[19] Between 1988 and 1993, sixteen violent deaths were registered in this municipality, the majority of which were caused by sharp-pointed weapons. As of 1995, violent deaths have increased considerably and high-caliber weapons are being used.

An analysis of death certificates shows that violence is not used against women except in cases of witchcraft and domestic violence. Previous to Acteal, there is no record of mass aggression toward women. Bodily mutilations of pregnant women had never previously been recorded, not even in the colonial history of highlands Tzotziles.

There is no cultural practice that would allow establishing any links between the Acteal massacre and indigenous cosmology or war rituals. The same researcher points out that the most violent murders on record in the highlands region have been against the *akchamel* (sorcerers), when it is believed that they have caused harm to a member of the community, and these murders took place once the akchamel recognized his guilt. What becomes evident in Acteal is a new manifestation of violence, which has very little to do with traditional ways of resolving conflicts among the highlands Tzotziles. However, testimonials from victims are very similar to those collected by anthropologist Ricardo Falla among Guatemalan Indians in the Ixcan jungle. In his book *Masacres de la selva* (1992), Falla describes the body mutilations performed by the *kaibilies* or elite Guatemalan troops: opening of pregnant women bodies, mutilation of corpses, destruction of fetuses appear to be common "rituals" among those who practice this "culture of terror."

The cry "we have to exterminate the seed," which was the banner for paramilitary forces in Acteal, is very telling of what these war practices are. The shared ideology that women are sources of life par excellence makes them into an important war target. Similar war practices in different parts of the world, which tend to make women the center of violence, have been analyzed by several academics that specialize in what is now known as war anthropology. Carolyn Nordstrom, an anthropologist specializing in military violence, has noted in different parts of the world the local impact of a global war industry ranging from sale of weapons to training for low-intensity wars. In her recent book on Mozambique, the author reflects upon something that might well be worthwhile to consider in the analysis of paramilitary violence in Chiapas:

> Having conducted on-site research at the epicenters of wars over three continents and a decade and a half, I have learned that the whole concept of local wars, whether central or peripheral, is largely a fiction.
>
> Massive interlinked and very international war-related industries make war possible in any location in the world. I have seen the same weapon vendors, mercenaries, military advisors, supplies, and military training manuals—both illicit and formal—circle the globe, moving from one war to the next. . . . And in all this a powerful set of cultural prescriptions develops around the concept and conduct of war. It is at once international and localized: as peoples and good move from war to war, through multinational industries. . . . [C]ultures of militarization, violence, resistance, humanitarian aid, and peacebuilding move fluidly around the globe, dipping deep into the most central and remote corners of war and politics alike. This global flux of information, tactics, weapons, money, and

personnel brokers tremendous power throughout the war zones of the world. The examples supporting this are legion. To give but one, when a new torture technique is introduced in a country, that same technique can be found throughout the world in several days' time. Obviously, transmitted with the physical techniques of harming bodies is a complex culture that specifies who can and should be targeted for torture, how and for what reasons and to what end." (Nordstrom 1997: 5)

Mexican anthropology has little experience in the analysis of war violence, and other countries' experiences can help the development of our own investigations. The relationships between local, national, or global levels are basic methodological premises for any analysis that attempts to recognize the complexities of the violence in Chiapas. Anthropological functionalism, which has attempted to present the indigenous communities as closed corporate communities, has been questioned and challenged by Mexican anthropological critics for decades.

Now is a good time to take the historical and anthropological contributions that have been made toward the contextualization of indigenous cultures into the political and economic frameworks at the national and global levels. Only by placing "interfamilial" struggles in wider contexts will we become able to account for the complexity of the violence in Chiapas, and from our professional practice perhaps be able to contribute to put a stop to ethnocidal strategies that have brought so much pain and death to the indigenous women of this region.

NOTES

1. The term *neoliberal* is used in the Mexican context to refer to a set of policies based on the diminished importance of the state, privatization, and economic and financial deregulation, together with the promotion of the export of manufactured goods. This economic model replaced the statist model, which was protectionist and based on import substitution industrialization, prevailing since the 1930s to the beginning of the 1980s. In the economic terminology of international organisms, these policies have also been called "structural adjustment programs" and became generalized throughout the developing world at the beginning of the 1980s.

2. NAFTA, known in Mexico as the TLC (Tratado de Libre Comercio), was one of the main initiatives promoted by Carlos Salinas's government in order to lock in economic reforms, especially commercial and financial liberalization. It is the first agreement of commercial liberalization in the world signed between two developed countries, the United States and Canada, and a developing country, Mexico.

3. This charter was created in consultation with Tojolabal, Chol, Tzotzil, and Tzeltal women and was made public on January 1, 1994. It includes the rights of indigenous women to hold local posts of authority, inherit land, and have control over their own bodies, among other rights. For an English version of the Zapatista's Women's Revolutionary Law see Hernández Castillo 1994.

4. There were two rounds of peace talks that ended optimistically in February of 1996 with the signing of the San Andrés Accords on Indigenous Rights and Culture by the Mexican

government and the EZLN. The euphoria following the signing of the accords was short-lived when it became evident that the Zedillo administration had no intention of implementing them. It wasn't until Vicente Fox took office in 2000—ending more than seven decades of PRI party rule—that there was any movement in legislating the accords. The final outcome was a bitter disappointment to indigenous peoples throughout Mexico (see Hernández Castillo, Paz, and Sierra 2004 for a description of the outcome).

5. These are armed groups with direct or indirect links to the state, which perform specific actions to debilitate dissidents who oppose the current regime. Their actions always take place at key political moments and have clear objectives and perpetrators. For a detailed description of the low-intensity war and paramilitarization of Chiapas, see the bulletin *Chiapas al Día* published by the Centro de Investigaciones Económicas y Políticas de Acción Comunitaria A.C. (CIEPAC—Center for Economic and Political Research for Community Action)., no. 139, 140, 144, 154.

6. The massacre of Acteal took place in the Tzotzil municipality San Pedro Chenalhó, where forty five Maya political refugees, mainly women and children, were killed on December 22, 1997. Executed by paramilitary villagers with logistic support from both the police and the military, the massacre has been denounced by human rights organizations as a part of planned low-intensity warfare.

7. I use the term *orientalize* following Edward Said (1978) to refer to the way in which academic and popular discourses construct a sense of "otherness" that objectifies non-Western societies and denies them an historical dimension, resulting in their stigmatization, or at best converting them, through the myth of the "noble savage," into a Western utopian ideal.

8. *Cacique* is a term used during the colonial period to refer to the native ruler of a community. In modern times the term is applied to the political boss of a community, usually considered an authoritarian traditional boss. This style of community government is known as *cacicazgos*.

9. Porfiriato refers to the dictatorship of Porfirio Díaz (1888–1910), during which no state policy toward indigenous peoples existed, other than state laws to legitimize extreme economic exploitation in the plantations.

10. Mestizo is the term used to designate a decendant of a mixed Indian-white parentage, but is used more generally to refer to the Mexican population, which culturally does not identify itself as Indian.

11. This narrative is extracted from witness's declarations presented by the author in "Before and after Acteal: Voices, Remembrances and Experiences from the Women of San Pedro Chenalhó" in Hernández Castillo, 2001. It is reproduced here because of the importance these experiences have for a wider consideration of gender and violence issues in chiapas.

12. Las Abejas (The Bees) is an organization of civil society founded in 1992 in the community of Tzanembolom, municipality of Chenalhó, with support of the Dioceses of San Cristóbal. One of the main objectives of the organization from the very beginning was to defend agrarian rights of indigenous peoples. After the Zapatista uprinsing they assumed as one of their objectives the struggle for peace and justice.

13. *Caxlan* is the local term to refer to nonindigenous people.

14. Oxytocin is a prescription drug to stimulate uterine contractions, used in hospitals, in special cases, to induce and accelerate labor, and is administered, postpartum, to prevent

uterine hemorrhage. In the communities of the highlands, they are being used as a matter of course before the birth, to "make things quicker."

15. In 1997, the women's group Grupo de Mujeres de San Cristóbal Las Cases A.C. (COLEM) began a campaign against maternal fatalities. As a part of this campaign, an interdisciplinary and interinstitutional group was formed to study this problem.

16. The Chiapas Mission was an intensive campaign to promote birth control in Chiapas in 1995.

17. For a legal analysis of the case, see Figueroa Mier 2001.

18. This narrative is extracted from Hernández Castillo, "Before and after Acteal."

19. *Pedranos* is the term used to refer to the Tzotzil inhabitants of San Pedro Chenalhó, Chiapas.

REFERENCES

Aramoni, Dolores. 1992. *Los refugios de los sagrado.* Mexico City: CONACULTA.

Centro de Derechos Humanos, Fray Bartolomé de las Casas. 1996. *Ni paz, ni justicia: Informe general y amplio acerca de la guerra civil que sufren los choles en la zona notre de Chiapas.* San Cristóbal de las Casas: Editorial Fray Bartolomé.

CIEPAC. http://www.Laneta.apc.org/cdnbcasas.

Collier, George. 1944. *Basta! Land and the Zapatista Rebellion in Chiapas.* Oakland, Cal.: Food First Books.

Collier, Jane. [1973] 1995. *El derecho zinacanteco: Procesos de disputar en un pueblo indígena de Chiapas.* Mexico City: CIESAS/UNICACH.

———. 1992. "Problemas teórico-metodológicos de la antropología jurídica." Paper presented in the conference "Orden jurídico y formas de control social en el medio indígena." Fortin de las Flores, Veracruz.

Dette, Denich. 1995. "Of Arms, Men, and Ethnic War in (Former) Yugoslavia." In *Feminism, Nationalism and Militarism,* edited by Constance R. Sutton. Arlington, Va.: American Anthropological Association.

Falla, Ricardo. 1992. *Masacres de la selva, Ixcán Guatemala (1975–1982).* Guatemala: Editorial Universitaria.

Figueroa Mier, Martha. [1998] 2001. "From Aggravated Homicide to Genocide: Legal Questions Surrounding the Acteal Massacre." In *The Other Word: Women and Violence in Chiapas, before and after Acteal,* edited by Rosalva Aída Hernández. Copenhagan: IWGIA.

Freyermuth, Graciela. [1998] 2001. "The Background to Acteal: Maternal Mortality and Birth Control, Silent Genocide?" In *The Other Word: Women and Violence in Chiapas, before and after Acteal,* edited by Rosalva Aída Hernández. Copenhagan: IWGIA.

Gall, Olivia, and Rosalva Aída Hernández. Forthcoming. "La historia silenciada: El papel de las campesinas indígenas en las rebeliones coloniales y postcoloniales de Chiapas." In *Voces Disidentes: Nuevos Debates en Estudios de Género,* edited by Patricia Ravelo. Mexico City: Taurus-CIESAS.

García de León, Antonio. 1985. *Resistencia y utopía.* Vol. 1. Mexico City: Editorial Era.

———. 1996. "El costo de la guerra." In *Militarización y violencia en Chiapas.* Mexico City: Producción Editorial SIPRO.

Garza Caligaris, Anna María, and Rosalva Aída Hernández Castillo. [1998] 2001. "Encounters and Conflicts of the Tzotzil People with the Mexican State: A Historical-Anthropological Perspective to Understanding Violence in San Pedro Chenalhó, Chiapas." In *The Other*

Word: Women and Violence in Chiapas, before and after Acteal, edited by Rosalva Aída Hernández. Copenhagen: IWGIA.

Hernández Castillo, Rosalva Aída. 1994. "Reinventing Tradition: The Women's Law." In *Akwe: Kon: A Journal of Indigenous Issues* 11.2 (Summer): 67–71.

Hernández Castillo A., Sarela Paz, and Maria Teresa Sierra. 2004. *El estudio y los indigenas en tiempos del PAN*. Mexico: CIESAS-Porrúa.

———. 1996. "From the Community to the Women's Sate Convention." In *The Explosion of Communities in Chiapas*, edited by June Nash. Copenhagen: IWGA.

———. 1998. "Between Hope and Despair: The Struggle of Organized Women in Chiapas since the Zapatista Uprising." In *Journal of Latin American Anthropology* 2.3: 77–99.

———. ed. [1998] 2001. *The Other Word: Women and Violence in Chiapas, before and after Acteal*. Copenhagen: IWGIA.

Human Rights Watch/Americas. 1997. *Implausible Deniability: State Responsibility for Rural Violence in Mexico*. New York: Human Rights Watch.

Jaulin, Robert. 1973. *La paz blanca: Introducción al etnocidio*. Buenos Aires: Tiempo Contemporáneo, Colección Análisis y Perspectivas.

Lebot, Yvon. 1995. *La guerra en tierra Mayas: Comunidad, violencia y modernidad en Guatemala, 1970–1992*. Mexico City: Fondo de Cultura Económica.

Millán, Margara. 1998. "Zapatista Indigenous Women." In *Zapatista! Reinventing Revolution in Mexico*, edited by John Holloway and Eloína Peláez. Londres: Pluto Press.

Morquecho, Gaspar. 1992. "Los Indios en un proceso de organización: La Organización Indígena de los Altos de Chiapas, ORIACH." Bachelor's honor thesis in Social Anthropology, Universidad Autónoma de Chiapas, San Cristóbal de las Casas: Chiapas.

Nash, June. 1993. "Maya Household Production in the Modern World." In *The Impact of Global Exchange on Middle American Artisans*, edited by June Nash. Albany: State University of New York Press.

Nelson, Diane Michele. 1999. *A Finger in the Wound: Body Politics in Quincentennial Guatemala*. Berkeley: University of California Press.

Nordstrom, Carolyn. 1997. *A Different Kind of War Story*. Philadelphia: University of Pennsylvania Press.

Olivera, Mercedes. [1998] 2001. "Acteal: Effects of the Low Intensity War." In *The Other Word: Women and Violence in Chiapas, before and after Acteal*, edited by Rosalva Aída Hernández. Copenhagen: IWGIA.

Ong, Aihwa. 1995. "Postcolonial Nationalism: Women and Retraditionalization in the Islamic Imaginary, Malaysia" In *Feminism, Nationalism and Militarism*, edited by Constance R. Sutton. Arlington, Va.: American Anthropological Association.

Osomañczyk, Jan. 1976. *Eciclopedia mundial de relaciones internacionales y naciones unidas*. Mexico City: Fondo de Cultura Económica.

Parker, Andrew, Mary Russo, Doris Sommer, and Patricia Yaeger. 1992. *Nationalisms and Sexualities*. New York: Routledge.

Robledo, Gabriela. 1987. *Disidencia y religión: Los expulsados de San Jua Chamula*. Bachelor's honor thesis at Escuela Nacional de Antropología e Historia, Mexico City.

Rojas, Rosa. 1996. *Chiapas ¿Y las Mujeres Qué?* Vols. 1 and 2. Mexico City: La Correa Feminista, Colección Del Dicho al Hecho.

Rosaldo, Renato. 1991. *Cultura y verdad. Una propuesta de análisis social*. Mexico City: CONACULTA and Grijalbo.

Rovira, Guiomar. 1997. *Mujeres de maíz*. Mexico City: Editorial Era.

Rus, Diana. 1990. "La crisis económica y la mujer indígena. El caso de San Juan Chamula, Chiapas." In INAREMAC Papers, San Cristóbal de las Casas.

Rus, Jan. 1994. "The Comunidad Revolucionaria Institucional. The Subversion of Natives Government in Highland Chiapas (1936–1968)." In *Every Day Forms of State Formation: Revolution and the Negotiation of Rule in Modern Mexico*, edited by James Scott, Gilbert M. Joseph, and Daniel Nugent. Durham: Duke University Press.

———. 1995. "¿Guerra de castas según quién?" In *Chiapas los rumbos de otra historia*, edited by Juan Pedro Viquiera and Mario Humberto Ruz. Mexico City: IIF (CEM)–UNAM, Coordinación de Humanidades-UNAM, CIESAS, CESMECA–UNICACH, U. de G.

Said, Edward. 1978. *Orientalism*. New York: Pantheon.

Sanford, Victoria. 2003. *Buried Secrets: Truth and Human Rights in Guatemala*. New York: Palgrave Macmillan.

Taussig, Michael. 1987. *Shamanism, Colonialism, and the Wild Man*. Chicago: University of Chicago Press.

Viqueira, Juan Pedro. 1993. *María de la Candelaria, india natural de Cancuc*, Mexico City: Fondo de Cultura Económica.

———. 1996. "La causa de una rebelión india: Chiapas 1712." In *Chiapas los rumbos de otra historia*, edited by Juan Pedro Viquiera and Mario Humberto Ruz. Mexico City. IIF (CEM)-UNAM, Coordinación de Humanidades-UNAM, CIESAS, CESMECA-UNICACH, U. de G.

Wood, Davida. 1995. "Feminist Perspectives on Palestinian Political Culture under Occupation." In *Feminism, Nationalism and Militarism*, edited by Constance R. Sutton. Arlington Va.: American Anthropological Association.

9

Indigenous Women and Gendered Resistance in the Wake of Acteal

A Feminist Activist Research Perspective

SHANNON SPEED

Images of Resistance

The images are dramatic: In Xo'yep, a Tzotzil woman pushes back a heavily armed soldier. She is small; the top of her head barely reaches his chest. But her arms reach up, one hand on the strap of his backpack, one on his neck, her gesture one of pent-up anger. His expression, of surprise and something like helplessness, is counterbalanced by the huge weapon at his side. In Yalchiptic, 400 Tojolobal women wearing ski masks and bandannas and holding wooden sticks confront the army and close the road with their bodies, forming a solid human blockade against the military's incursion. In Morelia, sixty Tzeltal women, many barefoot and carrying babies on their backs, run after more than hundred hastily retreating soldiers, chasing them several kilometers down the road to make sure they do not return.

Dramatic images of dramatic actions, in dramatic times. All of these events took place in the two weeks following the massacre at Acteal, in which twenty-seven indigenous women (four of whom were pregnant), ten children, and nine men were brutally slain by a pro-government paramilitary group. In the wake of the massacre, the Mexican government redoubled the federal army presence in the communities of the Zapatista base areas, which were already suffering high levels of military occupation. In this context of escalating violence and militarization, the mobilizations by women to block the military incursion into their communities—blocking the soldiers with their bodies, chasing them out with sticks and stones—represents bold collective actions. These acts, the images of them, and the public discourse about them, have much to tell us about women's political participation and gendered resistance since the Zapatista movement began.

As a feminist, an anthropologist, and a human rights activist working in Chiapas, I was following the events, and the public discourse about them, closely.

I had been coordinating the San Cristóbal office of Global Exchange, a U.S.-based nongovernmental organization (NGO) for about a year, concentrating our efforts on human rights accompaniment and documentations of violations. I was also conducting my doctoral research on human rights as a globalized discourse and its local meanings and uses in indigenous communities, both positive and negative. I was seven months pregnant. Each of these aspects of my life affected how I experienced the events at Acteal and afterward. It can perhaps be said that all researchers' life experience fundamentally shapes how they perceive their field experiences—this is feminism's basic insight about the "situated" nature of all knowledge production. I want to emphasize this point, and perhaps take it further by suggesting that an activist, feminist engagement with our research communities can lead to a richer gender analysis.

Gendered Experiences: Women and (Para)Militarization

"The majority of us had never seen soldiers before. Since we've had to live with the military so close to our community we have had so many problems. . . . For the women, it has been hard . . . our suffering is different."[1]

Since the Zapatista uprising began in January of 1994, and particularly since the first major military invasion by the Mexican federal army into Zapatista-held territory in February of 1995, the base communities have suffered an onerous level of military occupation. In December of 1997, when the Acteal massacre took place, one-third of the Mexican federal army—approximately 65,000 troops—was stationed in the conflict zone of Chiapas. In some areas, the ratio of troops to community members was as high as three to one, meaning concretely that a community of four hundred people could be living with twelve hundred soldiers camped permanently on its edges. In order to understand the specific kind of women's resistance discussed in this chapter, it is important to recognize how this large-scale militarization is experienced in distinct ways by men and women.

The direct occupation or close proximity of military bases has taken a heavy toll on the social and economic fabric of the communities, creating a situation of constant fear and tension among the populace, complicating or impeding normal sowing and harvesting cycles, as well as introducing or exacerbating a gamut of social problems, including alcoholism, drug abuse, prostitution, and sexually transmitted diseases. Maricela, a woman from the Cañadas region, notes a number of these problems: "Since the soldiers came, it has been very hard. They set up their camp where we have to pass through to get to our coffee fields. Of course, it is impossible to go by their camp everyday because they harass us and accuse the men of being Zapatistas, so our crops have failed. They cut the wires that fence in our cattle, so they escape. Also, the women are afraid to go down to the river where they always washed, because the soldiers are nearby. And, they have brought prostitution with them, and this is very bad for us."

Much of our work at Global Exchange at that time centered on facilitating the work of volunteers to staff the "peace camps" that had been established by the Fray Bartolomé Human Rights Center in militarily occupied communities. The volunteers' job was to monitor the military's adherence to the Law on Peace and Reconciliation, which established the rules for military occupation. Also, volunteers gave attention to the effects of military occupation on community life. My position as both a volunteer in the camps and as a coordinator of other volunteers gave me privileged access to information about these effects in a wide range of communities. My position as a feminist anthropologist made me acutely aware of the gendered nature of those effects. For example, since federal army occupation began, prostitution had been introduced into hundreds of indigenous communities. Local women are lured into prostitution through economic necessity, or at times through fear and intimidation. Prostitution was contributing directly to marital breakdown, social disharmony, and to the spread of sexually transmitted diseases. Women were becoming victims of diseases they did not know existed and had no defense against, their recovery impeded by their lack of access to information and health care, which, never optimal, was exacerbated by the military presence (see Physicians for Human Rights 1997).

In some communities that had previously respected the EZLN—the party of the Zapatistas—prohibition of alcohol use, soldiers reintroduced alcohol. Whereas a decrease in domestic violence with the decrease in alcohol use had been documented (Garza 1999), health providers were beginning to note an increase in domestic violence against women in militarily occupied communities where alcohol use had returned (Global Exchange 1998). The relationship between alcohol and domestic abuse was apparent to women. For example, Maricela commented, "My husband has hit me, yes. But only when he comes home drunk. For a while, he wasn't drinking because the community has prohibited alcohol, but now some are drinking again. . . . The soldiers sell it to them, that's what they say."

The increase in domestic violence may have been tied to more than just an increase in alcohol abuse in militarily occupied communities. Although it would require further research to conclude as much in Chiapas, analyses of other militarized states have demonstrated that concepts of "honor" and "masculine strength" or "courage" are made vulnerable by the presence of "enemy" male occupiers, resulting in a perceived loss of control, and a concomitant increase in control over women and in many cases an increase in domestic violence (Denich 1995). It seems probable that similar dynamics are at work in the heavily militarized areas of Chiapas.

Another aspect of women's experience of militarization is that they suffer sexual harassment and violence by soldiers. This can range from lewd comments made in passing to the rape of three Tzeltal women at a military checkpoint in Altamirano in 1994. Direct harassment and the potential for violence against them provoke fear and anxiety. Adelina, also of the Cañadas region, commented, "The women are afraid to go to the river where we used to bathe, because the soldiers would come and watch us and make ugly comments. Also, they make comments when they walk through [the community] and pass by us. We are afraid to go out walking, because we know that they could attack us." Thus, women in the communities must deal with fear on a daily basis, and it alters the routine and normality of their daily lives.

The effects of militarization have been amplified by the growth of paramilitary groups throughout the conflict zone. Beginning in the northern zone of the state with the groups called the Chinchulines and Desarrollo, Paz y Justicia, paramilitarization spread to the highlands and then to the jungle with groups like Mascara Roja and MIRA. They are often shadowy, and it has been difficult to document their relationship with the government and the military. However, their stance supporting the ruling party and a few high-profile connections—like a local congressperson who openly formed and directed Desarrollo, Paz y Justicia, and an ex-governor who, while still in office, formed the Coordination for State Security through which money and training were channeled—have led a number of analysts to argue that they are state sponsored (CDHFBC 1996; Olivera 1998; Ramirez 1997). The government's own human rights commission (CNDH) made damning conclusions about collusion between state security forces, state government officials, and the paramilitary violence in the Acteal case (CNDH 1998). Many people believe that the paramilitary groups form part of a campaign of low-intensity warfare, a divide-and-conquer strategy designed to exhaust and terrify the rebellious population into submission (Global Exchange 1998; Olivera 1998; Ramirez 1997). June Nash notes that low-intensity warfare has gendered effects: "In this kind of warfare, women are targets of hostility in part because their very presence in the spaces controlled by the military is an assertion of the right to remain there and live. This is itself an act of warfare punishable by rape or killing" (Nash 2003). Paramilitarization functions within low-intensity warfare by making it appear that the conflict is not with the state but rather within or between indigenous communities, and justifying further military presence as necessary to maintain control. In addition to some of the same problems provoked by militarization, the paramilitary presence increases even further the levels of tension and fear, since these forces are less visible and far less accountable for their actions than the federal army or state security police.

As with militarization, the experience of paramilitarization and paramilitary violence was lived differently by women and men. The exacerbation of intracommunity conflict has caused the displacement of tens of thousands of people since 1996 (CDHFBC 1996). Testimonies of displaced women tell us that the experience is devastating. Beyond the fear of fleeing for one's life and leaving everything behind, there is the pain of family separations, of seeing their children go hungry, and the loss of the home, the principal space of their daily existence and the formation of their identities as women (Olivera 1998). Physical effects of these stresses present themselves: women lose their milk because of stress and can no longer breastfeed their babies; they suffer headaches, fail to menstruate, and experience other kinds of malaise. Candelaria, a displaced woman from a highlands community, said, "My chest hurts all the time; I feel that I can't breathe. Sometimes I think I will die. It is because my heart is in pain since we left [our home] community."

But in a consideration of the gendered experience of paramilitarization, the terrible events at Acteal stand out for the dramatics of the violence toward women. Testimonies of women survivors tell of a particular cruelty toward women and a perverse use of the symbolics of maternity in the massacre. Many of the women who had been praying in the church in the refugee camp when the attack began, rather than fleeing and saving their own lives tried instead to protect their children by covering them with their own bodies. They were shot in the back. Testimonies of survivors tell of the paramilitaries hacking up the bodies of the dead women with machetes, cutting off their breasts and carving the fetuses out of their bellies (Hernández Castillo 1998). Some tell of the para-militaries tossing the fetuses from machete to machete, laughing and saying, "Let's do away with the seed" (Hernández Castillo 1998; Nash 2003). Many of these facts are documented in the public record.

The violence at Acteal was gendered violence. In reflecting on this, Mer-cedes Olivera writes, "By viciously massacring unarmed women as they did in Acteal, they sent a message to all rebels in the symbolic announcement of gen-eralized death. Destroying the mother, the children, and the lives still gestating was an announcement of the total elimination of the people, the ideas, the future of indigenous people who support the Zapatistas, but above all, the future of indigenous women who increased the forces of the insurgents by exer-cising their citizenship rights." Feeling my daughter move in my womb, I felt physically ill with the horror of what had happened. Perhaps being pregnant at the time made me intensely sensitive to the gendered symbolics as they were wrought on the mother's bodies. Although the violence at Acteal was a message to all, the threat to women specifically pushed forcefully to the front my con-sciousness. The violence against women in Acteal was not incidental; its moti-vation was the silencing of political opposition, and its logic and symbolism rendered women most vulnerable to attack.

The gendered violence was almost certainly connected to the fact that indigenous women had gained some prominence in the public eye since the Zapatista uprising had begun several years earlier. Decades of experience in organizing with the Catholic Diocese of San Cristóbal and with social organiza-tions in different regions of the state had prepared many indigenous women to step into new roles of authority and to challenge patriarchal relations within their communities, relations that limited their personal autonomy to make decisions about their lives and their participation in political decision making in the community, and left them toiling under staggering workloads. Some women's participation in armed opposition also focused attention on the patriarchal nature of the Mexican state and the violence suffered by women within it.

In sum, militarization and paramilitarization of the indigenous communities have had detrimental effects on community cohesion and livelihood, and individual psychological and physical well-being. This clearly affects all community members. However, the particular negative impact on women reflects the gendered nature of the experience of military occupation and war. The paramilitary violence perpetrated at Acteal had women as a particular target. This was part of a larger government strategy of low-intensity warfare, intended to "take the water from the fish" by diminishing active support for the Zapatistas, including that of women. This was articulated with tensions about women's increasing challenges to the gender status quo. The violence at Acteal was designed to force women into submission, perhaps in a variety of senses. It provoked a gendered form of resistance.

Resisting Militarization

Following the Acteal massacre, the Mexican government dramatically increased militarization, arguing that all armed groups in the state (not just the progovernment paramilitary groups of the kind that carried out the massacre) were to be eliminated. The army began a systematic process of incursions into Zapatista support areas. It is worthwhile to note that the events at Acteal did not directly involve Zapatistas or their supporters. Those killed were members of the organization Las Abejas, who, although they have been supportive of Zapatista goals at times, reject armed struggle and violence. At the time of the massacre, relations between the Zapatistas and the Abejas in the area were tense.[2] Nevertheless, within ten days of the massacre, six thousand new troops were introduced into the highlands, military patrols in the eastern Lacandón region tripled, and random house-to-house searches began in numerous pro-Zapatista communities.[3]

On January 1, 1998, the army entered the community of Nueva Esperanza, destroying personal and communal property while residents fled to the nearby mountains. There, the women organized and, leaving the men in hiding, returned to their community to demand that the soldiers leave. Women from several neighboring communities joined them to support the resistance to the military's intrusion.

Two days later, the army entered Morelia, taking the community by surprise. The women quickly organized and, while the men hid in the mountains, sixty of them drove out close to two hundred federal soldiers who were conducting house-to-house searches. The women then set up a round-the-clock roadblock to make sure the soldiers did not return. When they did, on January 8, the women not only prevented their entrance to the community but also chased them several kilometers down the road.

The following day, in the small community of 10 de Mayo, a lookout alerted the community that soldiers were approaching. Forty-five women, many carrying children on their backs, attempted to block soldiers and state police from entering their community. When they asked the army to turn back, the soldiers first verbally attacked the women, calling them "dirty Indian whores," then physically attacked them, beating them with rifle butts, shovels, and stones. Sixteen women and nine children were injured, including a seven-month old girl and a one-year old boy, both of whom lost consciousness from blows to the head. Several of the injured women were pregnant. Despite this disastrous outcome, the women did succeed in keeping the soldiers from entering the community.

The same day, in La Galeana, soldiers attempting to invade the community were driven back by residents—again, almost entirely women.

All of the above incidents took place in the three weeks following the massacre at Acteal. But over the following months, as the Mexican government broadened its interventions to joint military-police raids designed to dismantle the autonomous municipalities in Zapatista zones of support, women's role in resisting also expanded. A notable case is that of the community of Nicolas Ruiz, invaded on June 3, 1998, by over a thousand judicial police and federal soldiers. Women again put themselves on the front lines, attempting to physically block the entrance of security forces into the community. They were eventually overwhelmed by tear gas fired by the agents. Several dozen men, along with one woman, were detained and the community's *títulos primordiales*, papers fundamental to its collective identity as well as its 150-year-old land claims, were taken away by state police. They have never been recovered.

I followed the events in Nicolás Ruiz from California, where I was attempting to focus on my doctoral exams despite unfolding events at home in Chiapas. I didn't know that a short time later, through my work with a new human rights organization (I left Global Exchange when my daughter was born, six weeks after the massacre at Acteal), I would establish a relationship with the community of Nicolás Ruiz that would alter the course of my research and, more important for this chapter, my analysis of the gendered nature of violence and resistance. As an advisor to the Chiapas Community Human Rights Defenders' Network, a recently formed organization dedicated to training indigenous people in human rights defense work, I met Rubén Moreno and Herón Moreno, the newly appointed "defenders" of the community of Nicolás Ruiz. As I learned more about dynamics in Nicolas Ruiz through Rubén and Herón, I became interested in studying human rights in the community as part of my doctoral dissertation. I ended up doing research there over the course of nearly six years.

In one of my first interviews in the community, I talked with Doña Graciela, the only women arrested on the day of the raid. Her comments led me to a new perspective on women's resistance to militarization. She began, "We knew the state police were going to come. There had been rumors for days, and we were all tense and waiting. We women gathered and agreed to block their entrance, as the women had in other communities. We had seen videos and photos of the women who kept the soldiers out of their communities, and we agreed we would do the same here, that we would not let them enter." Graciela's comment indicates that the women's actions in Nicolas Ruiz in June, five months after women first went out to block the army from entering the community of La Esperanza, were openly inspired by images of the earlier women's actions. Photographs taken by reporters and printed in the national and state press regularly make their way into the community, which was located in the central zone of the state and relatively close to both the capital, Tuxtla Gutierrez, and to San Cristóbal, the old colonial capital and current seat of most NGOs and the Catholic Diocese. The video footage they had seen was apparently shared with them by activists from "civil society," here a blanket term for activists not directly linked to the Zapatistas. The actions to block army incursion had thus had a demonstration effect, even in communities that could not have witnessed them first hand, engendering further women's resistance.

Although it might seem intuitively logical that, fed up with the threat of ever-increasing militarization, women in various communities were motivated to carry out these defiant acts of resistance. Yet many of us were impressed at the time precisely because it was indigenous women, in many respects the most vulnerable of the vulnerable, that took the front lines in these actions. It might have seemed just as logical if they had fled (as had happened in many communities during the military mobilization two years earlier). On another occasion in Nicolas Ruiz, women's comments again led me to realign my thinking, and consider the possibility that the fact that these actions took place in the period right after the massacre at Acteal was due to more than just the accelerated rate of militarization. One woman, talking about her participation in blocking security forces from entering the community, said something striking. After mentioning a number of offensive acts carried out by the state security forces during the raid, she paused then said in a low voice, "And you know that they massacred women and little children. They say that all you could hear were the cries and screams of women and little children as they died. We won't let that happen here. Now we are angry." She was talking about Acteal. At the time, what I noted was that she so clearly connected the state security police and the paramilitaries who had committed these crimes in Acteal. But, on later reflection, I focused on her anger. As a human rights activist, as a feminist, and perhaps more than anything as a new mother, the events at Acteal provoked a rage in me that was difficult to quell. I was tremendously moved by the images of women, face-to-chest with the taller and heavily armed soldiers, screaming them down and chasing them away. They expressed all of our wrath. I realized that for these indigenous women, rage had turned to power—the power to resist not just military incursion but also the strategies of terror waged against them. The rage was provoked by the violence at Acteal. And this suggests that sometimes strategies of terror, which the Acteal massacre clearly was a part of, can have an effect contrary to their purpose. Such strategies, designed to generate fear that is paralyzing to rebellious populations, in this case engendered resistance. The gendered violence of Acteal, in which the majority of those killed were women, their bodies mutilated and babies torn from their wombs, deepened the anger and antimilitary sentiment of many women, who in turn responded with gendered resistance.

Political Spaces: Women's Participation and the EZLN

It is difficult to talk about the women's resistance to militarization without including a discussion of the EZLN itself in some way, not only because most of the communities that carried out this kind of resistance are base-support communities and all suffer militarization and/or paramilitarization related to the Zapatista uprising but also because the Zapatistas have made women's rights and women's participation central to their political program.

Since the first days of the Zapatista uprising, close attention has been paid to the significance of the Zapatista movement for issues of women's rights. The appearance of the EZLN, with a rank and file made up of 30 percent women, the issuance of the Revolutionary Women's Law, and the generally high visibility of women within the movement, generated hopes that the Zapatista movement might give new impetus to the struggle for women's rights in Mexico. In the Revolutionary Women's Law, the Zapatistas put forward their demands for women's "equality and justice," among them the rights to control their fertility, choose their partners, be free from rape and physical aggression by strangers and family members, and participate in positions of authority in both the EZLN and in their communities. These were direct demands that held the promise of dramatic change for indigenous women in Zapatista areas, and raised hopes of a movement committed to feminist struggle for participants in the women's movement—indigenous and mestiza, in Chiapas and beyond.

However, not long after the uprising began, criticisms of the Zapatistas' gender discourse and practice surged. Some pointed out that the Revolutionary Laws and other public statements by Zapatista leaders lacked a critical feminist consciousness, because they did not call for the elimination of the patriarchal system of oppression and simply inserted women into hierarchical structures of violence contrary, in their view, to feminist sensibilities (Bedregal 1994; Hernández et al. 1994). Others pointed to the notable disjuncture between the Zapatistas' discourse of women's rights and their practice "on the ground" (Rojas 1995).[4]

My own position as both an indigenous rights activist and a feminist made me cognizant of the complex and at times contradictory situation in Zapatista communities. As an activist who worked with Zapatista base communities and sympathized with the Zapatistas' struggle, I recognized the contribution of the movement to redefining gender norms, or at least opening debate about them. But as a feminist, I could not fail to recognize and feel frustration about ongoing gender inequality in many regions. The uneven nature of change made it hard to analyze in broad terms, and I was at times disconcerted by the fact that it was women—Zapatista women—who were arguing for maintaining such gendered practices as the payment of bride wealth, which they saw as cultural practices positive for women. Other critical but sympathetic feminist observers have argued that "changes in the subordinate position of women, although significant, have been few, and processes of transformation slow and difficult, but . . . never, until now, has the inclusion of specific demands of indigenous women in a revolutionary movement been achieved" (Olivera 1995: 176). This inclusion, it is argued, has real symbolic power. Further, the Revolutionary Women's Law, "like all laws, is an ideal to achieve, rather than a lived reality," and the Zapatistas' expressions of gender sensitivity represent only "the seed of a new culture which has yet to be constructed" (Hernández Castillo 1998: 140). From this perspective, precisely what is important about the Zapatista movement is that it is not a finished product that is set to be imposed, but rather a social process that opens the possibility for many to incorporate their struggles and contribute to the ongoing construction of a more pluralistic and just society.

The discourse of women's rights certainly did not spring spontaneously from the Zapatista uprising. It was built on a history of women's organizing that allowed the Zapatistas to articulate this discourse, which includes work by the Diocese of San Cristóbal, NGOs, campesino organizations, artisan's cooperatives, and women's health projects that opened spaces of reflection about inequalities and rights, these had begun to be reappropriated by women in questioning gender inequalities and their individual rights (Garza 1999).[5]

However, the Zapatista discourse of women's rights at the center of their political project did affect women—even women not involved in (or even aware of) previous organizational efforts. The Zapatista uprising importantly broadened the parameters of the democratization movement in the indigenous communities. Its high-profile discourse of women's rights brought the discussion of indigenous women's political participation to a broader public, both national and international—and resignified it as positive, necessary, and natural. Although in many areas the women in indigenous communities are not familiar with the details of the Revolutionary Women's Law, its existence has for many women become a symbol of the possibility of a better life. Anna María Garza suggests that the Zapatistas' discourse regarding women's rights, and concretely the Women's Law, have contributed to creating what Karl-Brand (1990: 2) calls a cultural climate that "generates a specific sensibility for certain problems, narrowing or broadening the horizon of what seems socially or politically possible." She notes that "the EZLN with its Women's Law had known how to harness a climate firmly embedded in the daily lives of the indigenous communities and the breaking of previous consensus about the manner in which masculine authority was exercised in those communities."

Thus in the Zapatistas' discourse of women's rights, the resignification of indigenous communities as the space of democratization and indigenous women as political actors created a cultural climate, or an opening of political spaces of expression. Escobar and Alvarez (1992) argue that the opening of political spaces by new social movements represent one aspect of their "transformative potential." That is, although they are not pursuing immediate and revolutionary transformation of society, new social movements do contribute to social transformations through the opening of spaces of political participation. Within these spaces, new types of participatory citizenship can be recognized, which, not restricted to efforts to redefine the political system, instead encompass struggles to redefine social and cultural practices (Alvarez et al. 1998). The concept of opening political space in which new forms of political participation emerge is helpful in understanding the relationship between the Zapatista movement and women's collective actions, such as the mobilizations to resist militarization, which I interpret as a form of political participation in the broad definition given by Alvarez.

In Nicolás Ruiz, women tied their actions directly to the EZLN uprising and an evolution of their consciousness. For example, one woman explained:

> After 1994 (the beginning of the uprising), we began to become more aware (*tomar consciencia*). In 1994, we were all Priistas [affiliated with the ruling party, the PRI]. But we saw what the Zapatistas were doing and saying, and we began to say, "they are right," and we entered the struggle. That was when people from what we call civil society started to come, and they wanted to work with us, with the women. We started several projects . . . and we began to see that we shared a lot of suffering with women in other places. . . . And they [presumably women from "civil society"] showed us the videos [of women in other communities resisting military incursion] and we said, we will do this, too, if we have to.

This comment shows a clear relationship in this woman's mind between the community becoming Zapatista, the arrival of outside activists interested in organizing women, growing consciousness of a shared oppression as women, the viewing of images of women resisting, and eventual participation in blocking the army and police incursion into their community.

In sum, whether or not the EZLN as an organization has actively pursued a change in women's roles and levels of political participation within the base communities, their rhetorical advocacy of such change created the cultural climate and opened that political space in which these women undertook this form of political action.

Understanding Women's Collective Action:
Practical Goals, Strategic Effects

As mentioned above, some feminists, in analyzing events in Chiapas, have argued that the EZLN itself—both in its discourse and its practice—retains fundamentally patriarchal forms of organization and social interaction (Lagarde 1994; Rojas 1995). From this perspective, the women's struggles associated with the EZLN are not "feminist," in that they "only put forward a few claims for women, and not a proposal from a critical and conscious female experience" (Bedregal 1994). Though these specific critiques were not made in relation to the women's mobilizations against army incursion, which had not yet taken place, the authors would not be likely to revise their statements in light of these actions, given that they were directed to one specific and limited goal, and certainly were not tied to an analysis of patriarchy and the pursuit of new forms of social relations.

The distinctions these analysts draw are consistent with a long-standing differentiation in Latin American women's movements between "feminist" and "feminine" movements, in which struggles for specific goals related to women's lives (such as access to health care, direct investment for women's cooperatives, and so on) are understood as "feminine" projects, whereas "feminist" projects involve a questioning of women's position in the current configuration of social relations (Sternbach et al. 1992). There is thus a perceived dichotomy between "practical" feminine goals and "strategic" feminist goals (see Molyneux 1986).

In her study of women and social movements in Latin America, Stephan (1997) concludes that such dichotomies are difficult to apply to movements "on the ground," arguing instead that many movements are simultaneously seeking practical goals and challenging accepted norms about women's roles in society. This insight seems crucial to understanding the recent women's mobilizations against militarization in Chiapas. Their resistance was directed to a practical goal: keeping the army and state security forces out of their communities. It seems clearly not directed at a strategic goal of challenging systemic gender inequality. Nevertheless, by mobilizing as wives and mothers to protect home, family, and their right to continue to work and live their lives (however oppressive these may be), they are simultaneously overthrowing the male role of protector of partner and community, and inserting themselves into the traditionally male role of physically opposing an armed invader. Within the logic that places emphasis on men's ability to protect "their" women, and subjects women to physical attack as symbols in male struggles against male enemies (see Denich 1995, cited in Hernández Castillo 1998), their actions do challenge culturally inscribed norms about male and female roles of dominance and subordination. This form of collective action thus blurs the line between "practical/feminine" undertakings and "strategic/feminist" ones.

Public Discourse: Hidden Transcripts of a Gendered World

The official discourse of the Mexican government portrayed this as a "Zapatista strategy" of putting forward "their" women to ward off the army, while making retaliation politically difficult. The president himself claimed that "exemplary soldiers are being insulted and hit by women and children *who are sent to do this*" and chastised "those who shamelessly do not hesitate to use *indigenous women and children for their own provocations*, and would not stop short of using them as cannon-fodder."[6] In a similar vein, one military police commander stated, "[the Zapatistas] are cowards, *they* put their women and children first. I want the leaders to show their faces."[7] The "clever Zapatista strategy" interpretation got broad play in the press, even in some articles highly celebratory of the women's courage and determination. In this reading of events, it is understood that "the Zapatistas" (or at least those who make the strategies) are by definition men, and that women are little more than pawns to be moved by the Zapatistas when politically expedient. Once again, indigenous women's agency as political actors is negated, erased.

Significantly, the testimonies of the women involved in these mobilizations contradict such interpretations. The following, from a variety of sources including my own interviews (see note 1, above), are a few examples:

MARCELINA: We women decided among ourselves that the army would not enter our community. We told them, go ahead and kill us, but we don't want you here.

ADELINA: [The soldiers] said they were looking for weapons, they were asking who had guns. . . . We women got together and said we've got to get them out of here. *Que se vayan.*

MATILDE: The women here are organizing to defend our community. We are tired of running away from them. When they came in 1995, they destroyed everything, they killed our three *compañeros*. We don't want that to happen again, so we organized ourselves and decided to stay here, with our work.

DOLORES: It's the men the soldiers come to take. We said, we don't want them to take our husbands. We don't want our husbands to die. . . . We won't let [the soldiers] return.

MARIA: The Army destroyed all of our crops, everything in the *milpa*. . . . We think it is more dangerous for the men, be we also know that the soldiers could attack us or rape us. We were frightened, but then anger got a hold of us.

JUANA: We had heard the word that women in communities were organizing to defend their homes. And we decided we would do this too. The army only comes to steal and to frighten our children. So we said, we won't let them in.

These testimonies illustrate these women's strength, courage, resolve, and anger. They tell us that women decided among themselves to defend their communities, their children, and their men. There is no indication that they were given orders or were in any way persuaded by others to take part in such actions. In fact, when asked explicitly about this issue, women in one community said that not only were they not ordered by the Zapatistas to take action, but rather that they had asked the EZLN to support their actions after the fact (see Flinchum 1998).

While the implication that women are not capable of acting on their own without the direction of their male "leaders" is overt in the rhetoric of the government and implicit to differing degrees in that of others, the fact that these women's actions were so often conceived of in this manner makes evident a hidden transcript that reads all women as subordinate to men. I refer here to Scott's (1990) concept of hidden transcripts, or covert ideas contained in popular culture as signs of resistance. Stephan (1997) applies this concept to social science paradigms and resistance to change within them. In this same sense, I use the term here to refer to signs of resistance to change by both Mexican government representatives and journalists and others involved in the production of public discourse. The hidden transcripts that come through in official and unofficial discourse about the women's mobilizations to resist army invasion are universal, unstated assumptions about how the world is gendered.

It is worth noting that this gendered hidden transcript has its race and class corollaries. Official statements abound that imply or state openly that the indigenous Zapatistas are controlled and manipulated by nonindigenous outsiders—most often Sub-Commandante Marcos, a middle-class, educated ladino from Mexico City. The hidden transcript reads, of course, that a bunch of Indians would not be capable of organizing or leading themselves, or doing much of anything other than following the orders of a non-Indian man. The infantilization of innocent indigenous males controlled by Marcos bears a similar message to that of the discourse which portrays women Zapatistas as controlled by men—that is, their inferiority and subordination.

Thus the hidden transcripts contained in official discourse respond to a double challenge: the political challenge of an insurgent group, and the implicit challenge to gendered social norms by women. The official discourse, perpetuated in some media, serves to undermine the credibility of the EZLN and to reproduce hierarchical relations of race, class, and gender through popular cultural forms. Official discourse diverted attention from women's agency, and thus kept many from focusing on the potential "real story": that indigenous women had not been terrified into political and social submission by the violence at Acteal, but rather had been so enraged by it that they were motivated to action.

Fortunately, the images of the women's actions also make up part of the public discourse. These images were widely circulated, and although women's versions of what happened were often silenced in favor of the official story of their manipulation, the images reached many and spoke volumes about the women's anger and their ability to act on their own. Among those the images reached were other indigenous women, who found in them the inspiration to act similarly when it became necessary. They also reached the public at large, and undoubtedly had some effect on the collective imaginary about indigenous women. Consider for a moment the few images of indigenous women that are most often seen in Mexico or abroad: La India María, tourist ads showing women as bearers of a cultural past, or, worse yet, the foolish and illiterate servants on the extremely popular television soap operas. In this context, the images of indigenous women confronting the army also confront hidden transcripts of a gendered world, reinscribing indigenous women in the collective imaginary as powerful and courageous, as the defenders of home and hearth, and as the protectors of their men before a powerful enemy.

In Favor of Engaged Observation: Reflections on Feminist Activist Analysis

When I sat down to begin this essay one year after the events at Acteal, I was surprised to find myself struggling with my emotional responses to the dramatic material, my own subjective reading, intimately linked to my political affinities and allegiances, as well as the heightened sensitivity of new motherhood. I was surprised at myself because I had gone to the field with an explicitly activist research project, firm in the belief that research on human rights and women's rights in places where violations of both were endemic ethically required an activist commitment. Further, I believed strongly in feminism's basic insight about the situated nature of all knowledge production: from my perspective, an explicit activist commitment made my own "situatedness" central to the research. Perhaps it was the introduction of motherhood, so deeply ingrained in my consciousness as a "personal" aspect of women's experience, that caused me to question myself. I am glad that I did. Questioning my perspective motivated me to interrogate the manner in which my role as an activist, as a feminist, and as a mother, had shaped my analysis.

I experienced the events at Acteal and the women's mobilizations against military incursion as researcher and a woman committed to changing the situation of violence that they formed a part of. Because I was actively engaged in working for change, I felt the events more personally than might a researcher working in the area without an explicit commitment. A researcher friend who was in Chiapas at the time, in spite of being a progressive person who clearly was morally outraged by the massacre, nevertheless implored me to "Please stay out of [the conflict zone]; they [meaning Indians] are killing each other and you could easily get drawn in to their conflict." In his expression of concern for my personal safety, he also revealed a tendency to distance himself from the events in a way that made them manageable: you just have to stay clear of the area and you will be all right. Importantly, distancing did not provide him a better understanding of the social dynamics, but rather a skewed one. My commitment to social justice in the region did not allow me this distance: the loss of indigenous men, women, and children at Acteal was a loss in a struggle I considered my own (even as I recognized my own privilege in being able to "stay away" if I so chose). This intense engagement, heightened perhaps by the connection I felt with the mothers involved as a pregnant woman and new mother, allowed me to identify intensely with the anger and rage they felt, and this fed my understanding of the relationship between events at Acteal and the blockages of the military. Further, my past activism allowed me access to and the trust of certain women involved, which is no small thing in a polarized conflict situation where distrust was running high.

My political positionality also affected my understanding of the significance of the women's mobilizations in the larger scheme of women's organizing in Chiapas. It was my commitment to social justice that led me to align myself with Zapatista supporters, and to feel a strong sympathy for the movement. But my commitment to gender equality as a feminist also compelled me to recognize ongoing gender inequality and injustice in many Zapatista base communities. Direct political engagement with communities I worked in made the contradictions and complexities of women's situation clear to me, and led me away from easy assertions of either Zapatista intransigence on gender or celebratory assertions of gender equity. And finally, my critical feminist reading of the public discourse about the women's mobilizations was joined with direct knowledge of the way the mobilizations had been carried out; knowledge that could only have been gained by engaged interaction with the participants themselves.

In short, I believe that an explicit activist engagement as part of the research process can be important for several reasons. First, in situations where the rights of the protagonists of the processes we are observing and analyzing are being violated, it is ethically untenable to observe and gain information about them, and thus benefit from them, without any commitment to their well-being or future survival. Second, in a practical sense, it may be impossible to conduct research in areas that are conflicted or politically polarized without demonstrating political commitment. But the point I wish to make here is that the kind of engagement that may be ethically and/or practically necessary is also beneficial to our analysis. Based on my own experience, I suggest that the kind of engagement an activist commitment entails, while full of challenges, also provides insights that might not be gleaned from simple observation. A feminist activist engagement doesn't mean ceding our critical analysis to political partisanship: far from it. As I understand it, it means combining critical analysis with engaged research to produce knowledge that is empowering to women and that contributes to the struggle for gender justice.

NOTES

1. The testimonies included in this paper were collected by Robin Flinchum, Hilary Klein, and the author. All translations of testimonies and citations from texts are mine. The names of women quoted have been changed out of concern for their safety and their privacy.

2. Many people have questioned why the paramilitaries attacked members of the Abejas, rather than Zapatistas. It has been speculated that the paramilitaries simply interpret all groups that oppose the hegemony of the PRI, and especially those linked to the Diocese of San Cristóbal, as the Abejas are, as being Zapatistas. Others have speculated that the massacre was an attempt to provoke the Zapatistas to violence, thereby justifying an all-out military attack on them (Olivera 1998).

3. *La Jornada*, February 2, 1998; January 3, 1998.

4. In many of the base communities, women's subordinate position remained unchanged, and women continued to be excluded from community meetings and decision-making processes. Women in the base communities who do organize and become active have faced both state-sponsored violence from the army and paramilitary groups, and domestic violence from their own partners, who are jealous or resent their loss of control over their women (see Hernández Castillo 1998). The lack of organizational response from the EZLN to incidents of violence against women, and the apparent tolerance of exclusionary practices, quenched the initial optimism of many women activists about the possibilities for change (Bonilla 1994).

5. It is also important to note that although I am addressing specifically the emergence of a discourse of women's rights and modern political action, there is a long history of women's participation in resistance in Chiapas, much of which has been ignored by historians and ethnographers (Hernandez Castillo and Gall 1999). Notably, the women's actions to impede the military were apparently not without precedent. Oral histories are told in Zinacantan of women in neighboring Chamula lifting up their skirts and mooning Ladino soldiers to "cool their weapons" during the caste war of 1869 (Laughlin and Karasik 1996), and of a woman who led the soldiers to a cave and made them disappear (Witold n.d.).

6. President Ernesto Zedillo, quoted in *La Jornada*, February 13, 1998, 12, and February 20, 1998, 6. Italics mine.

7. Quoted in *La Jornada*, January 4, 1998, 5. Italics mine.

REFERENCES

Alvarez, Sonia, Evelina Dagnino, and Arturo Escobar, eds. 1998. *Cultures of Politics/Politics of Cultures: Re-Visioning Latin American Social Movements.* Boulder: Westview.
Brand, K-W. 1990. "Cyclical Aspects of New Social Movements." In *Challenging the Political Order*, edited by R. Dalton and M. Kuechler. New York: Oxford University Press.

Bedregal, Ximena. 1994. "Reflexiones desde nuestro feminismo." In *Chiapas, ¿y las mujeres, qué?* Vol. I, edited by Rosa Rojas. Mexico City: La Correa Feminista.

——. 1996. *Ni paz, ni justicia.* San Crístobal de las Casas: CDHFBLC.

——. 1998. *Esta es nuestra palabra: Testimonios de Acteal.* San Crístobal de las casas: CDHFBLC.

Bonilla, Adela. 1994. "Nuestro primer entusiasmo estrellándose con la realidad." *Correa Feminista* 15.

CDHFBC (Centro de Derechos Humanos Fray Bartolomé de las casas). 1996. *Ni Paz, Ni Justicia: InForme amplio acerca de la querra civil que sufien los chíoles en la zona norte de chiapas.* CDHFBC: San Cristóbal de las casas.

CNDH (Comision Nacional de Derechos Humanos). 1998. *Recomendacion 1/98.* Mexico City: CNDH, January 8.

Denich, Dette. 1995. "Of Arms, Men and Ethnic War in (former) Yugoslavia." In *Feminism, Nationalism, and Militarism,* edited by Costance R. Sutton. Arlington, Va: American Anthropological Association.

Escobar, Arturo, and Sonia E. Alvarez, eds. 1992. *The Making of Social Movements in Latin America: Identity, Strategy, and Democracy.* Boulder: Westview Press.

Flinchum, Robin. 1998. "The Women of Chiapas." *The Progressive.* March, 30–31.

Garza, Anna Maria. 1999. "El género entre normas en disputa: San Pedro Chenalho." M.A. thesis, Instituto de Estudios Indígenas, Unach.

Global Exchange. 1998. "On the Offensive: Intensified Military Occupation in Chiapas Six Months since the Massacre at Acteal." http://www.globalexchange.org/campaigns/mexico/OntheOffensive.html.

Global Exchange, CIEPAC, and CENCOS. 2000. "Always Near, Always Far: The Armed Forces in Mexico." http://www.ciepac.org.

Hernández Castillo, Rosalva Aída. 1998. "Construyendo la utopía: Esperanzas y desafíos de las mujeres chiapanecas de frente al siglo XXI." In *La otra palabra: Mujeres y violencia en Chiapas, antes y despues de Acteal,* edited by Rosalva Aída Hernández Castillo. Mexico City: CIESAS, COLEM, CIAM.

Hernández Castillo, Rosalva Aída, and Olivia Gall. 1999. "Un historia desde las mujeres: El papel de las campesinas indígenas en las rebeliones coloniales y poscoloniales en Chiapas." In *Voces disidentes: Debates contemporáneos en los estudios de género en México.* Mexico City: CIESAS-Porrúa.

Hernández, Gloria, Adela Hernández Reyes, and Salvador Mendiola. 1994. "Guerra y Feminismo." In *Chiapas, ¿y las mujeres, qué?* vol. I, edited by Rosa Rojas. Mexico City: La Correa Feminista.

Hidalgo, Onesimo, and Gustavo Castro. 1999. *Poblacion desplazada en Chiapas.* San Cristobal de las Casas: CIEPAC and Consejeria de Proyectos.

Lagarde, Marcela. 1994. "Hacia una nueva constituyente desde las mujeres." In *Chiapas, ¿y las mujeres, qué?* Vol. I, edited by Rosa Rojas. Mexico City: La Correa Feminista.

Laughlin, Robert M., trans., and Carol Karasik, ed. 1996. *Mayan Tales from Zinacantán: Dreams and Stories from the People of the Bat.* Washington, D.C.: Smithsonian Institution Press.

Molyneux, Maxine. 1986. "Mobilization without Emancipation: Women's Interests, the State, and Revolution." In *Transition and Development: Problems of Third World Socialism,* edited by Richard Fagen, Carmen Diana Deere, and José Luis Coraggio. New York: Monthly Review Press.

Nash, June. 2003. "The War of the Peace: Indigenous Women's Struggle for Social Justice in Chiapas, Mexico." In *What Justice? Whose Justice? Fighting for Fairness in Latin America,* edited by Susan Eckstein and Timothy Wickham-Crowley. Berkeley: University of California Press.

Olivera, Mercedes. 1995. "Práctica Feminista en el Movimiento Zapatista de Liberación Nacional." In *Chiapas, ?y las mujeres, qué?* Vol. 2, edited by Rosa Rojas. Mexico City: La Correa Feminista.

———. 1998. "Acteal: Los efectos de la Guerra de Baja Intensidad." In *La otra palabra: Mujeres y violencia en Chiapas, antes y despues de Acteal*, edited by Rosalva Aída Hernández Castillo. Mexico City: CIESAS, COLEM, CIAM.

Physicians for Human Rights. 1997. *Health Care Held Hostage*. Mexico City: December.

Ramírez, Jesus. 1997. "Mapa de la contrainsurgencia." *Masiosare*. January 13.

Rojas, Rosa. 1995. "De la primera convención nacional de mujeres a la consulta nacional del EZLN." In *Chiapas, ¿y las mujeres, qué?* Vol. 2, edited by Rosa Rojas. Mexico City: La Correa Feminista.

Rosenbaum, Brenda P. 1993. *With Our Heads Bowed: The Dynamics of Gender in a Maya Community*. Albany: Institute for Mesoamerican Studies, State University of New York.

Rovira, Guiomar. 1997. *Mujeres de maíz*. Mexico City: Era.

Scott, James. 1990. *Domination and the Arts of Resistance: Hidden Transcripts*. New Haven: Yale University Press.

Stephen, Lynn. 1997. *Women and Social Movements in Latin America: Power from Below*. Austin: University of Texas Press.

Sternbach, Nancy, Marisa Navarro-Aranguren, Patricia Chuchryk, and Sonia Alvarez. 1992. "Feminisms in Latin America: From Bogota to San Bernardo." In *The Making of Social Movements in Latin America: Identity, Strategy, and Democracy*, edited by Arturo Escobar and Sonia Alvarez. Boulder: Westview Press.

Witold, Witik. n.d. Unpublished manuscript in possession of the author.

10

It's a Hard Place to be a
Revolutionary Woman

Finding Peace and Justice in Postwar El Salvador

IRINA CARLOTA SILBER

> When we first started organizing,
>   they used to tell us "In 24 hours
>   the country is going to be
>   liberated." . . . But you can see that
>   war is quite painful and it doesn't
>   last from night to morning. . . .
>   Many have to struggle and die. . . .
>   So that was a big lie . . . the costs
>   are too high to liberate a country.
>
> −Author interview with a resident of a repopulated community

Like many protagonists of the Salvadoran civil war (1980–1992), thirty-year-old Chayo, seamstress, former guerilla supporter, wife of a demobilized combatant, adult literary teacher, seventh grader, shop owner, community council member, and mother of three, often commented on the continued injustice and sadness of postwar times.[1] This chapter is based on seventeen months of ethnographic research in El Salvador on the challenges of postwar reconciliation and reconstruction in the department of Chalatenango, a former conflict zone. Chalatenango was the site of various consciousness-raising projects, from liberation theology to a militant revolutionary movement during a twelve-year civil war, to a historic repatriation movement, and now to a negotiated transition to rebuilding.[2]

My argument is this: while the transition to democracy has opened up new political spaces for previously silenced actors, in everyday life, democratization processes create a gendered violence that remarginalizes women survivors of the civil war. This argument builds from a body of work that has explored the postwar role of Salvadoran women.[3] By tracing the aftermath of revolutionary struggle, however, I address a lacuna in the literature on the demoralization of women who participated (see Paley 2001) and offer a corrective to more celebratory work on women's social movements.

As recent feminist research makes clear, it is critical to explore the "extra-official" spaces of women's activism (Alvarez et al. 2002). The stories I tell of two single mothers, Sandra and Martina, and a mother and her teen daughter, Elsy and Flor, suggest that we must be attentive to the possibilities, challenges, and uneven power of a polyphonic feminist movement (Alvarez 1998). The ethnographic material that follows emerges from my engaged research practices that privileged women's stories describing the ways in which they seek to make meaning of their past sacrifices and a present political economy that continues to marginalize them. These stories occur in the "in-between" of heroic and tragic memories of wartime activism, and a postwar disillusionment where women's everyday agency of "desires, agendas and projects" (Ortner 2001: 83) is constrained or limited by structural violence (Farmer 2001).

Background

The department of Chalatenango, located in the northeast of El Salvador, is a rural, mountainous region, historically a frontier land and marginalized department of the nation (Browning 1971). By the late 1970s, the new teachings of liberation theology grew throughout the region. This progressive movement of the Catholic Church with its focus on social and economic justice contributed to organizing rural residents into nonviolent collective action. Many have suggested that it formed part of a larger consciousness-raising project that radicalized and "reawakened" popular movements organized around land rights, increasing wages, and access to education and health care.[4] These movements were met with increasingly violent repression, and by the early 1980s the military and paramilitary presence in Chalatenango was brutal. The department became one of the key conflict zones and a strong site of oppositional mobilizing, and a salient characteristic of this period was women's prominent involvement in organizing for justice.

As a result of the twelve-year civil war (1980–1992) that claimed the lives of 80,000 people, left 8,000 "disappeared," and displaced one million of El Salvador's five million people, most community residents in Chalatenango were forced to flee their homes (Montgomery 1995). Many joined guerrilla forces and formed a militant revolutionary movement; others became internally displaced; but most civilians crossed the border into Honduras and lived in refugee camps for varying amounts of time. Scholars, development practitioners, and activists have documented this phase of the war and tracked the historic repatriation that began in 1987, as refugees mobilized to return to their place of origin while the war was still ongoing.[5]

Today, these repopulated communities (*repoblaciones*) have been resettled for more than a decade, and residents have shifted from wartime organizing to peaceful rebuilding, within a complicated postwar context in which the root causes of the war have not been resolved. Political and economic power relations have not changed dramatically, and structures of inequality continue to marginalize places like Chalatenango, as the majority of Salvadorans still suffer from lack of access to resources, political participation, and social services (Spence et al. 1997).[6] And although in the early postwar period the region received internationally sponsored relief and emergency assistance, and subsequently reconstruction projects, El Salvador as a "cause" has receded from the international mapping, as war and catastrophic relief and development work shifts globally.

Women in the Transition to Democracy

The growth of a strong though diverse women's movement born from oppositional politics of the war (Stephen 1997: 13), and the mainstreaming of gender and development in national reconstruction, place "women's issues" in the national public sphere. During the course of my fieldwork, the media began highlighting women's multiple roles as mother, wife, worker, politician, "deviant," survivor, and sufferer. The conservative newspaper *Diario de Hoy* often had sections devoted to women's "reality." Articles covered stories on women in politics (powerful and on the right), such as "Mujeres, madres y políticas de primera" (*Diario de Hoy*, July 7, 1997), juxtaposed with many that focused on the poor undifferentiated masses of women working in the informal economy, such as "Con ahínco, esfuerzo y sacrificio" (*Diario de Hoy*, March 21, 1997), and on other women who were "deviant" and in prison (*Diario de Hoy*, July 28, 1997).

The government of El Salvador has also begun to address gender concerns. As NGOs and international agencies privilege women in their postwar reconstruction plans, the government has made official statements promising to improve Salvadoran women's access to resources and power in a range of spheres such as health, education, labor, and politics. Indeed, in February 1996, the legislative assembly passed decree no. 644, which created the Instituto Salvadoreño para el Desarrollo de la Mujer (ISDEMU—the Salvadoran Institute for Women's Development). This institute was founded to facilitate Salvadoran women's development, and as a first step produced an official government political platform in 1997—"La Política Nacional de la Mujer" (Women's National Political Plan). This placed women and development on the map as a national issue. The platform, signed by then president Armando Calderón Sol and his wife Elizabeth Aguirre de Calderón Sol, delineates a series of problem areas and offers specific objectives that are intended to promote gender equality. The plan was promoted as "one more step that guarantees women equal access to opportunities to develop and progress, meeting the objectives of the government's

social plan" (ISDEMU 1997: 5). La Política Nacional de la Mujer importantly recognizes the discrimination Salvadoran women continue to face in the many
areas of their lives, and adds that although legal reforms have been made, their
application lags far behind (ISDEMU 1997: 6).

Although the government did not create an official national development
plan with the negotiated peace, there was a large influx of internationally backed
development projects, particularly in former conflict zones. A portion of this aid
focused on empowering women economically and politically (see Stephen et al.
2000). From the capital to historically isolated and remote rural communities,
NGOs addressing women's issues have taken hold. Groups include organizations
working to protect the rights of sex workers, and others that continue the wartime
activism of consciousness raising and empowerment in rural places. Behind much
of this focus on women lies a strong and diverse women's movement. Although
the revolutionary mobilization of the recent past subordinated gender equality
under an ungendered struggle for social justice (see Molyneux 1985; Aguilar et al.
1997; Vázquez et al. 1996), feminist scholars have recently documented the
diverse ways in which Salvadoran women negotiate their multiple identities and
obligations—balancing partnerships and motherhood with participation in
social movements—and how existing gender relations and ideologies limit their
social action (see Stephen 1997).[7] The strength of the movement is evidenced in
the ways in which it has organized around key issues.

For example, in 1994 the movement joined forces to develop a political platform for the election, and in 1997 it elaborated another highly detailed platform
that delineated specific ways in which to combat gendered injustices in the
nation. The Plataforma de las Mujeres Salvadoreñas 1997–2000 (Salvadoran
Women's Platform), published by Las Dignas, a leading radical women's group,
challenged the government's own proposal on social change. The platform
delineated the multiple spheres of women's marginalization and discrimination:
in education, health, violence, sexuality, labor, and representation. It provided a
detailed and specific critique of the legal reforms made to the constitution in the
recent past, indicating that the systems are not in place to apply the reforms. For
instance, although a 1981 pact was ratified to eliminate all forms of discrimination against women (DIGNAS 1997: 7) and several other articles were ratified in
the constitution in 1994—for example, pacts to guard against women's discrimination in labor, laws to protect women against domestic abuse, and a legislative
decree declaring November 25 Women's Day against Violence—La Plataforma
argues for a more aggressive and radical legislative reform. It offers 102 specific
points that range from addressing women's roles in sustainable development to
demands for equalizing women's political and economic power.[8]

Although these two platforms index a historic growth of democratic spaces
in the nation, the present and future for many Salvadoran women and men
across the nation remains frighteningly uncertain. There are many questions

that emerge regarding women in the transition to democracy, for as Fitzsimmons acutely summarizes in a review essay on Latin American women's movements in the 1990s, "Under democracy, oppression now looks different, as do the oppressors and circumstances in which women might win or loose. Similarly, the reasons why women mobilize, how various women's groups interrelate, and how women and the state interact have also changed" (Fitzsimmons 2000: 216).

Chalatecas: Living (Post)War Violence

In Chalatenango, as in many former conflict zones such as Morazán, Usulutan, and Cabañas, women's involvement during the civil war was a critical factor in organizing successes. In the postwar period, women's mobilizations have shifted from revolutionary activism to a negotiation of home and community politics. Scholars, activists, international development practitioners, and local NGOs and grassroots organizations[9] have recently shifted away from women-centered discourses and practices in an attempt to institutionalize a gender focus in their work.[10] But current mobilizing efforts continue to build almost exclusively on women's identities: as former revolutionaries, as survivors of everyday poverty, as single heads of households, as survivors of structural and family violence, and as contestors of repressive regimes of the past and oppressive neoliberal regimes of the present. These efforts are a continuation of a wartime gendered consciousness-raising project, taking place in a shifting context where women's participation, a key signifier of empowerment, has come to mean a multiplicity of roles—community leaders, micro-entrepreneurs, and FMLN militants.

Because of the legacies of violence, displacement, widowhood, and abandonment—and the ebbs and flows of mobilizations—women engage in a complicated weaving of their productive, reproductive, and community work that remarginalizes them as they are cast as either agentless victims or heroic mother fighters. The stories told below erase this binary opposition by demonstrating the gendered limitations in postwar Chalatenango. For many women the future remains uncertain; their children are underfed and undereducated, and daily life is full of the violence of a gendered poverty. Moreover, as Philippe Bourgois poignantly shows, there is no morally "worthy" violence. His reinterpretation of a brutal military operation he experienced with rural Salvadorans in 1981 leads him to state: "People do not simply 'survive' violence as if it somehow remained outside of them, and they are rarely if ever ennobled by it. Those who confront violence with resistance—whether it be cultural or political—do not escape unscathed from the terror and oppression they rise up against. The challenge of ethnography, then, is to check the impulse to sanitize and instead to clarify the chains of causality that link structural, political, and symbolic violence in the production of an everyday violence that buttresses unequal power relations and distorts efforts at resistance" (2001: 29–30).

It is to this challenge that I now turn as I provide the commentary of two women, survivors of both the war and of a more elusive and ambiguous marginalization in the present.

Single Mothers in El Rancho

On October 24, 1997, after I had pursued a year of fieldwork in a municipality of Chalatenango, two women I had come to know well agreed to speak with me in El Rancho about their lives, particularly about how they struggled as single mothers.[11] Both Martina and Sandra were women in their mid-thirties, the protagonist generation of the recent civil war. Both women were raising four young children alone, and rumor had it both were pregnant again. Although they each had received direct benefits from the negotiated peace, such as small, distant, and poor-quality land through the land transfer program (PTT), their households were desperately poor, barely surviving. As a result, each considered selling these plots of land. Martina, with kin in the community, did not receive much support from either her parents or her economically better-off sister, Chayo. Her fifteen-year-old son, who was old enough to work the land, had recently left her, seduced away by his father, who had not contributed to raising him. Community gossip added that he was fed up with his mother's sexual practices, which brought more young mouths to feed. Sandra and her four girls lived with her aging and sickly father, who between fainting spells continued to travel long distances to work in the fields. He was unable to produce enough for subsistence. She, like Martina, did not receive much assistance from her kin or the girls' fathers.

Three nights before our conversation, under the pouring rain, Martina, Sandra, and I had returned from a credit meeting. Here an altercation took place between Martina and another woman regarding the paternity of Martina's *chelito*—her four-year-old blond-headed boy.[12] The father of the child, according to Martina, was the woman's husband.

In postwar Chalatenango, one of the legacies of the civil war is a generation of women without partners and children without fathers. Though the pattern of multiple fathers of children to a single mother predates the war and reflects a historical pattern of male labor migration to the coast and coffee regions, this pattern was exacerbated during the war as many men tragically lost their lives. The extremes of war also created a historic sexual freedom for both women and men that was liberating at the time, "transforming" gender relations. However, in the present the ramifications of these practices are mixed. Many men and women abandoned their partners. Families were uprooted because of the violence, and when relocated to refugee camps, many people formed new partnerships. In some cases a series of partnerships formed as *compas* (guerilla soldiers) moved in and out of the camps.[13] During the war, fatherhood and motherhood were circumscribed by the logistics of battle. However, in the present many fathers do not take responsibility for the children born during the war and during repopulation. In El Rancho, there are many single women raising children by many fathers. These women bear the full brunt of productive, reproductive, and community work. They engage in the backbreaking work of cultivating corn and beans; they labor in the informal sector, for example selling home-grown cucumbers or weaving fishnets; they are the primary child care givers and providers; and they are expected to participate in community politics.

As Martina and Sandra sat on hammocks, speaking softly into the tape recorder so that neighbors could not overhear, I realized that I was engaged in a special and uncommon moment, for it is rare for Chalateca "deviant" women to speak so freely. For many single mothers, their very position in the community has come to marginalize them further. Martina and Sandra's narratives demonstrate that their practices as single women are a threat to "married" women's households.[14] Both Martina's and Sandra's stories tell of their involvement with their neighbors' partners, the subsequent birth of illegitimate children, and the violence that ensues as they pursue legal reparation through the new postwar human rights institution—La Procudería de Derechos Humanos. The ability to make claims with this institution marks a profound postwar advance for women's rights.[15] From the hidden, private acts of the night emerges a public shaming and violence. This is a situation that positions woman against woman, neighbor against neighbor, and man against woman. For Martina and Sandra, these survival practices, born from historically constituted gender relations and ideologies, in the end construct them as "deviant" community women. The years of consciousness raising to create women's solidarity is seemingly unable to combat their marginalization.

During our long exchange, Martina and Sandra juxtapose the past and the present. They construct a past of unity amid wartime horror, and a present marked by a very different sort of social injustice. For Sandra, her marginalization is a recent phenomenon. She explains how in the past, many were alone but not forgotten. There was solidarity. She explains that she did not choose her status, but rather the circumstances of war, the destruction of family, the male migration—all of these were factors in *la mala suerte de uno* (one's bad luck—to be abandoned). Thematically, this exchange was unexpected (for me). As I asked them both to describe their experiences and thoughts as single mothers, the conversation repeatedly focused on oppressive and violent gender relations at the community level, perhaps a legacy of "the ways violence follows gendered fault lines and becomes an accepted way to solve community anxieties in wartime" (Bourgois 2001: 20). Theirs is a discourse marked by male violators, "bothering" women (*molestar*),[16] and of women vulnerable to men's lies because of their desire to rebuild family. From interview transcripts, Martina and Sandra's narratives illustrate the obstacles confronting gendered social change in the nation and also explain why so many NGOs working to empower women focus on issues of sexuality and self-esteem.

Sandra, abandoned by multiple partners, sets the tone for the exchange. She aggressively analyzes the reasons why she is, like so many other women, in such a dire living situation.[17] She explains this in terms of the power men have over women, a situation that is often repeated, as women swallow a series of men's lies:

> Mirá, Look. The reality of things here is that we were a big group of single women. Not because we want to be alone but because bad luck surrounds us. All the men, what they like is to have a woman on the side, in secret, so that no one else realizes that a woman is with him. Then he gets her pregnant . . . after a while, up to two or three women can get pregnant by the same man. . . . Then comes another man, maybe two or three years after the first man abandoned you. This other man comes to bother you too. And you end up believing his lies too.

With the displacement caused by the war, many women like Martina and Sandra fled to refugee camps in Honduras and through the years formed new couples. In Martina's case, while in Mesa Grande she left her partner and had two girls by a second partner, who subsequently left her during the repopulation movement. The waves of male migration have not stopped in postwar times. In some cases, households in Chalatenango receive the economic benefits of their kin's remittances. But for many, as the years pass, this influx of dollars dwindle and this negatively impacts household economies. Martina explains that the father of two of her children no longer sends remittances. Her explanation is framed by a discourse of deceit: "At first he started helping us, not with very much, with a little, the most he sent me was 400 colones. But now, I don't know what's going on with him, but now he only lies to us. Saying he doesn't have anything. . . . And I cultivate my little plot of milpa and not even with a dime to buy fertilizer. . . . So I feel as though I haven't had any help from anywhere. It's to say I haven't had any help in raising the children that I have."

As mentioned above, the sexual practices of single women become the topic of community gossip. The personal pain, suffering, and too often physical abuse of these women enters the public domain. During the war, problems between people were dealt with at the community level through the institutions of the community council and general assemblies, where democratic practices were the norm. At least this is how past community practices are constructed in the present. In postwar times, however, many people have lost faith in the community councils (that is, the councils have been accused of corruption), and Chalatecos have turned to new postwar institutions to find redress. But as legal strides to protect women and children's rights have been made in El Salvador, for example, through the creation of human rights offices in each department of the nation, the ramifications of these efforts are mixed. In Chalatenango, many women traveled to the Procudería de Derechos Humanos to denounce their former partners and request child support. This was a bureaucratic process, often met with no res-olution as the mechanisms to implement reforms were not fully in place. Most often women initiated the action covertly and the accused men refused to partic-ipate, many refusing to arrive at the Procudería, ultimately violating women's right to child support. Martina recounts: "I went to the Human Rights Office. My little boy was eighteen months old. Well, they called him [his father] to present himself many times, and he never came . . . like she says about the fathers here, when they get you pregnant, when they hear that you are pregnant, they retreat and start saying that it is someone else's baby."

Rather than empowering women through an institutionalized avenue of redress, in many cases as women seek to defend their rights they are met with increasing marginalization in their everyday lives. In the transition to democ-racy these new spaces become a "threat" to established gender relations and patterns. As abandoned women begin to contest their position, they become easy targets of community gossip (*chambre*) in what they identify as a series of offensive lies (*mentiras*) that indeed move beyond the local community through a dense social network of kin and ritual kin. This gossip constructs them as deviant women whose resentment can cause illness and threatens community life. Ultimately this construct provides the rationale for their victimization by the men and their kin, who in "self-defense" publicly humiliate, threaten, insult, and marginalize the women they have abandoned.

Martina and Sandra both recount how they have been accused of evil actions, of leaving poisoned food, such as bananas and chiles, for their former partners. Martina was even accused of giving the evil eye (*mal de ojo*) to her for-mer partner's infant son by his new legal wife: "And then his little boy got the evil eye. His little baby boy died. . . . What he says is that I gave him the evil eye. And I tell you, if he goes around saying that, he is insulting me, and I don't deserve that. So, that really affects me."

For Martina and Sandra, their anger at being abandoned and the redress they seek is decontextualized and used to legitimate violence against them. Sandra explains: "So the father of my little boy said, 'she's nothing but a great big nobody, she's the only one who is mad at me.' 'It's true,' I said, 'I was mad.' I was mad. But I'm angry because he doesn't help me. . . . How am I going to greet him and talk to someone who doesn't help me and who spreads lies about me? That doesn't please me."

Word often reached Sandra, sometimes through kin, that her former part-ner was planning vengeance: "My mother heard that he was walking through the campo, enraged, when he came across another person and told him that he better not find me along the way in the street or else he was going to cut me up into little pieces."

Martina's stories of violent encounters are many. In each narrative she tells, her attempts at redress, whether through personal appeals to her former lover, through the *directiva* (community council) or through official government channels, are met with violence. Martina attempts to contest the community gossip against her through the directiva and the local *juzgado de paz*.[18] Although her former lover does not refute her accusations, he later responds with violence:

> So he said to me . . . that he had friends that could come out to the streets or on pathways and beat me up. So, after that, I held a meeting. I called all the members of the directiva, I called the judge in order to present my case. So then, I called him and they held a meeting. He accepted the charges and he did not deny that the child was his. . . . Well, I never thought that he was going to stay angry. But he was determined to stay angry. He came to tell me that he had friends, that he would send them after me on the streets, which he did.

Despite this painful experience, Martina explains how it was that she became embroiled with yet another married man and how he too abused her. In this narrative she constructs herself as victim to a man's lies and his violent words and actions:

> Four years after having this child, maybe I believed this other young man. I believed him, he lied to me, and I believed him . . . the father of this little girl, and I was with him for around seven months. Well, during the first month when I started going out with him, he bothered me . . . when he bothered me I didn't want to do it. Because I told him that I didn't want to have him because I didn't want to end up with more children. I told him this. So, after seeing his great need, he would tell me that I wasn't going to get pregnant. That I should take birth control, right. Well, so that's when I trusted him, I was going to use birth control, but then I trusted him and I had two relations with him without taking anything.

In this situation as well, Martina's attempts to have the younger man accept the paternity of her daughter and provide child support are futile and the results oppressive. She explains that despite his constant violence, she continued seeing him with the hopes that he would eventually provide for the child: "After he got mad at me, he came back to bother me, he came back because he had no shame . . . and I kept accepting him, seeing that I was already pregnant, I kept accepting him to see if he would help me. That's why I did it."

Martina discovered that she was not the only woman to bear this man's child, but that her neighbor, also a single mother was expecting at the same time. She reflects: "That was news to me. That's when I said, 'if I had known that,' I said, 'that he was with another woman I wouldn't have fallen so easily.' That was the deceit. He deceived me. He deceived me and I wasn't able to 'un-deceive' myself that he was with another woman."

While Martina's narratives express with an urgency the daily violence of being abandoned, Sandra's commentaries tend to be more political. Her stories of gendered violence are framed by an analysis of past and present injustices, of locally hegemonic memories of a past of unity, and a present focused on individual gain:[19]

> Look, I feel that there's a big change. I feel a big change. Because look, during the war, we were incorporated, we were not five or ten people, we were thirty, sixty, ninety people in one unit. If there were problems, a meeting was held and the problems were worked out. And everyone worked well. . . . Well, I felt that there was A LOT of unity. A lot of support among people. During the war and then during the repopulation their was a lot of unity and organization to help children, women, everybody. Problems were worked out. . . . I feel that it is different now. Everybody is out for themselves, to advance themselves, and they don't care if five people work and four are left with nothing, and that one gets ahead. . . . That's why I feel there is a great injustice, a great injustice . . . those of us who have nothing, well, we have to resign ourselves to the fact that others have things. And you can't complain because then you become enemies, and sometimes if you complain they threaten you with death. So, there is a great change. Back then, there was a lot of support.

Sandra's political analysis and interpretation of her past involvement in the revolutionary movement occurs in a present of extreme poverty, on the borderline of survival, her children greatly underfed and underclothed:

> I feel a great deal of suffering. Weeks pass without even tasting beans. We get by only with the small help that we get from the municipality. In the clinic they give us rice, a bottle of oil, and with that we make it until they give us more the next month. . . . So for me it is a great deal of suffering, because I'm always worried. Sometimes fifteen days have gone by and I have a huge load of clothes in the bucket but I have no soap to wash with, and no money. So, I start to really worry. If I made a list of all the things I need, I'd probably go crazy. Because you can't sleep from worry . . . you just keep thinking about it. And if you have small children and you say you are going to work it's a lie.

For women like Martina and Sandra, despite over a decade of consciousness-raising projects, few community spaces exist for them to articulate, exchange, or address their painful suffering. Whether privately or openly, they are easy victims of gossip that remarginalizes them. Although the interview context perhaps created a more positive and shared moment to speak of common problems, it also created a space that opened up unhealed wounds. This is a central contradiction of engaged research. And this project portends no easy answers. It does however, enter in conversation with a wide ranging body of literature on reconciliation,[20] although it does not offer conventional examples of human rights research, such as the documentation of regional massacres by Salvadoran military and paramilitary forces. This study focuses on women's stories of violence and threats of violence, a violence that is often apologetically voiced as not of the war. By being open to what is perhaps best described as women's ambivalent and uncertain embracing of the postwar period, engaged research in El Salvador does offers the multiple, competing, frustrating, and frustrated interpretations of women's experiences that do not fit easily in a human rights paradigm.

Both Martina and Sandra explain that marginalized women did not have the power to meet and discuss their lived realities, adding that exchanges such as ours could very easily become weapons used against them. I conclude with a transcript from the session:

IRINA CARLOTA: Do you feel supported by the women's community council? Do you feel support among yourselves?

SANDRA: Not really, there is no support from anybody. They leave us totally abandoned.

MARTINA: Because when there is resentment, they don't call you to talk about it, like we're doing right, to express yourself, because you don't tell anybody your suffering, how you've had to ensure the future of your children. Nobody knows what they've done to you. You only know, and you carry it with you in your heart. . . . Because you can't trust anybody here to tell them your story. Because if I tell somebody, that person ends up doing more harm.

And so while Martina and Sandra live only four houses away and survive under very similar circumstances, they do not support each other for fear of community attacks. Sandra states: "Here between the two of us, I feel that we are in the same situation, equally poor. The same situation, we are facing the same problem. So, I feel really bad for her, poor her that she has nothing. And poor me also. And I'm embarrassed to go bother her. . . . Sometimes we communicate, even if it's only once a year . . . we don't get in touch once a week or anything, every once in a while to avoid problems."

Suffering, Witnessing, Change

This engaged anthropological account fits well with recent transnational feminist theorizing and practice. Specifically, it calls attention to the underbelly of Latin America's vibrant women's and feminist movements—the uncertain participants that leadership hopes to embrace. As Alvarez (1998) reminds us, though Latin American feminisms have gone "global" they have done so unevenly, often following, I suggest, the fault lines of neoliberal economic policies. Highlighting

Martina and Sandra's interpretations, and exploring the socialization of Elsy's teen daughter Flor below, provide an often unexamined perspective. This can enrich both social theory regarding expectations of subaltern gendered experiences and suggest practical models for change. As Ready (2003) clearly demonstrates, it is often the exigencies of international funders that complicate an increasingly fragmented movement along lines of race, class, rural, urban, sexuality, and education.

Martina and Sandra's expressive voices articulate the desperation of postwar times at a very personal level of suffering. While they, like many residents, live in a historic moment of new possibilities, their daily life is circumscribed by a new set of constraints. Though women now have the public space to struggle for gendered social change (such as paternity laws), contradictions continue to occur, as in practice the implementation of reforms to the legal system lag far behind. Throughout the nation there are still many ambiguous spaces where social injustices take place. For wartime survivors, on the right and the left, negotiating this complicated landscape characterizes day-to-day life. Although the road to democratization has offered access to new resources, this unknown territory is littered with bureaucracy that is often overwhelming and frustrating for wartime survivors, who find that their intended benefits are elusive. And in general, grassroots groups and nongovernment organizations have not focused on facilitating this complicated trajectory—for example, of collectively organizing orphans, through their kin, to receive available government benefits.[21]

During a formal interview with Beatrice, a director of the womens' programming of a human rights NGO based in the capital of San Salvador and working in wartorn areas, we discussed the challenges of postwar times. Beatrice typifies the emergence of a Salvadoran women's movement. Her analysis and practice come primarily from her longtime involvement in revolutionary struggle, and her present is marked by a search for implementing newly learned concepts such as gender mainstreaming in development and human rights work. Her analysis of the obstacles facing women in Chalatenango centered on the women's movement's unclear vision, theoretically and methodologically, during the early postwar period. She said that the question back then was, *¿que vamos hacer las mujeres?* (what are we women going to do?) with a vague answer, *nos tenemos que organizar* (we need to organize). Here we can hear still the wartime rhetoric of struggle, of organization, together with the beginning movement of women's rights. Although women's groups throughout the nation discussed women's problems and tried to find solutions, development and empowerment directed specifically at women in the repopulated communities was unclear. In Beatrice's analysis of the evolution of this work, the lack of a clear gendered project resulted in the dominance of more "extreme" and "radical" perspectives that were circulating through the women's movement in El Salvador—here she made reference to self-identified feminist organizations such as Las Dignas.[22] She argues these "failed" by increasing tension between women and men in communities. Beatrice's anecdotal information voices how men understood self-esteem workshops as vehicles for women to leave them. Empowerment, for example, became synonymous with women charging for each sexual exchange with their partners. As a result, many women, encountering resistance from their male partners, ceased participating in gender-specific projects. In the later postwar period, Beatrice says that the vision is clearer though the methodology still not sufficiently defined. The vision: Lift a woman's self esteem, change her traditional mindset, help her form a new vision of the world and her reality, and empower women to participate in decision making in the community and in the party. However, she voices the limitations of this project of political, gendered empowerment—the long road ahead to reeducate men to understand that gender relations as they stand are unacceptable.

Ilja Luciak, focusing on the FMLN, documents how many women leaders began their gendered consciousness-raising projects only after the end of the war (2001).[23] His case study of repopulated communities in Chalatenango supports my work on the disillusionment of everyday life, the feelings of indemnification born from suffering, the unmet expectations of a long struggle as people's standards of living and prospects for the future have not changed dramatically (93). Still, the majority of women and men in Chalatenango's repopulated communities continue to self-identify through a politics and ideology of opposition (that is, they ultimately support the FMLN and the various grassroots and NGO links to them). For example, in my conversations with Elsy, a "community leader" of a repopulated community, we discussed what many of her neighbors described as *estamos peor que antes* (we are worse off than before[the war]); their kin were dead, their bodies injured, their families altered, and neoliberal national economic policies were resulting in even further reduction in social services and a shift away from supporting a rural agricultural economy. Elsy's response was honest (and sad), voicing the limitations of a negotiated revolution in the present. She said, "It's true we lost my brother, but we know that in order for there to be victory compañeros had to die in order to achieve it. Sometimes I think, despite the fact that I'm an old woman, now with the kids, and that I suffered so much during the war, at least I'm with Avel. I'm well, my parents are well, and despite the war with all of its suffering, at least we are alive." She followed after a pause with the comment: "The objective of organizing was to have social change in the country." Then after another pause: *Quedé con las manos buenas y los pies buenos*—"I have both my hands and my feet."

Recent scholarship importantly points to how there is "often a traumatized silencing of the brutal events by witnesses who blame themselves for what they had to do to survive" (Bourgois 2001: 14).[24] This leads Bourgois to assert that "the question, too painful to ask, that was raised implicitly in most of my conversations during this visit revolved around whether all the suffering and violence of the guerilla struggle had been in vain" (19). In my research, it was precisely this question, always painful, that was raised explicitly and frequently in the daily conversations of family and community life, and answered differently in shifting contexts.

I end this chapter by turning to the next generation of Chalatecos, the future protagonists to build peace. To do so I weave the stories of a mother-daughter dyad to illustrate the uncertainties of a gendered justice.

Socializing the Next Generation of Women Fighters?

Elsy, age thirty-five, is a self-identified "women's community leader" and former participant in the revolutionary social movement. Her daughter Flor, age fifteen, is her eldest child, bright, shy, and in the fifth grade. Both mother and daughter, although differently, constitute generations socialized under a militarized society characterized by institutionalized violence. Elsy, like many parents and local grassroots activists, expresses her concern for the next generation, the generation for which she has struggled. Concerns range from the limits of children's education, underemployment in a now nonagriculture-oriented economy, increasing alcohol and marijuana consumption, and the increasing crime in communities, committed by their very own local teen boys and young adults—something generally absent during the war. These concerns are often expressed in a gendered language of crisis, and I suggest that their practices center on the surveillance of teen girls, their sexuality, and their bodies, reproducing what some term as "traditional" gender relations in the next generation. Despite more than a decade of women's involvement in revolutionary movements, and the growth of a strong Salvadoran women's movement, today many of these women have decreased their activism and "retrenched" to the social space of the home, putting their energies into social reproduction. Elsy's sacrifices and trauma of the war affect her daughter's socialization, Flor's practices and life choices. Despite Elsy's waxing and waning activism in radical social movements and in postwar gendered, local development efforts, Flor takes a different turn.

Elsy's stories range from the imprisonment she felt in the refugee camps to the freedom she felt as a young teenager within the armed movement. She carries the suffering of her youth with her and reproduces it in the raising of her children. And so I suggest we look at her narratives of the war as gendered coming-of-age stories. These tell of a transition from childhood to womanhood through both her empowered participation in the armed movement and her sexual freedom within a context of terror. Her stories recount her own trajectory through her relationship with young men. This is a trajectory of child to woman as *mujer de un hombre* (a man's woman), which is precisely what she struggles to protect Flor from, and a story of a series of losses, as one after another her compañeros die.

Elsy explained one of her first traumatic events, the death of her first compañero when she was just fifteen, the same age as her daughter when she told me these stories. She told me how she went looking for his remains at the site of his death. A story she tells me most do not know, a story she has not told her daughter. She says: "I picked up a handful of his curly hair and some bones from his feet and others from his hands and like that little bits of bone. And the shirt, the shirt was red and dried hard by his own blood. I cut a piece of the shirt and put all of that in it, put it in a bag and I carried that bag with me in my knapsack. No one knew. Only my friend Lupe. And I carried them with me until I met Rolando and then I went to bury the bones in the cemetery."

This story was followed by many others, by her childhood friend's violent death and the horrific display of her decapitated head on a stick, her head paraded through the municipality; Elsy's premature labor and the death of her first child while she was fleeing from a military operation; and the death of her next two compañeros, Ricardo and then Domingo—Flor's father.

This selective process of remembering and its telling, imparted to the next generation, informs Flor's socialization, as Elsy tries to rebuild her life and negotiate a modernizing project of development and the associated consumption. Repeatedly, almost obsessively, Elsy contrasted her past to Flor's present, often doing so in earshot of her daughter. She says,

> My youth, I didn't enjoy it like Flor is enjoying it. Our youth, well we didn't enjoy it neither in schooling nor in things. Because imagine when I was that young, we didn't even have shoes. She is really having a good time. That's what I think because it may be hard, but if she says, "I want those shoes, that skirt" she gets them little by little. And she doesn't have to worry that the planes are after her, she doesn't have to suffer what I did during those times. What I want for Flor is that she not be like I was, after I had the children, because I suffered for so long when I was alone with them.

It is interesting that in my seventeen months of research and extensive interactions with Elsy and Flor, most of my ethnographic data on Flor consists of her actions. While her mother is outspoken, Flor is very quiet. *Soy penosa* she tells me, which is the cultural gloss describing women who are "not empowered": the efforts of consciousness raising—teaching women how to speak and have self-esteem—is still in process. During my research, I watched Flor's transformation from child to a young teen fully displaying her sexuality. Along with Elsy, Flor wears makeup and perfume, goes to community festivals and dances with boys, wears tight short skirts and tops, as marketed on TV. She performs well these new transnational practices of fashion-conscious teens.

But her life is complicated. She also remembers the war, has her own traumatic memories, and recalls the struggles of extreme poverty that only recently have diminished for her family since her mother's new partnership with a salaried civilian police officer. She remembers how her father Domingo died when she was seven, how from one day to the next life changed, and her father could no longer hold her. She remembers washing clothes one afternoon at the *pila* with her mother and seeing all the compañeros come up the dirt road, except for her father. As Elsy learns that Domingo was one of three men ambushed and killed in the early morning hours of combat, Flor remembers saying "now mamá, who will buy me dresses and shoes?" And she carries the picture of her father with his dark, curly hair and dark skin just like hers in her trendy black backpack along with a few colones, perfume, and a hairbrush. Along with carrying this childhood trauma, in day-to-day life it is Flor who has the obligations and responsibilities of taking over most of the household labor and care for her younger siblings. This allows Elsy in a sense to continue, although in limited ways, with a life of "activism."

Toward the end of my research, rumors began circulating about Flor and her sexual practices, how she was Chepe's woman. Her mother challenged this transition from teen girl to *mujer de un hombre* and denied the relationship. However, the rumors were true, and Flor moved into Chepe's house. Elsy's attempts were futile: beatings with a leather belt, keeping her from joining community youth projects—because they allow for less supervised interactions, as they often take place in the evenings, under cover of the dark—did not work. Shortly after the move, Flor's newborn baby died and she was left shattered. She stopped participating in community youth events, dropped out of the fifth grade; when I heard her second child was baptized she had moved from maintaining her mother's household to building her own.

I present Flor's story as neither representative nor atypical. Along with other teen girls in the community, she embodies, I suggest both a "failed" job of mothering for many women and a "failed" job of politicized consciousness raising in the formation of a new generation of citizens.[25] In Chalatenango, democratization is an ambiguous and often contentious process. Ultimately, for many teen girls and young adult women, this continued consciousness-raising project has not translated into the participation that the current generation desires, for as many parents and activists explained to me, *ya estamos cansados*—we are tired.

Conclusion

Today, Flor is a young adult living in Los Angeles. She is learning how to speak English; like many Salvadorans she sends money home to her close kin, and she has bought a car. Her experiences inspired her stepfather, Elsy's partner, and he too migrated to the United States, though to the East Coast. I have not seen Flor, though pictures show a beautiful, healthy, and happy young person.[26] I am left wondering about the meaning of her trajectory.

Taken together, my reflections provide a complementary account of a transition to democracy. My focus on the everyday, on narratives of violence and threats of violence add to the important work on comparative truth commissions (Hayner 2001), on human rights work and the search for truth (Sanford 2003), on commemorative practices (such as Silber 2004b), and on the negotiations between remembering and forgetting (i.e. Minnow 1998; Silber 2004c). This is timely, as El Salvador reenters the headlines of leading U.S. newspapers such as the *New York Times* and the *Washington Post* with clear connections between El Salvador and Iraq—"The Salvadorization of Iraq?" (Maass 2005). As journalists begin to report on the importation not only of 1980s counterinsurgency models from Central America but also the bodies of Salvadoran men, and some women, to Iraq as private security forces (Sullivan 2004), we must be attentive to how these new narratives will intersect with the quieter and uncertain stories of Martina, Sandra, Elsy, and Flor that search for justice.

NOTES

1. In this chapter, I provide pseudonyms, as requested by most people who agreed to share their time and experiences with me. See Silber (2000: 16) for further discussion of this point. Edelman (1999) also provides a concise summary of the anthropological debates on maintaining anonymity/protection of ethnographic subjects. Unless otherwise indicated, translations are mine.

2. Wood (2000) provides a convincing argument for focusing on the local logic of conflict resolution and the local challenges of constructing an enduring peace.

3. Dignas 1993, 1997; Luciak 2001; Rivera et al. 1995; Stephen et al. 2001; Vásquez et al. 1996.

4. Berryman 1984; Cabarrús 1983; Hammond 1998; Pearce 1986; Peterson 1997.

5. Cagan and Cagan 1991; Compher and Morgan 1991; Edwards and Siebentritt 1991; MacDonald and Gatehouse 1995; Schrading 1991; Thompson 1995.

6. Other scholars, though, do describe a national situation characterized by democracy in some areas (Montgomery 1995), made evident in sweeping victories by the FMLN in the March 1997 elections.

7. See Fitzsimmons (2000) for a general discussion of the contradictions of Latin American womens' movements in terms of class positioning, debatable democratic practices between "leaders" and the women they represent, strategic mistakes, political infighting, and factioning.

8. This document provides a detailed analysis of what the women's movement envisioned as still needed for gender equality—from equal pay, better working conditions, equal access to credit and land, to free education, gender training for teachers, women's literacy, to a national education campaign to address violence against women, the creation of hotlines to improving women's health, to finally assuring gender equity though a reform that would call for women to fill 50 percent of political positions from the local to national level.

9. These are not mutually exclusive categories, but rather the overlapping and blurred nature of these positions tend to characterize work on El Salvador.

10. They defining gender relations as culturally and socially constructed through time.

11. El Rancho is a pseudonym for a community in northeastern Chalatenango. The data for this section come from many ethnographic encounters during the course of my fieldwork. The quoted material is from a five-hour taped conversation on October 24, 1997. Translated transcripts appear neater than the spoken word (that is, I have cleaned up some of the repetition in the spoken language).

12. Chelito is an expression referring to the many light-skinned people in El Salvador. Chalatecos are sometimes referred to as *los indios cheles* (the white Indians).

13. Compas is a shortened version of the word *compañero*, which in English translates as *comrade*. In Chalatenango it refers to guerrilla soldiers and more generally to those supporting the struggle for justice.

14. Because of the war, many couples have not been married through the church. Rather many men and women say that they are *acompañados*. There is a recent shift by some partners to legitimize their unions as some men and women who have been together for years are turning to the Church to be married.

15. This part of the study helps to fill a gap in the literature on women's use of new democratic legal systems in their pursuit for social justice (Fitzsimmons 2000: 228). See Ready (2003) for a cogent analysis of the work of La Asociación de Madres Demandantes in organizing for women's rights in collecting child support and the tension that emerges between organizers and their constituency.

16. Meaning to engage in sexual relations with degrees of force.

17. In El Rancho, several of the single women heads of household I met during preliminary research in the summer of 1993 had by 1996 found partners—some significantly older, some younger.

18. Justice of the Peace with more duties of maintaining community conflict.

19. See Silber (2000a) for an analysis of the politics of memory.

20. Borneman 2002; Hayner 2001; Minnow 1998; Sanford 2003; Skidmore 2003.

21. For example, the fund for orphaned children covered children until their eighteenth birthday. Elsy (discussed below) had been mobilizing for her daughter since the signing of the accords in 1993. By 1997, when her daughter was already fifteen years old, she still had not received the funds as she struggled to have the legality of her case recognized. This involved getting the death certificate of her daughter's father (a cost of 300 colones), three "originals" of her daughter's birth certificate, again more money, and the father's birth certificate; he was born in another department, so she made several trips to the mayor's office there, also quite an expense from San Salvador, not to mention very tiring, having to leave her children while she did so. She also needed two witnesses and, she explained, twelve copies of everything.

22. Mujeres por la Dignidad y la Vida (Women for Dignity and Life). See Ready (2003).

23. See Molyneux (1985) for a classic and early study on how revolutionary struggles subordinate gender equity.

24. The Holocaust literature provides comparative work on this (see Langer 1991).

25. Here I engage in recent debates on the meaning of childhood, and by extension I suggest adolescence. In particular I begin to question assumptions about "lost youth" and how structural violence "reproduces a generation of children without childhood" (Scheper-Hughes, Sargent, and Sargent 1998: 15).

26. Personal communication with international human rights activist.

REFERENCES

Aguilar, Ana Leticia, et al. 1997. *Movimiento de Mujeres en Centroamerica*. Managua, Nicaragua: Programa Regional la Corriente.

Alvarez, Sonia E 1998. "Latin American Feminisms 'Go Global': Trends of the 1990s and Challenges for the New Millennium." In *Cultures of Politics Politics of Culture: Re-Visioning Latin American Social Movements*, edited by S. Alvarez, E. Dagnino, and A. Escobar. Boulder: Westview Press, 1998.

Alvarez, Sonia E., et al. 2002. "Encountering Latin American and Caribbean Feminism." *Signs* 28.2: 537–579.

Berryman, P. 1984. *The Religious Roots of Rebellion: Christians in Central American Revolutions*. Maryknoll: Orbis Books.

Borneman, John. 2002. "Reconciliation after Ethnic Cleansing: Listening, Retribution, Affiliation." *Public Culture* 14: 281–204.

Bourgois, Philippe. 2001. "The Power of Violence in War and Peace: Post–Cold War Lessons from El Salvador." *Ethnography* 2: 5–34.

Browning, D. 1971. *El Salvador: Landscape and Society*. Oxford: Clarendon Press.

Cabarrús, C. R. 1983. *Génesis de una revolución: Análisis del surgimiento y desarrollo de la organización campesina en El Salvador*. Mexico: Ediciones de la Casa Chata.

Cagan, B., and S. Cagan. 1991. *This Promised Land, El Salvador*. New Brunswick: Rutgers University Press.

Compher, V., and B. Morgan. 1991. *Going Home, Building Peace in El Salvador: The Story of Repatriation*. New York: Apex.

DIGNAS. 1993. *Hacer política desde las mujeres: Una propuesta feminista para la participación política de las mujeres salvadoreñas*. San Salvador: DIGNAS.

———. 1997. "Plataforma de las Mujeres Salvadoreñas 1997–2000." pamphlet.

Edelman, Marc. 1999. *Peasants against Globalization: Rural Social Movements in Costa Rica*. Stanford: Stanford University Press.

Edwards, B., and G. Siebentritt. 1991. *Places of Origin: The Repopulation of Rural El Salvador*. Boulder: Lynne Rienner.

Farmer, Paul. 2001 [1999]. *Infections and Inequalities: The Modern Plagues*. Berkeley: University of California Press.

Fitzsimmons, Tracy. 2000. "A Monstrous Regiment of Women?: State, Regime, and Women's Political Organizing in Latin America." *Latin American Research Review* 35.2: 216–229.

Hammond, John. 1998. *Fighting to Learn: Popular Education and Guerrilla War in El Salvador*. New Brunswick: Rutgers University Press.

Hayner, Priscilla. 2001. *Unspeakable Truths: Confronting State Terror and Atrocity*. New York: Routledge.

ISDEMU. 1997. *Politica nacional de la mujer*. San Salvador: Gobierno de El Salvador.

Langer, Lawrence. 1991. *Holocaust Testimonies: The Ruins of Memory*. New Haven: Yale University Press.

Luciak, Ilja. 2001. *After the Revolution: Gender and Democracy in El Salvador, Nicaragua, and Guatemala*. Baltimore: Johns Hopkins University Press.

Maass, Peter. 2005. "The Way of the Commandos." *New York Times Magazine*, May 1, pp. 38–47.

MacDonald, M., and M. Gatehouse. 1995. *In the Mountains of Morazán: Portrait of a Returned Refugee Community in El Salvador*. New York: Monthly Review Press.

Minnow, Martha. 1998. *Between Vengeance and Forgiveness: Facing History after Genocide and Mass Violence*. Boston: Beacon Press.

Molyneux, Maxine. 1985. "Mobilisation without Emancipation? Women's Interests, the State and Revolution in Nicaragua." *Feminist Studies* 11.2: 227–254.

Monge, José Osmin. 1997. "Mujer y trabajo: Con ahínco, esfuerzo y sacrificio." *Diario de Hoy,* March 21, pp. 97–98.

Montgomery, T. S. 1995. *Revolution in El Salvador: From Civil Strife to Civil Peace.* 2nd ed. Boulder: Westview Press.

Ortner, Sherry B. 2001. "Specifying Agency: The Comaroffs and Their Critics." *Interventions* 3.1: 76–84.

Paley, Julia. 2001. *Marketing Democracy: Power and Social Movements in Post-Dictatorship Chile.* Berkeley: University of California Press.

Pearce, J. 1986. *Promised Land: Peasant Revolution in Chalatenango, El Salvador.* London: Latin America Bureau.

Peterson, Ann. 1997. *Martyrdom and the Politics of Religion: Progressive Catholicism in El Salvador's Civil War.* Albany: State University of New York Press.

Ready, Kelley. 2003. "Child Support as a Strategic Interest: La Asociación de Madres Demandantes of El Salvador." *Gender and Development* 11.2: 60–69.

Rivera, K., et al. 1995. *¿Valió la pena?: Testimonios de salvadoreñas que vivieron la guerra.* San Salvador: Editorial Sombrero Azul.

Sanford, Victoria. 2003. *Buried Secrets: Truth and Human Rights in Guatemala.* New York: Palgrave Macmillan.

Scheper-Hughes, Nancy, and Carolyn Sargent. 1998. "Introduction: The Cultural Politics of Childhood." In *Small Wars: The Cultural Politics of Childhood,* edited by N. Scheper-Hughes and C. Sargent. Berkeley: University of California Press.

Schrading, R. 1991. *Exodus en América latina: El movimiento de repoblación en El Salvador.* San José, Costa Rica: Instituto Interamericano de Derechos Humanos (IIDH).

Silber, Irina Carlota. 2000. "A Spectral Reconciliation: Rebuilding Post-War El Salvador." Ph.D. dissertation, New York University.

———. 2004a. "Mothers/Fighters/Citizens: Violence and Disillusionment in Postwar El Salvador." *Gender and History* 16.3: 561–587.

———. 2004b. "Commemorating the Past in Postwar El Salvador." In *Memory and the Impact of Political Transformation in Public Space,* edited by Daniel J. Walkowitz and Lisa Knauer. Durham: Duke University Press.

———. 2004c. "Not Revolutionary Enough?: Community Rebuilding in Postwar Chalatenango." In *Landscapes of Struggle: Politics, Society, and Community in El Salvador,* edited by A. Lauria-Santiago and L. Binford. Pittsburgh: University of Pittsburgh Press, 2004.

Skidmore, Monique. 2003. "Darker than Midnight: Fear, Vulnerability, and Terror Making in Urban Burma (Mynamar)." *American Ethnologist* 30: 5–21.

Spence, J., et al. 1997. *Chapúltepec: Five Years Later: El Salvador's Political Reality and Uncertain Future.* Cambridge, MA: Hemisphere Initiatives.

Stephen, Lynn. 1997. *Women and Social Movements in Latin America: Power from Below.* Austin: University of Texas Press.

Stephen, Lynn, Carol A. Ready, and Serena Cosgrove. 2001. "Women's Organization in El Salvador: History, Accomplishments and International Support." In *Women and Civil War: Impact, Organizations and Action,* edited by Krishna Kumar. Boulder: Lynne Reinner Press.

Sullivan, Kevin. 2004. "Poor Salvadorans Chase the 'Iraqi Dream': U.S. Security Firms Find Eager Recruits among Former Soldiers, Police Officers." *Washington Post,* December 9, A24.

Thompson, M. 1995. "Repopulated Communities in El Salvador." In *The New Politics of Survival: Grassroots Movements in Central America*, edited by M. Sinclair. NY: Monthly Review Press.

Vázquez, Norma, et al. 1996. *Mujeres montaña: Vivencias de guerrilleras y colaboradoras del FMLN*. Spain: Horas y HORAS la Editorial.

Wood, Elisabeth J. 2000. *Forging Democracy from Below: Contested Transitions in South Africa and El Salvador*. Cambridge: Cambridge University Press.

PART FOUR

The Engaged Observer, Inside and Outside the Academy

11

Perils and Promises of Engaged Anthropology

Historical Transitions and Ethnographic Dilemmas

KAY B. WARREN

Scandals tell us as much about the present as they do about the past.[1] Anthropology's scandals at the turn of the twenty-first century—including the Tierney-Neel-Chagnon-Turner dispute about research ethics in the Amazon, the David Stoll exposé questioning the veracity of Nobel Peace Prize winner Rigoberta Menchú's personal accounts of state violence, and David Price's historical critique of the American Anthropological Association's policies toward the alleged involvement of anthropologists in espionage and covert research—have something in common, even as their particulars differ.[2] Each is marked by traces of the Cold War and ipso facto makes the case that legacies of the past live on in the present (see also Chomsky et al. 1997).

These and other contemporary debates provide windows onto the issue of engaged anthropological research. Today's engagement for many cultural anthropologists involves investigations that consider such issues as social justice, inequality, subaltern challenges to the status quo, globalization's impacts, and the ethical positioning of our field research in situations of violent conflict. In addition to raising more general questions about Cold War legacies, this chapter considers the dilemmas faced by anthropologists of different historical generations who write about state and rebel violence, rights struggles, poverty, and the divergent politics of social movements in Latin America, particularly in Guatemala. My hope is that this approach will resonate in interesting ways with those working elsewhere.

This analysis affirms as integral aspects of our ethnographic project the importance of examining our roles as anthropologists and assessing the political and intellectual contexts in which we pursue our research and teaching. It discusses the underappreciated work of public intellectuals and scholars in the societies we study, a history of engagement that has been obscured in mainstream

Western accounts of anthropological thought and ethics. I conclude that we have much to learn from refusing to idealize twenty-first-century engaged anthropology even as we celebrate its rich possibilities.

There are important epistemological issues for anthropology at this historical juncture, given the diffuse influence of postmodern framings of anthropological field research and writing. Many anthropologists now embrace a more fluid, nonessentialized view of identity and recognize the partiality and interestedness of any observer's account of social life. As a result, our studies incorporate the observer within the scope of the study. No longer is there an authentic or comprehensively true image of social and cultural groups, no singular language of protest and revindication, but rather partial, shifting, and clashing representations, each with its own paradoxes and erasures. As Mona Rosendahl and Steffan Löfving reminded me in our discussions of these issues at the University of Stockholm in 2004, it has become problematic to assert a unitary solution for a "cultural whole" that does not exist.

Cold War Legacies and Historical Generations

The period since the late 1980s has been a time of remarkable transition for global politics, the discipline of anthropology, and Latin American countries. Finding new critical positionings after the Cold War has been an issue for scholars and activists across the political spectrum. The polarized wartime grammar of revolutionary socialism versus violent anticommunism has given way in many quarters to a grammar of transnationalism, antiglobalization movements, and rights and identity struggles at odds with elite-driven nationalism (Trouillot 2001; Nash 2004; Jackson and Warren 2005). This has also been a time of social fragmentation, economic instability, and mounting everyday violence.

The end of the Cold War did not mark a linear or definitive shift to a new world order. Rather, much unfinished business was left for the practice of anthropology in the United States, the dynamics of the societies we study, and American domestic politics. Michael Kearney (1996) argues that regional studies and peasant studies—both formative aspects of cultural anthropology—owe much of their genesis to U.S. responses to the Cold War. The shorthand anthropologists most often use to signal the political context of the face-to-face communities they study—the nation-state within regionalized systems of nation-states—was a product of decolonization negotiated in a world characterized by U.S.-Soviet Union polarization (Falk 2001). This state- and region-centric discourse has profound ramifications for scholars as national borders define what we read ("I do Mexico, Guatemala, and Peru but not . . .") and how we identify our special interests (as a colleague at another institution commented, "I don't really read outside Mesoamerica"). Or how graduate students specializing in one world region respond when they are asked to read literature on another area in a sustained way ("Do I really have to write about Japan?" worried a Latin Americanist in my Pacific Rim seminar).[3] There is an irony here, because many anthropologists are eagerly and critically consuming works on globalization and transnationalism.[4] From the 1960s on, cultural anthropology has been an intrinsically multisited field of inquiry.

Whatever our politics, my own historical generation, born at the close of WWII, and the generation above are veterans of the Cold War. It shaped our research agendas, what most of us felt we could study, and what we could not. It stigmatized certain topics and approaches. ("Where will I file that little red book on my bookshelves?" "Is so-and-so really a card-carrying communist?" "Will there be fallout from the mid-1970s government surveillance of our feminist protests in New Haven and elsewhere?") In the 1960s and 1970s, the leftist versus liberal democratic cleavage in academics and activism overdetermined norms of inclusion and exclusion in research networks operating in Latin America and beyond. Political and scholarly endogamy prevailed in many quarters. These norms informed tenure and promotion decisions, given that there was much partisanship and complex subdivisions multiplied on both sides in the social sciences. The thematic hybridity evident in individual anthropological works from that period—the concern with cultural issues on the part of some leftists and class issues on the part of some liberals—is evidence of individualized academic independence in the face of competing orthodoxies. This dynamic is perhaps best understood when it is historicized to reveal how the varying intensity of polarization made more or less room for heterodox approaches. There is ample evidence of damaged or ruined careers across these cleavages in both directions.[5]

I am fascinated by how unaware undergraduate students are of this history. For many of them, the Cuban missile crisis, communism, the Vietnam war, socialist experiments in Latin America, the contras, and scandalous moments of U.S. intervention to topple regimes it disagreed with in Latin America are ancient history at best. My first-year students at Harvard in 2002 were born in 1984; they would have had to been born a decade earlier to have experienced the fall of the Berlin Wall in their early adolescence.[6] Former Senator Bob Kerrey's pressured revelation in 2001 of his wartime massacre of Vietnamese civilians, including women, children, and old men, thirty-two years before as a twenty-five-year-old, is a powerful reminder of the haunting quality of repressed experiences from the Cold War period (Vistica 2001). So is Joseph Ellis's secret about the fictional quality of his Vietnam combat stories, recounted to generations of rapt undergraduates in his college course on the American war in Vietnam (Robinson 2001; Robin 2004).

The generation one belongs to is a crucial but often neglected aspect of anthropological analysis and our experience as teachers. This finding argues for a genealogical approach—not just to the study of key figures and concepts in anthropological theory but also for the ethnographic situations we study and our subjectivity as analysts. Although Kerrey's and Ellis's stories seem wedded to a distant past, Jacob Weisburg (1999) draws our attention to the day-to-day relevance long after the Cold War of polarized discourse on both sides of the U.S. conservative-progressive divide; this political language hides more than it reveals about contemporary domestic politics as it is repeatedly evoked. The self is objective, patriotic, and "with us," as opposed to the other who is a politicized, radical, and dangerous force "against us." The repeated eruption of "culture wars" in U.S. domestic politics, signaled by rightist attacks on progressives in the academy and journalism, has shifted from the struggle over custody of young Elián González, who in 2000 lost his mother as they fled from Cuba to Florida, to the questioning of the patriotism of individual professors during the Afghanistan war in 2001–2002, and on to the punishing repression of dissent during the Iraq War. Targeting of intellectuals as disloyal and dangerous is available as a political weapon whenever it seems useful to one or another faction of the self-constituted mainstream. This troubling face of nationalism can be seen outside the United States as well.

The post-Cold War transition has left complex legacies in the conflicts anthropologists study around the globe. For instance, Jennifer Schirmer (1998) crafted a new form of political ethnography to demonstrate how the Guatemalan army reinvented itself a decade after the anticommunist counterinsurgency war of the late 1970s and early 1980s. As a self-professed partner in national development, the army now holds fast to its early monopoly as the guardian of national security charged with identifying and combating enemies of the state. Discourses of "the enemy within" remain available whenever the army decides to evoke these powers.

In Latin America, social movements have played an important role in the transition to democracy (however problematic democracy has been) as they have developed social critiques and activism to challenge both the contradictory currents of neoliberal political and economic change and the limits on the inclusion of political minorities in liberal society. For example, in Guatemala, the Pan-Mayan movement has sought national reforms in government that officially recognize and empower the indigenous majority of the nation's citizens. The movement was shaped by the deep historical interplay of ethnic and class stratification in Guatemala, unfinished business from Central America's socialist revolutions, United Nations multicultural norms for participatory democracy, and Western pressures for neoliberal economic reforms.

Indigenous public intellectuals have generated new lines of research that defy disciplinary boundaries. Maya scholar-activists such as Demetrio Cojtí Cuxil (1995, 1996, 1997) and Victor Montejo (1999, 2005); linguistic research groups such as OKMA (1993); and editorial columnists in Guatemala's major daily newspapers, including Estuardo Zapeta (1999), Enrique Sam Colop, and Victor Montejo, have produced social criticism for different audiences. In seeking a wider role for the indigenous majority, Mayan critics have focused on the genocidal racism of the war and challenged conventional assumptions of a monocultural national society rationalized by ladino and elite Euro-Guatemalan nonindigenous racism. A younger generation, including Irma Alicia Velásquez Nimatuj (2005), is challenging these activists to refocus on the rural underclasses. These scholars certainly fit the definition of engaged researchers, and some of them, including Montejo, Zapeta, and Velásquez, are anthropologists.

Since the late 1980s, indigenous activists have confronted foreign researchers about their research practices, particularly scholarly conventions that cast indigenous peoples as informants and the objects of research rather than as protagonists and peer researchers. It is important to note that the pressure to reexamine research practices and ethics has come from politicized indigenous organizations rather than from foreign supporters. It has also come from anti-imperialist critics sympathetic to indigenous issues and research groups like FLACSO. This multifaceted pressure has lead to important changes in research methodologies, academic agendas, and modes of engagement by international investigators (Warren 1998; Warren and Jackson 2002; Hale 2005).

An important current of engaged anthropology that identifies with grass-roots left struggles and Mayan cultural revindication, however, criticizes polarized representations of ladino domination and Maya ethnic marginalization for their neglect of impoverished ladinos and erasure of elite Euro-Guatemalan power. At the heart of this critique is a concern with Guatemala's severe rural poverty (Casáus Arzú and Elena 1992; Arenas Bianchi et al. 1999; Smith 2005; Velásquez Nimatuj 2005).

Anthropology faces a stunning paradox, especially for those of us who have studied subaltern groups struggling for cultural recognition in the face of political and economic marginalization. As the deconstruction of ethnic polarities gains currency in the discipline, the question is how one works on racism, cultural and linguistic pluralism, fluid ethnic identifications, and many people's experience of what they perceive as ethnic polarization in their lives. At issue, beyond documenting the genesis and impact of racism's degradation and violence, is how to represent social movements and national policy in the post-dichotomized global context, when debates are no longer between socialist rebels and rightist authoritarian dictators (Warren 2002b; Warren and Jackson 2002; and Jackson and Warren 2005).

One school of thought, represented by Carol Smith's recent work (2005), argues that "elite-focused" research misses the authentic Maya, the illiterate rural poor, with their own strategies and revindications, who gained little or nothing from the economic opportunities of Guatemala's peace negotiations and internationally financed postwar reconstruction. International funding, in fact, supported indigenous efforts to promote diverse lines of cultural revitalization, indigenous rights, and multilingual education. Scholarships, specialized training, and white-collar jobs became available, as never before, to a small but growing class of Mayas with access to high school who aspired to university training and professional jobs in urban-based organizations, and their rural counterparts. Smith questions the legitimacy of research done on internationally funded urban Mayan activist groups, Maya social critics and research centers, and Maya involvement as public intellectuals in international forums—despite the fact that many groups had rural agendas. By contrast, other ethnographers such as Diane Nelson (1999), Quetzil Castañeda (2004), and myself (1998) have used a variety of social-historical and postmodern perspectives to argue that there are many ways of being Maya, that no single sector can represent the whole, and that the point of anthropology is to capture multiple views of subaltern groups rather than to freeze any community in a formulaic engagement with the world.[7]

Another perspective is that we need to move beyond the antagonisms of the past to grapple with new issues: gang violence, alienation, and the mass marketing to the urban underclasses of commodities from foreign clothing styles to mood-altering drugs; the globalization of popular culture that undercuts local authority and parental status in the eyes of many youths and their parents; and consumer expectations and forms of employment that, as they respond to transnational media and forms of production, are independent of local space (García Canclini 2000). These generational ruptures have been more acute in places like Guatemala as a result of the dislocations of the counterinsurgency war. Twenty percent of the national population was displaced from their homes between 1978 and 1985, most dramatically when the army took up its scorched-earth campaign designed to cut off incipient civilian support of the guerrillas (Manz 1988; Schirmer 1998; Montejo 1999). Many refugees from the rural communities of the Mayan western highlands fled to neighboring countries and ultimately to the United States. Others fled to the capital city or to remote communities of refuge where, without land or security, they faced terrible deprivation (Manz 1988). The trajectory of these social transformations is a multigenerational and a transnational one, with a proliferation of youth gangs in Guatemalan towns originating from established gangs in the United States and the flow of return migrants through countries such as El Salvador and Mexico (Wallace 2000).

This globalization is not an abstraction or product of the wonders of the Internet, but rather a reflection of concrete social histories. It has roots in the Cold War, when Guatemalan state policy sought to exterminate socialist rebels and preemptively punish civilians who were their potential recruits. The result of violent ethnic targeting and terrible economic instability was an international diaspora of Mayas, a significant number of whom found menial jobs in the United States. Their children are English-speaking Americans, who grew up translating for their parents. Refugee workers who endured American economic and social racism have contributed to a surging remittance economy directed to their hometowns. Others have brought home HIV from work sites in California to unprepared highland communities. Some children of the diaspora have found new religious support abroad and returned to convert Catholics to evangelical Christianity. This history also transcends the Cold War in that today's youth know little of their parents' war and, rather, exist in a world driven by a globalized experience of highly self-conscious haves and have-nots.

Given the globalization and urbanization of Guatemalan culture, some anthropologists now ask: Why get caught up in the past, the essentialized language of Maya cultural revitalization and rights, when the urgent issue for anthropology, if it is to be relevant, is rural poverty and urban violence for a youthful generation that has a weak commitment to Maya leadership norms, languages, and communal religion? Anthropology needs to engage land tensions, drugs, street children, urban poverty, prostitution, HIV. And perhaps to pursue the ironies of newly acquired coffee plantations and swimming pools—being developed in remote communities by return migrants with newly found wealth from pariah jobs in the United States, which in today's Guatemala trump the status and earnings of local professionals. Longer histories reveal the precariousness of that wealth, invested in local coffee farms that suddenly failed with the 2001 glut of cheaper Vietnamese coffee on the international market. If one is to focus on cultural issues in this environment, discontinuities not invented continuities are the rightful business of contemporary anthropology (Euraque et al. 2004; Hale 2004, 2005; Warren 2002b).

A third line of analysis argues that we still need to revisit the past to reveal hidden histories from the Cold War. For Guatemala and beyond, this project involves historical recuperation to document the full impact of state violence. Studies have centered on the truth commissions, set up by the state and by the Catholic Church (CEH 1999; REMHI 1998), and on forensic anthropology that has heroically sought to document massacres in order to create a historical record for the families of the disappeared and the military which has never taken responsibility (Sanford 2003). Now the complex history of the clandestine left, known but unreported by sympathetic foreign anthropologists, is being documented. This revisionism gained wider audiences after David Stoll's (1999) attacks on Rigoberta Menchú in the 1990s (replies to Stoll in Arias 2001; Warren 2001). Beatriz Manz (2005) and Carlotta McAllister (forthcoming), among others, have done important new field research on rural communities that produced rebel militants during the civil war of the late 1970s and 1980s. Just as notable are the oral histories of the former militants who speak more openly, as Mayas, of the racism within the guerrilla movement. These experiences were suppressed by wartime politics that called for ideological unity within the rebel opposition.

A final line of analysis seeks to show the relevance of earlier struggles for the present. Some of the most interesting currents of anthropology are coming out of Chiapas from anthropologists such as June Nash, Lynn Stephen, Shannon Speed, Aída Hernández, Christine Eber, Christine Kovic, John Watanabe, and Edward Fischer.[8] In these powerful contemporary accounts, land scarcity for rural families and communities is interwoven with the impact of neoliberalism, the ripple effects of NAFTA regionalization, state violence in the face of regional organizing, internalized violence in rural communities, and the stillborn status of serious peace negotiations during the Fox administration. June Nash (2001) narrates this transition in southern Mexico as the birth of the Zapatista post-Cold War Maya Left, which became a sophisticated post-Marxist global actor. Their alternative democratic politics incorporates the highly participatory norms of community consensus decision making and Maya cosmology with the global language of human rights. It has been created through a pan-community social movement that actively sought regional autonomy. Stephen (2001) narrates this as a case of rural opposition to state-focused counterinsurgency violence, corruption, and cynical land politics, negotiated through the powerful but contested imagery of the early revolutionary hero Emilio Zapata. It is fascinating that Eastern European democracy movements have seen the Zapatistas as exemplars of what they are trying to accomplish.[9]

Cross-cutting these projects has been a concern with retooling the interpersonal politics of research, with the growing sense that field research involves an engagement with local agendas, criticism of anthropological practices as they reveal wider structural asymmetries, the obligation to share findings with the communities studied early in the research process, and the self-reflexive commitment to include one's own presence as an object of ethnographic inquiry. Informed consent in this construction ideally becomes a much more interactive process subject to longer-term negotiation, reciprocities, and collaboration (see England and Elliot 1990; Warren 1998; Sanford 2003). Unfortunately, the bureaucratization and standardization of research ethics of state-controlled university research boards in the United States, which inappropriately use scientific clinical trials as their ethical template, renders these collaborative and politically responsive practices "unethical."

Challenges of Writing Engaged Anthropology

Let me now turn to a consideration of some of the challenges I see for engaged anthropology. Despite the use of demonizing discourses by President George W. Bush, the contrast between good and bad guys not as clear as it once appeared to be. For researchers, the issue is how we write credible, critical, sympathetic social science without reproducing older polarizing discourses, without idealizing social movements or demonizing and essentializing at least one party in our social analysis.[10] Some anthropologists warn against "humanizing power" or investigating the troubling micropolitics within social movements. In response, others have self-critically asked about the consequences of this analytic and political choice, this form of self-censorship. Does it meant that whole domains of social life have been, in effect, off the table for richer ethnographic analysis?

It is also time to come to terms with the romanticization of our own roles in situations of conflict. As the use of the exposé and *testimonio* genres increases, the temptation has been for anthropologists to position themselves heroically in ethnographic accounts. This self-positioning hides the reality that most of us are part-time observers who offer pieces of a puzzle that may collectively generate wider truths through a process of accumulating knowledge from multiple perspectives.

In ethnography, self-aggrandizing and heroic voices come from across the political spectrum and from anthropology's subfields. Used as a tactic to establish the narrator's authority, these portrayals stimulate reader fascination by tapping popular culture's fascination with the outlier. The relentless expository character of these works often limits their capacity for self-reflection, however—for questioning the neutrality of all observers, including themselves (Nichols 1994). When research thus becomes an individualized process of discovery, there is often a failure to acknowledge scholarly networks and lines of transnational solidarity that provide the basis upon which innovative findings and activism are constructed.

In the early 2000s, the tension in anthropology between activism and social science took a new turn with the Rigoberta Menchú and research ethics scandals. I noticed a linguistic shift during the Tierney/Neel/Chagnon/Turner debates and the Stoll exposé from "science" conceived of as noninterference versus "activism," to "science" versus a demeaned "moral" commitment to rights and "relativism" (the latter issues being cast as politically compromised and uncritical). This is a polarizing polemic for many of us who find ourselves in the middle, concerned with both politics and moral dilemmas, with bearing witness and seeking wider justice along with rigorous ethnography of the local (Warren 2001).

In the post-Cold War order, many anthropologists want to find forums for engaged anthropology that speak to issues of concern to wider audiences, not just to in-house scholarly debates. Each of us would make his or her own list of these issues. High on my list of topics would be ethnographies of international development with more complicated politics and goals than conventional discourse and structural analyses allow. Anna Tsing's *Friction* (2005) and Timothy Mitchell's *Rule of Experts* (2002) are provocative examples of the second wave of these issues in anthropology. I believe that there is an important place in anthropology for investigations of the great powers, emerging economic blocs of states, and transnational development strategies in this postnational moment, issues that in the past were ceded to other disciplines such as political science. Their incorporation raises important theoretical and methodological issues for the field.

Perhaps more of us should follow the lead of anthropologists who are studying the interrelation of liberal politics and neoliberal economics in order to understand in ethnographic terms the relation of cultural politics to poverty. Here Julia Paley's insightful work (2001) on the marketing of democracy in Chile comes to mind. In 2005, a group of anthropologists joined Paley at the School of American Research to pursue comparative and transnational studies of democracy, in order to decenter the issue of democratic ideals and investigate on-the-ground democratic practice in very different situations.

At issue is what anthropological analysis can reveal about the human cost and micropolitics of local experiences of poverty, political agency, and depoliticization, on the one hand, and the expectations and practices of development aid agents and governmental officials who market their yardsticks of international norms, on the other hand. The goal is to capture the heterogeneity of experience so that our interpretations are more than the reflection of our politics, be they on the left, right, or elsewhere. A younger generation of anthropologists, such as Clara Han and Miriam Shakow, is focusing on poverty's interconnectedness with democratic politics and neoliberalism through innovative field research on these issues.

Also on my list is the interrelation of weak states, which demonstrate the capacity for great violence, and globalization, which defies state borders and sovereignty (see the work of Carolyn Nordstrom 2004). The proliferation of violent regional crises has not only created donor exhaustion (Moeller 1999), as financially struggling progressive NGOs from the Cold War era tell us. It has also generated audiences for anthropological studies of what lies behind the "obvious" violence of cultural difference and fundamentalism.[11] The question is how we might find better ways to connect our readers to issues surging outside their immediate social world and interests—and how we might foster a more sophisticated consumption of works by commentators in the U.S. media. In an innovative move, Hugh Gusterson and Catherine Besteman (2004) brought together a group of anthropologists to publish critical readings of the works of major public intellectuals such as Samuel Huntington, Robert Kaplan, and Thomas Friedman. This work complements and updates other studies of mass media and their representations of culture, ethnicity, war, and political economy around the world (Allen and Seaton 1999).

Finally, for those who value engagement, it is time to come to new understandings of what makes good anthropology. Is it our contribution to high theory? Is it, as Rob Borovsky suggested in a lecture at Harvard in 2001, fighting over the same ethnographic evidence to find *the essential truth*? Is it, as generations of anthropologists have practiced, dismissive and decontextualized critiques that show the weaknesses of our elders in order to heighten our sense of accomplishment? Is it a zero sum game between competing perspectives and subfields? Is it poaching the issues of other fields in the sciences and humanities?

Alternatively, could one imagine engaged anthropologists taking on globally significant issues through comparative arguments, however partial and suggestive, so that others understand the wider significance of our particular findings? In this event, future success hinges less on changing what we do in terms of meaning-centered and politically informed field research than in developing a new self-consciousness about how we do it, and identifying new issues, powerful questions, and innovative framings through which to assert the salience of our well-honed approaches to real-world issues. Finally, we must wrestle with the ever-critical question of how to keep alive the pluralism that has been central to our intellectual project in the face of institutional insecurities about the academy's future in our society.

NOTES

1. My thanks to the participants in the 2000 AAA panel for stimulating discussions of this issue as it unfolds for different kinds of researchers throughout the world. Special thanks to Lynn Stephen for excellent feedback and to Mona Rosendahl and Staffan Lövfing for inspiring exchanges.

2. See Tierney (2000) for the initial journalist's account of unethical behavior on the part of scientists and social scientists, including biological anthropologists, in the Amazon; the University of Michigan and AAA Web sites for the controversy that exploded within the subdisciplines of anthropology; See Stoll (1999) for charges that Rigoberta Menchú falsified some events in her famous testimony of military violence against civilians during the Guatemala's counterinsurgency war of early 1980s, and Arias (2001) for a collection of responses to Stoll. See Price (2000) on the issue of anthropologists as spies, a scandal with deep historical roots that did not achieve much traction at this historical moment. Price criticizes anthropology for failing to develop an adequate institutional response to anthropologists who engage in secretive government research or espionage.

3. Later in the seminar, another student argued that cross-regional framings and comparative anthropology risk stripping regions of the specifics of their colonial histories and current political contexts.

4. On transnationalism, for example, see Appadurai (1996), García Canclini (2000), Escobar (1995), and Ferguson (1994), Ong (1999), and Nordstrom (2004). Cultural anthropology came early to the issue of globalization through studies of colonialism (Wolf 1982; Taussig 1980, 1987; and Stoller 1985, for example), through research on decolonization and the emergence of new states in the 1960s (Geertz 1973), and later with the study of multinational corporations and the *maquiladora* mode of production in the 1970s (Nash and Fernandez-Kelly 1983). Perhaps it is more accurate to say that cultural anthropology's fascination with the global has come in waves.

5. On the ethnography of historical generations, see Holland and Leve (2001), Warren (1998), and Reed-Donahay (1997).

6. This chapter raises painful issues, and I have decided purposely not to single out individuals by name at several key junctures.

7. Smith (2005) uses an interesting approach in this critique. On the one hand, she adopts postmodern analytical language common in anthropology (discourse analysis,

identity as a construction, and critiques of essentialism); on the other hand, she argues that there is one real (essential) movement, centered on the rural poor, and that focusing on other elements of Maya politics is a mistake that risks endangering the Maya. See Warren (2005) for a more sustained engagement.

8. See Eber and Kovic (2003) and Watanabe and Fischer (2004) for important collections.

9. Personal communication from Maple Razsa.

10. One of the best examples of this reassessment is the two-volume work on social movements in Latin America produced by Escobar and Alvarez (1992) and Alvarez, Dagnino, and Escobar (1998). See also Warren and Jackson (2002), Warren (2002b), and Gustafson (2001) on essentialism, subaltern political strategies, and micro-politics and self-censorship.

11. Of course "the obvious" phenomenon of violence is not a unmediated experience for the wider public, but rather represents views influenced by lines of argument such as Huntington's "clash of civilizations" argument (1996), Kaplan's "anarchy" without strong states argument (2000), and Beck's cognitive and social psychology argument (1999).

REFERENCES

Allen, Tim, and Jean Seaton, eds. 1999. *The Media of Conflict: War Reporting and Representations of Ethnic Conflict*. London: Zed Books.

Alvarez, Sonia, Evelina Dagnino, and Arturo Escobar, eds. 1998. *Cultures of Politics/Politics of Culture: Revisioning Latin American Social Movements*. Boulder: Westview Press.

Appadurai, Arjun. 1996. *Modernity at Large: Cultural Dimensions of Globalization*. Minneapolis: University of Minnesota Press.

Arenas Bianchi, Clara, Charles R. Hale, and Gustavo Palma Murga. 1999. *Racismo en Guatemala; Abriendo debate sobre un tema tabú*. Guatemala: AVANCSO.

Arias, Arturo, ed. 2001. *The Rigoberta Menchú Controversy*. Indianapolis: University of Indiana Press.

Beck, Aaron T. 1999. *Prisoners of Hate*. New York: HarperCollins.

Casáus Arzú and Marta Elena. 1992. *Guatemala: Linaje y racismo*. San José: FLACSO.

Castañeda, Quetzil. 2004. "We Are Not Indigenous! The Maya Identity of the Yucatan, an Introduction." *Journal of Latin American Anthropology* 9.1: 36–63.

CEH, Guatemalan Commission for Historical Clarification. 1999. *Guatemala: Memory of Silence Tz'inil Na'tab'al*. Washington: American Association for the Advancement of Science. hrdata.aaas.org/ceh/report.

Chomsky, Noam, et al. 1997. *The Cold War and the University: Toward an Intellectual History of the Postwar Years*. New York: New Press.

Cojtí Cuxil, Demetrio. 1995. *Ub'aniik Ri Una'ooj Uchomab'aal Ri Maya' Tinamit; Confirguración del pensamiento político del Pueblo Maya*. Part 2. Guatemala: Seminario Permanente de Estudios Mayas and Editorial Cholsamaj.

———. 1996. "The Politics of Mayan Revindication." In *Mayan Cultural Activism in Guatemala*, edited by Edward Fischer and R. McKenna Brown. Austin: University of Texas Press.

———. 1997. *Ri Maya' Moloj pa Iximulew; El movimiento Maya (en Guatemala)*. Guatemala: Editorial Cholsamaj.

Eber, Christine, and Christine Kovic, eds. 2003. *Women of Chiapas: Making History in Times of Struggle and Hope*. New York: Routledge.

England, Nora C., and Stephen R. Elliot, eds. 1990. *Lecturas sobre la lingüística Maya*. Guatemala: Centro de Investigaciones Regionales de Mesoamérica.

Escobar, Arturo. 1995. *Encountering Development: The Making and Unmaking of the Third World*. Princeton: Princeton University Press.

Escobar, Arturo, and Sonia Alvarez, eds. 1992. *The Making of Social Movements in Latin America: Identity, Strategy, and Democracy*. Boulder: Westview Press.

Euraque, Dario, Jeffrey Gould, and Charles R. Hale. 2004. *Memoiras del mestizaje: Cultura y política en Centroamérica, 1920 al presente*. Guatemala: CIRMA/Cholsamaj.

Falk, Richard. 2001. "Self-Determination under International Law: The Coherence of Doctrine versus the Incoherence of Experience." In *The Self-Determination of Peoples: Community, Nation, and State in an Interdependent World*, edited by Wolfgang Danspeckgruber. Boulder: Lynne Rienner.

Ferguson, James. 1994. *The Anti-Politics Machine: "Development," Depoliticization, and Bureaucratic Power in Lesotho*. Minneapolis: University of Minnesota Press.

García Canclini, Néstor. 2000. *Consumers and Citizens: Globalization and Multicultural Conflicts*. Minneapolis: University of Minnesota Press.

Geertz, Clifford. 1973. *The Interpretation of Cultures*. New York: Basic Books.

Gustafson, Bret. 2001. "Native Languages and Hybrid States: A Political Ethnography of Guarani Engagements with Bilingual Education Reform in Bolivia, 1989–1999." Ph.D. dissertation, Harvard University Department of Anthropology.

Gusterson, Hugh, and Catherine Besteman, eds. 2004. *Why American Pundits Are Wrong: Anthropologists Talk Back*. Berkeley: University of California Press.

Hale, Charles R. 2004. "Rethinking Indigenous Politics in the Era of the "Indio Permitido." *NACLA* 38.1: 16–20.

———. 2005. *Mas que un indio . . . Racial Ambivalence and the Paradox of Neoliberal Multiculturalism in Guatemala*. Santa Fe: School of American Research Press.

Holland, Dorothy, and Jean Leve, eds. 2001. *History in Person*. Santa Fe: School of American Research.

Huntington, Samuel. 1996. *The Clash of Civilizations and the Remaking of the World Order*. New York: Simon and Schuster.

Jackson, Jean E., and Kay B. Warren. 2005. "Indigenous Movements in Latin America, 1992–2004: Controversies, Ironies, and New Directions." *Annual Reviews of Anthropology* 34: 549–573.

Kaplan, Robert D. 2000. *The Coming Anarchy: Shattering the Dreams of the Post Cold War*. New York: Vintage.

Kearney, Michael. 1996. *Reconceptualizing the Peasantry: Anthropology in Global Perspective*. Boulder: Westview Press.

Manz, Beatriz. 1988. *Refugees of a Hidden War: The Aftermath of Counterinsurgency Guatemala*. Albany: State University of New York Press.

———. 2004. *Paradise in Ashes: A Guatemalan Journey of Courage, Terror, and Hope*. Berkeley: University of California Press.

McAllister, Carota. Forthcoming. *The Good Road: Conscience and consciousness in a Post-Revolutionary Maya Village*. Durham: Duke University Press.

Mitchell, Timothy. 2002. *Rule of Experts: Egypt, Techno-Politics, Modernity*. Berkeley: University of California Press.

Moeller, Susan D. 1999. *Compassion Fatigue: How the Media Sell Disease, Famine, War and Death*. New York: Routledge.

Montejo, Victor. 1999. *Voices from Exile: Violence and Survival in Modern Maya History*. Norman: University of Oklahoma Press.

———. 2005. *Maya Intellectual Renaissance: Identity, Representation, and Leadership*. Austin: University of Texas Press.

Nash, June. 2001. *Mayan Visions: The Quest for Autonomy in an Age of Globalization*. New York: Routledge.

———. 2004. *Social Movements: An Anthropological Reader*. Oxford: Blackwell Publishers.

Nash, June, and María Patricia Fernández-Kelly, eds. 1983. *Women, Men, and the International Division of Labor*. Albany: State University of New York Press.

Nelson, Diane. 1999. *A Finger in the Wound: Body Politics in Quincentennial Guatemala*. Berkeley: University of California Press.

Nichols, Bill. 1994. *Blurred Boundaries: Questions of Meaning in Contemporary Culture*. Bloomington: University of Indiana Press.

Nordstrom, Carolyn R. 2004. *Shadows of War: Violence, Power, and International Profiteering in the Twenty-First Century*. Berkeley: University of California Press.

Ong, Aihwa. 1999. *Flexible Citizenship*. Durham: Duke University Press.

———. 2000. "Graduated Sovereignty in Southeastern Asia." *Theory, Culture, and Sovereignty*. 17.4: 55–75.

OKMA (Oxlajuuj Keej Mayab' Ajtz'iib' [Ajpub', Ixkem, Lolmay, Nik'te', Pakal, Saqijix, and Waykan]) 1993. *Maya' Chii'; Idiomas Mayas de Guatemala*. Guatemala: Editorial Cholsamaj.

Paley, Julia. 2001. *Marketing Democracy: Power and Social Movements in Post-Dictatorship Chile*. Berkeley: University of California Press.

Price, David. 2000. "Anthropologists as Spies." *The Nation*, November 20.

Reed-Donahay, Deborah, ed. 1997. *Auto/Ethnography: Rewriting Self and the Social*." Oxford: Berg.

REMHI, Proyecto Interdiocesano de Recuperación de la Memoría Histórica. 1998. *Guatemala: Nunca Más*. Guatemala: Oficina de Derechos Humanos del Arzobispado de Guatemala (ODHA).

Riles, Annelise. 2001. *The Network Inside Out*. Ann Arbor: University of Michigan Press.

Robin, Ron. 2004. *Scandals and Scondrels: Seven Cases that Shook the Academy*. Los Angeles: University of California Press.

Robinson, Walter V. 2001. "Professor's Past in Doubt Discrepancies Surface in Claim of Vietnam Duty." *Boston Globe*, June 18, A1.

Sanford, Victoria. 2003. *Buried Secrets: Truth and Human Rights in Guatemala*. New York: Palgrave Macmillan.

Schirmer, Jennifer. 1998. *The Guatemalan Military Project: A Violence Called Democracy*. Philadelphia: University of Pennsylvania Press.

Smith, Carol. 2005. "Acerca de los movimientos mayas en Guatemala." *Mesoamérica* 47: 114–128.

Stephen, Lynn. 2001. *Zapata Lives! Histories and Cultural Politics in Southern Mexico*. Berkeley: University of California Press.

Stoll, David. 1999. *Rigoberta Menchú and the Story of All Poor Guatemalans*. Boulder: Westview Press.

Stoller, Ann. 1985. *Capitalism and Confrontation in Sumatra's Plantation Belt, 1870–1979*. New Haven: Yale University Press.

Taussig, Michael. 1980. *The Devil and Commodity Fetishism in South America*. Chapel Hill: University of North Carolina Press.

———. 1987. *Shamanism, Colonialism, and the Wild Man: A Study in Terror and Healing*. Chicago: University of Chicago Press.

Tierney, Patrick. 2000. *Darkness in El Dorado: How Scientists and Journalists Devastated the Amazon*. New York: W.W. Norton

Trouillot, Michel-Rolph. 2001. "The Anthropology of the State in the Age of Globalization: Close Encounters of a Deceptive Kind." *Current Anthropology* 42 (Spring): 1–27.

Tsing, Anna Lowenhaupt. 2005. *Friction: An Ethnography of Global Connections*. Princeton: Princeton University Press.

Velásquez Nimatuj, Irma Alicia. 2005. "Entre el cuerpo y la sangre de Guatemala." *Mesoamérica* 47: 105–113.

Vistica, Gregory. 2001. "What Happened in Thanh Phong." *New York Magazine* April 29.

Wallace, Scott. 2000. "You Must Go Home Again: Deported L.A. Gangbangers Take over El Salvador." *Harpers Magazine*, August, 47–56.

Warren, Kay B. 1998. *Indigenous Movements and Their Critics: Pan-Maya Activism in Guatemala*. Princeton: Princeton University Press.

———. 2001. "Telling Truths: Taking David Stoll and the Rigoberta Menchú Exposé Seriously." In *The Rigoberta Menchú Controversy*, edited by Arturo Arias. Minneapolis: University of Minnesota Press.

———. 2002a. "Epilogue: Toward an Anthropology of Fragments, Instabilities, and Incomplete Transitions." In *Ethnography in Unstable Places: Everyday Life in Contexts of Dramatic Political Change,* edited by Carol Greenhouse, Beth Mertz, and Kay B. Warren. Durham: Duke University Press.

———. 2002b. "Introduction: Rethinking Bi-polar Constructions of Ethnicity." *Journal of Latin American Anthropology* 6(1): 90–105.

———. 2005. "Los desafíos de representar los movimientos panmayas: respuesta a Carol Smith." *Mesoamérica* 47: 139–150

Warren, Kay B., and Jean E. Jackson. 2002. "Introduction: Theory and Politics in the Study of Indigenous Movements." In *Indigenous Movements, Self-Representation, and the State*, edited by Kay Warren and Jean Jackson. Austin: University of Texas Press.

Watanabe, John, and Edward Fischer. 2004. *Pluralizing Ethnography: Comparison and Representation of Mayan Cultures, Histories, and Identities*. Santa Fe: School of American Research.

Weisberg, Jacob. 1999. "Cold War without End." *New York Times Magazine*, November 29, 116–158.

Wolf, Eric. 1982. *Europe and the People without History*. Berkeley: University of California Press.

Zapeta, Estuardo. 1999 *Las huellas de B'alam, 1994–1996*. Guatemala: Editorial Cholsamaj.

12

Knowledge in the Service of a Vision

Politically Engaged Anthropology

DANA-AIN DAVIS

> We must never merely discourse on the present situation, must never pro-
> vide the people with programs which have little or nothing to do with their
> own preoccupations, doubts, hopes and fears . . . programs which at times
> in fact increase the fears of the oppressed consciousness. It is not our role
> to speak to the people about our own view of the world, nor to attempt to
> impose that view on them, but rather to dialogue with the people about
> their views and ours. We must realize that their view of the world, mani-
> fested variously in their action, reflects their situation in the world.
>
> —Paolo Friere

Thirty years after Dell Hymes articulated the anthropologists' dilemma concerning the discipline's commitment in and to the world, debates continue about
politically engaged anthropology.[1] Attitudes move along a continuum that incorporates both opposition to using the discipline to serve advocacy interests[2] and
supports for interventionists who view anthropology as capable of promoting
liberation (Harrison 1997). There are some who employ anthropology to challenge
the reproduction of structural inequality (Mullings 2000), and others whose
anthropological work reaches beyond the boundaries of intellectual endeavor,
influencing nonacademic spheres (see for example Sanjek 1987; Curtis n.d.). In
the tradition of those anthropologists, particularly Black feminist anthropologists who view the discipline's potential to disrupt authoritative discourse and
practice, I too, consider myself a politically engaged anthropologist. I conduct
research examining the lives of those who are most silenced in the public
sphere: namely, battered women, low-income and poor women and young girls
of color—especially those who are Black. They neither own nor control media

outlets to challenge distorted representations; nor do they have the means to counter claims highlighting their deficits. And, although these groups live at the center of public policy, their voices often go unheard. I investigate and document women's histories and views with the goal that their experiences will be strategically deployed in coalition and movement building. Consequently, I often ask myself "What did you do today in the service of the women and girls who are the subjects of your research?" I also ask myself, "In what ways have you ensured that the principles of Black feminist theory and practice have been realized toward the goal of promoting social justice?"

It has not been difficult to arrive at the place of being a politically engaged anthropologist. As a Black feminist anthropologist, I have been influenced by a number of contemporary Black feminist scholar/activists. Among them are Zora Neale Hurston, A. Lynn Bolles, Leith Mullings, Angela M. Gilliam, Audre Lorde, and bell hooks. My intellectual genealogy lays claim to interrogating and problematizing inequity and following those who have inspired me. I also seek to link thought, research, and action in my work. This chapter offers examples that shape the contours of what I call pracademics, the bridging of theory and practice, in an effort to illustrate the meaning of being politically engaged.

As debates continue regarding the efficacy of politically engaged anthropology, it may be argued that when research agendas address issues of inequity, there is a responsibility to use information in the service of social change. In the service of social justice, anthropological research on women's poverty requires that anthropologists make commitments to social change. Yet the process is as important as the outcome. Using three examples, I explore the content of being politically engaged: the first example explores my pedagogical approach. The second example draws on my use of a participatory research strategy with the women who were part of the project. Finally, I describe the dissemination of data to progressive organizations working on welfare reform issues. Theoretically grounded in Black feminist theory, this chapter seeks to shape the contours of pracademics, that is, using research for change.

Moving from Margin to Center

In January 1998 I began my dissertation research in a small city in upstate New York. The project centered on the impact of welfare reform on battered Black women living in a shelter. The research took shape shortly after welfare reform was legislated in New York State in August 1997. Activists, policy analysts, and the women with whom I did my work were reeling with concerns. The content of those concerns was shaped by the mandates of Personal Responsibility and Work Opportunity Reconciliation Act (PRWORA) of 1996 signed by President Clinton, which shredded the safety net of welfare. In large part this was achieved by devolving federal responsibility of providing for the poor to each state, and implementing policies that placed five-year lifetime limits on the receipt of cash assistance. At the time of my research in 1998, welfare reform policies ushered in new requirements for recipients, including having to work in order to remain eligible for benefits, mandates to find employment regardless of the type of work, and draconian sanctions against those who did not meet the mandates of the law. I witnessed women's degradation and resilience as they crept through the Kafkaesque maze of new laws and requirements. They desperately worked within and against the controls of the state, whose main interest was to ensure women's participation in the market economy—at almost any cost—even in the absence of opportunity and resources. They tried to find jobs, entered into training programs that were often meaningless or inappropriate, and were caught between a rock and a hard place as their desire to stay home with children was overruled by laws forcing them to work or be engaged in work-related activities (Davis, forthcoming; Davis et al., 2003). Take Sherita for example, a thirty eight-year old woman who left her batterer and had to participate in a training program to receive assistance: "I went and got training as a certified nursing assistant (CNA). What I really want to do is go to Community College and work toward getting a degree in social work or human services. But they [the Department of Social Services] won't let me do that. So I go and finish the training. I get a job at the Johnson Home [for the aged]. But the [the human resources people at the Johnson Home] tell me my CNA training is not applicable. I have to get retrained as a Personal Care Assistant. When am I going to be able to do that?" (Davis, forthcoming).

That year, 1998, was also an election year for the Senate. In New York, Charles S. Schumer and Geraldine Ferraro were running against the incumbent New York State senator, Alfonse D'Amato. On the national front anti-affirmative-action initiatives gained momentum, as did anti-abortion measures. Within this context it was fascinating to note that in the Department of Social Service (DSS) office, where I spent innumerable hours with battered women as they attempted to secure social supports, there was a table set up to register people to vote. One day, after having waited an entire day at DSS with Leslie, a pregnant eighteen-year-old young woman applying for benefits, I began to connect the ways in which the state co-opts civic participation. Over the next three weeks, Leslie spent approximately four days a week meeting social service mandates. At one point I asked her if she was going to vote and she did not respond. I thought to myself, "Why did I ask her that question? When will she get the chance to think about voting? When will she have the time to consider the candidates for office and their political perspectives?" I felt that the social services practices with regard to people who need assistance constituted a peculiar regulation of poor people, which prevented Leslie, as one example, from being an active citizen.

The regulations are "meticulous rituals of power" (Staples 1997: 3) that serve to discipline people into acting in certain ways. Participating in these rituals can also limit the peripheral vision of the subjects of control, in this case those on welfare, since much energy is expended responding to the demands of social services while simultaneously meeting one's daily needs. The regimes of power that regulated activity led to Leslie's hyperengagement with social services. This engagement included constantly reporting back to caseworkers, fear and actual denial of assistance, repeated attempts to reinstate suspended benefits, and being forced to live on what Susser (1992) has identified as "institutional time." These activities took up an inordinate amount of time; time lost to actually being an engaged citizen.

Iliana, a twenty-three-year-old mother of three described how much time she spent dealing with social services: "I lie awake at night trying to figure out what I'm going to do. They [the Department of Social Services] must have been thinking about me everyday. I would get a letter every week. They want me to get training, they want me to get a job. I do what they want, and the letters still keep coming. They still take stuff away from me" (Davis, forthcoming). Iliana had no time to herself. Meeting the mandates of welfare reform meant that she was up at five o'clock, walked her children to school regardless of the weather, went to her training program, participated in a work employment program (as mandated by the Department of Social Services), picked up her kids, walked home, and reported to her caseworker on a very regular basis.

Was this one way to regulate the participation of those at the bottom of the social and economic ladder in electoral politics? Could the logical conclusion of this control be to diffuse the ability of poor and working-class peoples to challenge hegemonic structures through acts of resistance, community organizing, and involvement in social movements and civic engagement?

Although these questions may smell like conspiracy theory, and although we know that poor and working-class people resist poverty-induced assaults on their integrity in a multitude of ways, being a poor Black woman who was battered and on welfare was certainly a roadblock to her engagement in any kind of civic participation. I considered what my role was in addressing these concerns when Sherita asked me what was I going to do with all of the information I collected. She made it very clear that she was only a "case file" at social services and that it was my responsibility to tell "people" how difficult life was and share the problems women faced while on welfare. What Sherita was asking of me was to move my work as an anthropologist from the margin of my own personal achievement, that of being awarded a degree and facilitating my employment as an academic, to a center of relevance, to the realm of policy. In return for the "gift" of her life story and the stories of other women, I was asked to do something that might make a difference. My work as a politically engaged anthropologist began at that moment. My accountability was a moral and political issue, not so much because I am in academia but rather because my responsibility as a moral agent is no different from the responsibilities of others, as Noam Chomsky

(2001) points out. He also notes that intellectuals do enjoy a degree of privilege and power and should seek out an audience that matters, which is precisely what Sherita asked me to do as a gesture of reciprocity to accommodate her perceived (and real) lack of power in influencing policy.

Shortly after completing my dissertation research in 2000, I applied for a one-year appointment in anthropology at Purchase College. I was asked to comment on my teaching philosophy and quickly responded that I taught to "transgress." Teaching to transgress is of course the title of a book by bell hooks (1994), which I have unabashedly adopted as a strategy to motivate students to explore social issues. These issues include exploring the parameters of inequality and the persistence of structural barriers with an eye toward students becoming politically engaged. Why? Because as hooks notes, "The academy is not paradise . . . the classroom, with all its limitations, remains a location of possibility. In that field of possibility we have the opportunity to labor for freedom, to demand of ourselves and our comrades, an openness of mind and heart that allows us to face reality even as we collectively imagine ways to move beyond boundaries, to transgress" (hooks 1994: 207). Using this pedagogical strategy, I reasoned, would help students recognize the possibilities of anthropology not only as a discipline concerned with intellectual inquiry, and not only as "a field for those who believe that if we can better describe the world, decision makers will listen to our well-reasoned positions and act accordingly," as Kirk Dombrowkski notes (Curtis n.d.).[3] I also embraced this pedagogy as a way for students to consider intellectual work as bridging theory and practice, what I call pracademics.

I lay the foundation for pracademics on the first day of class when I explain to my Anthropology of Poverty class that I live at the intersection of intellectual engagement and practice. I point out that the distinctions between research, service, and activism are not clearly defined if one is productively engaged in social justice work. And although each of those elements may constitute points against which tenure will be measured, I am, first and foremost, a person concerned about fairness and equity, concerned that the voices and rights of those on the margins be centered. Anthropology can shift equations by incorporating not only "culture talk" but also "rights talk." There are research tools that facilitate this process, as Mullings (2000: 20) points out. Anthropological research practices, she notes, including ethnography and community participation, can bring to the fore the voices of those who lie outside the centers of power. However, turning up the volume of under-represented voices is not enough. There are other commitments that we as anthropologists have. We must link research practices to critical inquiry and ultimately to action that will dislodge power. Roger Sanjek (1987) argues that we need to be concerned about the outcome of our work; an issue also raised by Hymes, who noted that the role of anthropologists is threefold: we are critics and scholars in the academic world; we work for communities, movements, operational institutions; and we are linked to direct action as members of a community or social movement. There is need for all three roles (Hymes 1972: 56). In other words, we can all be pracademicians if we choose to make our connections to all of these worlds explicit in our work.

Transforming Ideals of Equity and Democracy into Shared Research

Politically engaged anthropology is grounded in principles of inclusion, equal rights, and equal access. It is not limited to the application of knowledge gained; in other words, it aims not only to share our knowledge with elite policy makers but also addresses the process of gaining that knowledge. This can be achieved through participatory research, which fundamentally embodies fairness, respect, and encourages the broadest possible distribution of power by including the subjects of projects in the decision-making process and analysis. The challenge is in transforming the ideal of equity into a lived experience of shared power. Participatory research provides people with the analytic and practical tools to document their lives and offers a language for articulating the unique strengths of a group. Using this model, we can ensure that the voices and expertise of our constituents are not lost in the effort to achieve scientific validity (Fullwood, Davis and Debold, 2000). To that end I employed an interpretive community. This involved discussing themes with individuals who were part of the study. As themes emerged during my manual coding process, I asked some of the people interviewed to participate in the interpretation or elaboration of those themes. For example, I had coded the strategies that women used to survive welfare reform and the loss of access to material goods. One woman, in reading my list of strategies, and the chapter on strategies, noted that there was a way women used talking to get what they needed. I went back and reviewed all the data again and found that a number of women, in fact almost all the Black women, engaged in this practice that I subsequently called "Speech Acts" to secure goods and services. It was this woman's observation that motivated what essentially became a critical framework in understanding how people negotiate scarcity.

Partnering with study subjects requires that they be actively involved in all or various stages of the research design. At its most successful, participatory research extends beyond the idea that researchers are studying subjects, and invites them to produce more nuanced and profound analyses of the problems or issues with which they are faced and to improve the conditions of their lives (Park 1993).

Knowledge in the Service of a Vision

My research on battered Black women living in a small city in upstate New York represents an anthropological elaboration of the impact of the Personal Responsibility and Work Reconciliation Act of 1996.[4] Black women are at the center of this analysis for several reasons. First, historical constructions of inequity have challenged Black women's economic viability. Second, Black women have become the markers of women on welfare based on distorted representations of poverty. Third, Black women's receipt of institutional assistance in relation to violence has been complicated in part because of racialized ideologies, that frequently render it impossible for them to be viewed as victims.[5] As an ethnography of the particular, which Abu-Lughod (1991) argues is a powerful tool in subverting the process of "othering" and generalizing, my research on welfare reform and the strategies Black women use to make ends meet in the absence of, or threat of losing, what used to be entitlements is a project that seeks to reduce homogeneous views of women on welfare, Black women, and battered women.

One way to achieve this goal as a component of politically engaged anthropology emerges out of the insight of Sherita's charge, that I inform people about the problems facing Black women who are battered and on welfare. The first order of business after completing the dissertation was to send it to progressive organizations and advocacy groups. These included the Human Rights Project of the Urban Justice Center; the Women, Welfare and Abuse Task Force, the Applied Research Center in California; NOW Legal and Education Defense Fund, and the New York State Coalition against Domestic Violence, among others. These submissions were often follow-ups on contacts made at various meetings. I implored people to make use of whatever examples they chose in making a case against the egregious wrath against poor people, especially women of color, that various aspects of welfare reform policy represent. Typically I pointed out that the research highlights the microregulatory practices of battered women on welfare by social services. These practices are experienced differentially by Black as against other women. For example, there is an inequitable distribution of information to Black women with regard to support services and educational opportunities. For example, although many women were not fully informed about waivers for meeting certain mandates contained within the welfare reform, Black women were less likely to be made aware of those dispensations. Further, some of the women experienced a form of streamlining toward certain types of training programs and employment sectors. The point is that real people live at the crossroads of policy decisions and implementation.

Making the research available to the above-mentioned organizations, I hoped the material would be used to illuminate disparities. I am aware of two ways that the research embodied a pracademic approach. First, the Human Rights Project of the Urban Justice Center used the work as background material for a shadow report examining the compliance of the U.S. government with the International Convention on the Elimination of Racial Discrimination.[6] According to Ramona Ortega, the director of the Human Rights Project, such anthropological documentation brings real lives and real people to the framing of issues around economic and gender-based human rights violations. "Presenting local examples of how women and women of color in particular have been discriminated in the social and legal systems here is really important because while there is so much research out there, not enough of it relies on individual stories. It is hard to find detailed information on violations and to whom they occur, because the kind of data that is collected are not broken out by race and gender" (personal communication with author, June 6, 2003).

A second example comes from the Women, Welfare and Abuse Task Force (WWATF). The task force is composed of a broad coalition of domestic violence and welfare advocates from various counties in New York, whose mission is to encourage economic solvency for victims of domestic violence. Originally founded to advocate for the adoption of the Family Violence Option (FVO) in New York State, WWATF monitors legislation and policy initiatives as they affect survivors of violence. The Family Violence Option was an amendment to the PRWORA of 1996. The Option permits states to screen for domestic violence among those applying for and those being dropped from assistance programs. Further, a Domestic Violence Liaison can refer survivors of violence to counseling and may determine whether certain welfare requirements should be waived—requirements that would unfairly penalize women for mandates they may not be able to meet while in the process of leaving an abusive relationship (Kurz 1999). Clearly the central focus of the FVO is provide safety planning. However, the Office of Temporary Disability Assistance in New York proposed some amendments to the Option. The proposed amendments would shift the scope of services provided by the Domestic Violence Liaison from screening, assessment, and referral to developing employment plans following the basic work experience model that constitutes work mandates. That is, as a result of the amendments survivors of violence would have to be in the same location for up to thirty five hours each week, placing them at risk, since batterers often seek them out. The research I conducted on battered women and welfare discusses the ineffectiveness of the Family Violence Option for Black women versus other women. Implementation of the FVO in various counties in New York was inconsistent, and my research along with other analyses was cited as an example of a discrepancy in the execution of the FVO in New York State. More pointedly, evidence from the research showed that even without the proposed amendment, the FVO waivers were not being used in the safety planning process. If accepted, the amendment would further weaken the protections that battered women need.

A Final Note

In very concrete ways, what has been presented here represents a number of ways that commitment to politically engaged anthropology can be met, through participatory research, popular methodology, strategic use of material to organize, and dissemination of research to "user-friendly" groups. Commitment to these means is a reflection of accountability. As Cheryl Mwaria points out, Black feminist anthropologists are accountable to a number of constituents—among them ourselves, our informants, the general public, and those who work to influence policy (Mwaria 2001: 208). Knowledge production around issues of poverty and violence must be conducted in the service of some greater goal than just getting it done, because people's lives are often at stake. Research on particular issues, such as those that uncover persistent patterns of marginalization, should always be connected to emancipatory praxis.

In conclusion, I offer a cautionary observation, however. We must remember that although this is what Black feminist theory has sought to do, there are some differences between the activist practices of community workers and the ways in which anthropological research is used in the service of activism. Community activists and organizers are often looking for immediate and direct results from the methods they employ, such as public education campaigns and protests to bring about change. Anthropological research can be posited as a more indirect form of activism, more often with implications on long-term policy decisions. The measure of our success (when we succeed) is certainly less transparent than what is looked for among those whose profession is organizing.

At the same time, we can be comforted by the fact that anthropology and activism are not mutually exclusive endeavors. In fact, there appears to be a particular ease with which anthropologists and activists move across boundaries, boundaries which to the less critical may appear to represent a gulf of difference. My association with anthropologists and activists has revealed that some anthropologists may use their research as a stepping stone to direct engagement with activism. But just as commonly, I have found that many activists became anthropologists. Here I'll draw on the cumulative biographies of people for whom this is true—without naming names. Several alumni from my alma mater, the Graduate Center, City University of New York, came to the discipline from activist backgrounds, myself included. We worked on direct-action campaigns, community organizing, public education, and advocacy around issues of affordable housing, mental health, welfare, and violence against women. The discipline was a logical extension of community work, especially in linking the methodological tenets of the discipline to our skills as documentarians. Also, and importantly, faculty mentors showed us by example that being an academic did not mean we had to forgo our politics and supported our political commitments. Faculty were often highly regarded for their ability to synthesize activism and anthropology, and many of us learned that there is not a contradiction between the two.

NOTES

For her direction in identifying sources and her ongoing support, I would like to thank Leith Mullings. For their helpful comments, I thank Susan Hyatt, Sarah Orndorff, and the reviewers. I appreciate Susan Hyatt and Vin Lyon-Callo for originally asking me to write this article. And finally, I thank Sister Scholars and Asale Angel-Ajani for being pracademicians. This article is based on an earlier article "What Did You Do Today?: Notes from a Politically Engaged Anthropologist," *Urban Anthropology* 32.2: 147–173. Although I cannot find documentation of the quote in textual form, I recall a story once shared with me by a friend who had taken classes with Audre Lorde at Hunter College. She said that Audre often asked her students, "What have you done today?" I hope I have attributed this story appropriately and wish I had been there.

I.   Anthropology and its role in politics and advocacy was the organizing subject of the 2003 Society of Anthropology of North America meeting in Halifax, Nova Scotia. An ongoing symposium addressing this issue was "Intergenerational Perspectives on Anthropology and Social Advocacy/Activism: The 1980s and Forward." There was a roundtable titled "Politicizing Students in the Field: Pedagogies for an Activist Anthropology," and a session "Engaged Anthropology: Marginal Voices or? Cutting Edge?" during which the issue of anthropologists and political engagement reemerged.

2.   See, for example, Michael S. Billig, who is avowedly opposed to advocacy anthropology (n.d.).

3.   Ric Curtis of John Jay College discusses the meaning of an engaged anthropology, noting that Kirk Dombrowski framed the field of anthropology as an ongoing debate between two sides: those who are obsessed with "getting it right" and those who are pragmatic and engaged. See Ric Curtis (n.d.).

4.   The title of this section comes from Audre Lorde, who argued that we should not be afraid to speak out—in fact, our silence will not protect us. More precisely, she stated that "When I dare to be powerful, to use my strength in the service of my vision, then it becomes less and less important whether I am afraid." See Lorde (1980).

5.   Race plays an important role in institutional and social network response to Black women. For example, Mama (1989) points out that Black women in Great Britain experience abbreviated social service assistance due to race. Barbee (1991) argues that societal response to the abuse of Black women is enveloped in the belief that Black people are inherently violent. For other discussions on the link between race and violence, see Ammons (1995) and James (1996).

6.   The report that was put together was *Compliance with Article Five: Economic, Social and Cultural Rights under the International Convention on the Elimination of Racial Discrimination*, August 2001, Human Rights Project, Urban Justice Center. It was submitted to the Committee on the Elimination of All Forms of Racial Discrimination in Geneva 2001.

REFERENCES

Abu-Lughod, Lila. 1991. "Writing against Culture". In *Recapturing Anthropology: Working in the Present*, edited by Richard G. Fox. Santa Fe: School of American Research Press.

Ammons, Linda. 1995. "Mules, Madonnas, Babies, Bathwater, Racial Imagery and Stereotypes: The African-American Woman and the Battered Woman Syndrome." *Wisconsin Law Review* 5: 1003–1080.

Barbee, Evelyn L. 1991. "Ethnicity and Woman Abuse in the United States." In *Violence against Women: Nursing Research, Education, and Practice Issues*, edited by Carolyn M. Sampselle. New York: Routledge.

Billig, Michael S. n.d. http://www.fandm.edu/Departments/Anthropology/billig.html.

Chomsky, Noam. 2001. "The Moral Role of Intellectuals," Public Anthropology: Engaging Ideas, Intellectual, and the Responsibilities of Public Life: An Interview with Noam Chomsky. Public Anthropology Journals. http://www.publicanthropology.org/Journal/ Engaging–Ideas/chomsky.htm.

Curtis, Ric. n.d. "Adventures in Engaged Anthropology, or Why 'Getting It Right' Isn't Enough." http://www.sfa.net/committees/policy/curtispolicy.pdf.

Davis, Dana. Forthcoming. *Between a Rock and a Hard Place: Battered Black Women Surviving Welfare Reform.* Albany: State University of New York Press.

Davis, Dana, et al. 2003. "Working It Off: Welfare, Workfare and Work Experience Programs in New York City." *Souls: A Critical Journal of Black Politics, Culture, and Society* 5.2: 22–41.

Friere, Paulo. 1993. *Pedagogy of the Oppressed.* New York: Continuum.

Fullwood, P. Catlin, Dana Davis, and Elizabeth Debold. 2000. *The New Girls' Movement: New Assessment Tools for Youth Programs Healthy Girls/Healthy Women Collaborative Fund for Women.* New York: Ms. Foundation for Women.

Harrison, Faye.V. ed. [1991] 1997. *Decolonizing Anthropology: Moving further toward an Anthropology for Liberation.* 2nd ed. Arlington, Va: Association of Black Anthropologists and American Anthropological Association.

Hooks, bell. 1994. *Teaching to Transgress: Education as the Practice of Freedom.* New York: Routledge.

Hymes, Dell. ed. 1972. "The Uses of Anthropology: Critical, Political, Personal". In *Reinventing Anthropology,* edited by Dell Hymes. New York: Vintage.

James, Joy. 1996. *Resisting State Violence: Radicalism, Gender, and Race in U.S. Culture.* Minneapolis: University of Minnesota Press.

Kurz, Demi. 1999. "Women, welfare, and Domestic Violence." In *Whose welfare?* edited by Gwendolyn Minic. Itheea: Cornell University Press.

Lorde, Audre. 1980. *The Cancer Journals.* San Francisco: Aunt Lute Books

Mama, Amina. 1989. *The Hidden Struggle: Statutory and Voluntary Sector Responses to Violence against Black Women in the Home.* London: London Race and Housing Research Unit.

Mullings, Leith. 2000. "African-American Women Making Themselves: Notes on the Role of Black Feminist Research". *Souls: A Critical Journal of Black Politics, Culture, and Society* 2.4: 18–29.

Mwaria, Cheryl. 2001. "Biomedical Ethics, Gender, and Ethnicity: Implications for Black Feminist Anthropology". In *Black Feminist Anthropology: Theory, Politics, Praxis, and Poetics,* edited by Irma McClaurin. New Brunswick: Rutgers University Press.

Park, Peter. 1993. "What is Participatory Research? A Theoretical and Methodological Perspective." In *Voices of Change: Participatory Research in the U.S. and Canada,* edited by P. Park, M. Brydon-Miller, B. Hall, and T. Jackson. Westport, Conn.: Bergen and Garvey.

Sanjek, Roger. 1987. "Work at a Gray Panther Health Clinic." In *Cities of the United States: Studies in Urban Anthropology,* edited by L. Mullings. New York: Columbia University Press.

Staples, William G. 1997. *The Culture of Surveillance: Discipline and Social Control in the United States.* New York: St. Martin's.

Susser, Ida. 1992. *Norman Street: Poverty and Politics in an Urban Neighborhood.* New York: Oxford University Press.

NOTES ON
CONTRIBUTORS

ASALE ANGEL-AJANI is an assistant professor in the Gallatin School at New York University. She is the author of numerous articles on race, violence, and human rights. She is completing her manuscript about her work in Rebibbia Prison in Rome, Italy. She was the founder of Texas Prison Watch and has worked for Women Care, New York City, an organization assisting women returning home from prison.

PHILIPPE BOURGOIS is professor of medical anthropology at UC San Francisco's Department of Anthropology, History, and Social Medicine. He has conducted fieldwork in Central America (Costa Rica, Panama, Nicaragua, El Salvador, and Belize) and in the urban United States. He is the author of *In Search of Respect: Selling Crack in El Barrio* (2003) and co-editor with Nancy Scheper-Hughes of *Violence in War and Peace: An Anthology* (2004).

MICHAEL J. BOSIA is an assistant professor of comparative politics at Saint Michael's College, an activist, and former policy maker. His research has focused on the local forms of marginalization and citizenship that help explain how Ryan White in the U.S. and Ludovic Bouchet in France came to represent distinctively national AIDS movements.

ALDO CIVICO is a research associate at the Center for International Conflict Resolution at Columbia University and a doctoral student in applied anthropology at Teachers College. Currently, he teaches at the New School University and at the William Paterson University. For several years he worked as a freelance journalist for European media on the Mafia and organized crime. He was born in Trento (Italy) and lives in New York.

JOHN COLLINS is an assistant professor of global studies at St. Lawrence University in Canton, N.Y., where he teaches courses on Palestine, nationalism, media analysis, cultural studies theory, and the global politics of violence. He is the author of *Occupied by Memory: The Intifada Generation and the Palestinian State of Emergency*, an ethnographic study of the relationship between nationalism, memory, and generational identity in the context of the first Palestinian intifada. He is also the co-editor, with Ross Glover, of *Collateral Language: A User's Guide to America's New War*, a collection of essays critically interrogating the rhetoric used to justify U.S. military action after the September II attacks.

ROBERTA CULBERTSON is founding director of the Institute on Violence and Survival and Director of Research and Education at the Virginia Foundation for the Humanities(VFH). The VFH is affiliated with the University of Virginia. She received her Ph.D. and Masters in anthropology at the University of Virginia. She has worked with survivors of violence for more than twenty years, and has been recognized for her service to survivors. She is a poet and also the editor of *Sacred Bearings*.

DANA-AIN DAVIS is an assistant professor of anthropology at Purchase College, State University of New York. Her research interests include poverty, policy, violence against women, HIV/AIDS, and the role of community-based organizations in social justice and social change. She conducts research in the United States and Namibia.

R. AIDA HERNANDEZ was born in Ensenada, Baja California, on the northern Mexican border. She has worked and lived among Guatemalan refugees and Chiapas's indigenous peoples on the southern Mexican border since 1986. She is a researcher-professor with CIESAS (Center for Advanced Studies in Social Anthropology). She is the author of *Histories and Stories from Chiapas—Border Identities in Southern Mexico*.

VICTORIA SANFORD is an associate professor of anthropology at Lehman College—City University of New York and a senior research fellow at the Institute on Violence and Survival at the Virginia Foundation for the Humanities. She is the author of *Buried Secrets: Truth and Human Rights in Guatemala and Violencia y Genocidio en Guatemala*. She is currently completing *Markings: Violence and Everyday Life in Colombia*.

IRINA CARLOTA SILBER received her Ph.D. in cultural anthropology from New York University. Currently she is an assistant professor at City College of New York Center for Worker Education. She is working on her manuscript, "Desencanto Revolucionario" and two other projects: "From Solidarity to Development," which explores postwar shifts in Central American development work, and "The Color of Illness," which is a study of childhood genetic illness and disability.

MONIQUE SKIDMORE is a research fellow at the Center for Cross-Cultural Research at Australian National University. She is a medical anthropologist with a Ph.D. from McGill University who has been conducting research in Burma since 1994, funded by a number of grants, including Wenner-Gren, Rockefeller, and Australian Research Council grants. She was a 2002–2003 Rockefeller Visiting Fellow at the Joan B. Kroc Institute for International Peace Studies at the University of Notre Dame. She is the author of *Karaoke Fascism: Burma and the Politics of Fear*, editor of *Burma at the Turn of the Twenty-First Century*, and co-editor of the forthcoming *Women and the Contested State: Religion, Violence and Agency in South and Southeast Asia*.

SHANNON SPEED is an assistant professor of anthropology at the University of Texas at Austin. She holds an M.A. degree in Latin American Studies from the University of Texas and an M.A. and Ph.D. in anthropology and Native American studies from the University of California, Davis. For the last nine years, Dr. Speed's research has been carried out in Chiapas, Mexico. She has published numerous articles and is currently completing a book entitled *Global Discourses on the Local Terrain: Human Rights and Indigenous Resistance in Chiapas*, as well as co-editing two volumes, *Dissident Women: Gender, Ethnicity and Cultural Politics in Chiapas*, and *Human Rights in the Maya Region: Global Politics, Moral Engagements, and Cultural Contentions*.

KAY WARREN is the Tillinghast Professor of International Studies and professor of anthropology at Brown University, where she heads the Politics, Culture, and Identity Program at the Watson Institute of International Studies. She is the author of *Indigenous Movements and Their Critics*, and co-editor (with Jean Jackson) of *Indigenous Movements, Self-Representation, and the State*. She is currently working on a book entitled *Politics, Culture and Identity Abroad and at Home: A Multi-Sited Ethnography of Japanese Social Development Policy and Practice*, and co-editing (with David Leheny) *Remaking Transnationalism: Japan, Foreign Aid, and the Search for Global Solutions*.

INDEX

abandonment by sexual partners, 194, 195–199

Abejas, Las, 156, 161, 166n12, 175, 186n2

abortion, 230

abstractions, 119, 123, 124

Abu-Lughod, Lila, 234

academics, 12–13, 88n4, 232; and activism, 215; and Burmese scholarship, 47; and crime, 76–77; and HIV/AIDS, 126; and intellectuals, 216, 232. *See also* anthropologists; anthropology

accountability, 236

acculturation, 153, 160

Achi-Maya, 26–28, 30, 37n7

Acteal, 8, 151, 155–164, 186n2; analysis of violence in, 151, 162–164; genocide and, 158–159; as impetous for resistance, 177–178, 184; massacre description, 160–162, 166n6; maternity and, 174; paramilitaries and, 173; refugees in, 155–157; responses to, 170–171, 175

activism, 4, 8, 14, 85; and anthropology, 44–46, 55, 77–79, 171, 184–186, 215, 221; in Burma, 43, 47; and HIV/AIDS, 118, 120–121; and intifada as, 95, 98, 101; by proxy, 46; and witnessing, 81, 87; women and, 77, 190, 193, 203, 205

Act Up Paris, 120–121, 122, 124–126

adulthood, 10, 95, 97, 109

advocacy, 3–5, 14, 55, 81, 234

affirmative action, 230

Afghanistan war (2001–2002), 216

Africa, 151; Burundi, 80; Congo, 34; and HIV/AIDS, 117; Mozambique, 74, 174; Nigeria, 83; Rwanda, 63, 70; Tanzania, 80

Agamben, Giorgio, 25, 81

age, 85, 106, 109

agency, 30, 126–127; and Guatemala, 54; and HIV/AIDS, 114–116; political, 50, 52; women and, 182–184

Aguirre de Calderón Sol, Elizabeth, 191

AIDS. *See* HIV/AIDS

alcohol, 20, 153, 154, 172

Al Qaeda, 25

Altamirano, 172

Alvarez, Sonia, 180

Álvaro (Colombian paramilitary leader), 131–133, 136–144

Amazon, indigenous people of, 160

American Anthropological Association Code of Ethics, 3

Angel-Ajani, Asale, 6–7, 9, 12, 35

anger, 177, 197

anthropologists, 117, 184–185, 228, 232; and compartmentalization, 31; and mysticism, 72–74; privilege of, 6; relationships with informants, 131–132, 142–144; risks to, 48; and witnessing, 81–82

anthropology, 83–85, 87; and activism, 44–46, 55, 77–79, 171, 184–186, 215, 221; engagement and, 184–186; literature of, 190; metaphors for, 79–83; and policy, 231–234; and poverty, 232; and violence, 51, 150, 159, 160, 163–165. *See also* ethics; ethnography, research

Arafat, Yasser, 104, 105, 111n12

Arana Osorio, Efraín, 152

Aretxaga, Begoña, 84

Arias, Arturo, 54

Armenian genocide, 64

army. *See* military

ASEAN (Association of Southeast Asian Nations), 44